PENGUIN BUSINESS

REPUTATIONS OF VALUE

Over more than twenty-five years, Stephen (Steve) Thomas has led programmes designed to earn and protect corporate reputations.

In 2022, Steve established TAVO Advisory to help organizations achieve valued results by providing counsel on complex matters relating to reputation, trust, and stakeholder engagement.

Steve was Head of Group Brand and Communications at AIA Group from 2012 to 2021. AIA, which is listed and headquartered in Hong Kong, is one of the world's largest life insurers.

Prior to AIA, Steve was a Managing Director and Head of Corporate Affairs for Citigroup (Citi) in China.

Steve began his career at Burson-Marsteller (now Burson), a leading global public relations firm, working in the firm's Melbourne and Hong Kong offices.

Steve's professional recognition includes being named multiple times in PR Week's Power Book list of the world's most influential PR professionals as well as the Influence 100, PRovoke Media's annual compilation of the most influential in-house communicators around the world. In 2020, Steve was named the In-House Communications Professional of the Year by the Asia-Pacific Association of Communications Directors.

Steve is a Board Trustee of the Institute for Public Relations and from 2014 to 2020 he was Chairman of the Hong Kong chapter of the Arthur W. Page Society.

T0280096

ADVANCE PRAISE FOR *REPUTATIONS OF VALUE*

'Built around enduring principles and grounded in more than two decades of Steve's experience working with major multinational firms, this is an important book that demonstrates how companies can strategically navigate today's complex stakeholder society.'

—The Honorable Curtis S. Chin, U.S. Ambassador to the Asian Development Bank (2007–2010) and former Managing Director, Global Business Development and Managing Director, Asia-Pacific, Burson-Marsteller

'*Reputations of Value* by Stephen Thomas is an invaluable resource for senior corporate affairs executives, and indeed every single executive who is responsible for protecting their company's reputation. It is a well-written and highly enjoyable read, with fascinating insights into hot topics such as ESG, speaking up on social issues, the importance of media relations and how to best handle investor activists and even internal risks such as employee activists. This book is packed full of practical examples on safeguarding reputations that even the most seasoned professionals can learn from, and the author's extensive experience in this area is evident throughout each chapter. It explores each of the facets that can affect a company's reputation both negatively and positively, and offers insights across a range of industries and explores cultural nuances that are often forgotten or overlooked by multinationals operating in Asia. In business, trusted relationships are at the heart of everything we do and this book offers invaluable advice on how to maintain these relationships in an authentic and purposeful way. A must-read!'

—Lynne Mulholland, General Manager, Group Corporate Affairs, The Hongkong and Shanghai Hotels Limited (owner and operator of The Peninsula Hotels)

'Stephen Thomas has crafted a practical guide for anyone involved in helping companies navigate today's complex stakeholder landscape. Well-researched and highly readable, the book is a great resource for communications and brand marketing professionals, from students to seasoned business executives.'

**—Joe Cohen, Chief Marketing &
Communications Officer, AXIS**

'An authoritative playbook for anyone interested in understanding the critical aspects of earning and preserving corporate reputations in the complex business landscape of today and tomorrow. Steve Thomas relies on his incomparable experience in international business to combine real-world examples with insightful, actionable advice. This timely book is an invaluable resource for those working to earn and protect corporate reputation.'

**—Pat Ford, Professional-in-Residence, College of
Journalism and Communications, University of Florida**

'Stephen Thomas distils his tenure as an executive at some of the top global companies into a comprehensive guide to managing and building all aspects of corporate reputation, including emphasizing the influence of the often-overlooked workforce. This book navigates the complex terrain of reputation management, coupling insightful stories and experiences from top executives with practical strategies, and enriching each chapter with cases and key takeaways. For leaders aiming to understand and enhance their organization's most invaluable and precarious asset strategically, Thomas offers not just a lens but a roadmap, making this a must-read for leaders impacted by an ever-changing social and business landscape.'

**—Tina McCorkindale, PhD, APR, President and
CEO, Institute for Public Relations**

REPUTATIONS OF VALUE

Winning with
Corporate Reputations in
an Unpredictable World

Stephen R. Thomas

BUSINESS
An imprint of Penguin Random House

PENGUIN BUSINESS

Penguin Business is an imprint of the Penguin Random House group of companies whose addresses can be found at global.penguinrandomhouse.com

Published by Penguin Random House SEA Pte Ltd
40 Penjuru Lane, #03-12, Block 2
Singapore 609216

First published in Penguin Business by Penguin Random House SEA 2024

ISBN 9789815127805

Typeset in Garamond by MAP Systems, Bengaluru, India

www.penguin.sg

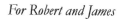

For Robert and James

Contents

Introduction

My career—first in consulting and then in-house—has afforded me a bird's-eye view of the aspirations and challenges of a range of companies. I have witnessed numerous corporate strategies, thorny issues, and proud milestones. For example, my tenure at Citi, from 2005 to 2012, gave me the chance to be part of the bank's programme of investment in, and expansion across, China. During my first few years with Citi, we led a consortium to acquire a controlling stake in Guangdong Development Bank (now known as China Guangfa Bank), locally incorporated, rolled out a consumer banking business, expanded to new cities, and launched a credit card business (among many other activities). Later, during the global financial crisis, the focus was reassuring clients and other stakeholders regarding the ability of the bank to continue operations and then to demonstrate its recovery.

I joined AIA Group in the first half of 2012, less than two years after its IPO on the Hong Kong Stock Exchange to spin the company off from AIG. In its new era, AIA had become an independent company headquartered in Hong Kong with an exclusive focus on the Asia-Pacific region. Over the nine years I spent with the Group, AIA was in a mode of dynamic growth. As it defined a new vision, operating philosophy, and ultimately its purpose, AIA entered markets such as Sri Lanka and Cambodia, struck major bancassurance partnerships, launched a comprehensive new health and wellness proposition, and made acquisitions in markets including Malaysia and Australia.

Throughout my career, I have been fascinated by the role that the ethereal concept of reputation plays in the success or otherwise of business. Reputations cannot be controlled, but they can be shaped. And any progress made in earning reputations has been traditionally problematic to measure. These factors have meant that the considerable effort involved in earning and protecting reputations usually falls into ambiguous territory in the context of running a business.

This is personal: I have dedicated my working life to helping companies to communicate and interact with their various constituencies in a way that contributes to the success of the business. The work has been rewarding, stressful, and never dull! Throughout it all, at the back of my mind, was this question: Am I doing something that is truly valuable to the company? Early on, I would wonder if I was just there to work around the edges, to help announce a completed project (rather than being involved from the beginning), to receive calls from the press, to take instructions rather than offer advice. Over time, however, I have satisfied myself that the endeavour to build and protect reputations sits at the core of the company's success.

Perhaps it has always been the case, but society today seems to have been engulfed by a particularly immense degree of unpredictability and complexity. A range of megatrends have placed a high degree of stress on the ability of companies to operate to optimum effect. There is greater global interconnectedness than ever before and more volatile geopolitical tensions. Technology continues to advance at breakneck speed. Climate change is arguably the biggest threat of our era. Income, racial, and gender inequalities continue to cause distress and suffering around the world. And of course, there has been the global pandemic. At the same time as these influences, among others, have converged, there has been a drop in confidence around the world in the ability of governments to find solutions. Society has placed an increased onus on corporations to drive transparency, to demonstrate accountability, to tell the world what they do and why that activity is aligned to the achievement of greater societal value.

To respond accordingly, companies need specialized advice and support. The process of earning reputations is the responsibility of the business itself, however the Corporate Affairs[1] team has a crucial role to play in helping the organization operate on a sustainable basis. One of the key responsibilities of the best-run Corporate Affairs teams is to advise the business on which reputations are important among which stakeholders in the short- or long-term, and therefore what the business needs to do to achieve and keep them. Doing so encompasses far more than the act of communications. Rather, it is also about decisions and actions. Whether a company is a public one or privately held, whether it is large or small, how that business makes decisions, and acts accordingly, is the way trust between the company and its stakeholders is created and how its reputations will be defined. I seek to uncover some of the decisions a company needs to make in the course of doing business that impact this process. These include how it defines its purpose, engages with its employees, when and how it should speak up on social issues, how it should react when targeted by shareholder activists, among many other areas of much needed support.

This book explores some of the key risks that companies face to their reputations from various sources, and what they can do to better protect themselves. However, the book is not intended to be solely about risk management and what to do when things go wrong. While this is critical, done well, taking

---

[1] There are several terms to describe those teams that help organizations engage with their various constituencies—Corporate Affairs, Corporate Communications, Public Relations are some of the common ones. Which term is more apt is a question that generates debate among some who work in the field. For the sake of consistency and simplicity, this book will use the term 'Corporate Affairs'.

an informed approach to earning reputations provides any company with a distinct source of competitive advantage—it's not just about playing defence, but rather finding new ways to *win* through earning accurate and positive reputations with specific stakeholders. Numerous benefits are available to those firms that take this process seriously, which in turn supports their sustainable success.

While many aspects of reputation are universal in nature, having worked in Asia for more than twenty years, I am mindful that cultural nuances matter a great deal. Not every learning from the West is transferable to other regions of the world. Despite the world getting smaller through our collective connectivity, significant cultural, socio-economic, demographic, and political differences remain—all of which can have an impact on how stakeholders perceive a particular corporation. I have tried to include perspectives from Asia in different sections of the book.

Finally, I wrote this book as someone who does not know all the answers. Rather, I wanted to further educate myself by seeking out experts and specialists in their respective fields and capturing their insights into the topics at hand. I am most grateful to all of the individuals who shared their thoughts with me. I have interviewed specialists around the world—from Singapore to London, from Tokyo to New York, from Beijing to Sydney—and weaved their insights into each chapter. As well as helping me to better understand this expansive topic of how to earn and protect corporate reputations, my hope was to articulate a set of principles that will be enduring in nature. Principles that those involved in the running of companies (or advising them) can rely on, now and in the future.

The degree of focus on Artificial Intelligence (AI) in the book is something I thought long and hard about. On the one hand, there is no doubt that technological developments are having, and will continue to have, a vastly profound influence on levels of trust and on corporate reputations. The curiosity and in some cases, fear, that AI is sparking around the world is palpable. The advent of AI has many positive and negative ramifications in this context—new and efficient ways to inform decision making, the ability to better predict how announcements and developments will be received by audiences, improved measurement capabilities, the extreme dangers of disinformation and fake news, the delivery of unintentional biases, and the list goes on. On the other hand, this is such a fast-evolving space that anything put forward in a single chapter about the subject matter will soon be redundant. There will continue to be advancements and a rapid process of trial and error. The threats and opportunities posed by AI to corporate reputations will need to be understood and countered or leveraged. There will be disruptions that by their nature, are difficult to forecast. I will leave it to others to provide an informed view of how the age of AI will impact the shaping and protection of corporate reputations.

I trust that readers of this book find it valuable to their own efforts to better understand the subject of corporate reputations, and to support the success of their respective companies or clients. I hope you enjoy reading it as much as I have enjoyed the process of writing it.

Part One

Understanding Corporate Reputations

1

The Implication of Multiple Reputations

Reputation: the multiple perceptions of an entity made by different stakeholders, based on their evaluations of the past capabilities and character of the entity, and their assessment of its ability to provide future contributions[1]

There is a tendency to talk about corporate reputation in singular terms. Apple is known for technology design. Singapore Airlines is known for customer service. Patagonia is known for sustainability. Louis Vuitton is known for luxury fashion. In media reporting, and perhaps just in general, companies (and people for that matter) are placed into a box with a neat and single label.

There is nothing inherently wrong with being known for something in particular—to stand for something in the minds of your stakeholders, or least some of them. In fact, there can be significant benefits. But a singular reputation belies the far more nuanced realities of life. The fact is that companies do not have one reputation but multiple reputations. These reputations can be conflicting in nature, reflecting the different perceptions of different stakeholders at different times. Company A might have an excellent reputation for the quality of its products, but a muddied reputation regarding its treatment of suppliers. Or it might be known as a generous supporter of, for example,

---

[1] Will Harvey, *Reputations at Stake* (Oxford University Press, 2023), page 17.

higher education, but with a dubious reputation regarding its environmental track record.

Further, the same stakeholders of a company, say customers, may have a different perception of a company depending on their geographic location and local culture. Scott Kronick is an American who has lived and worked in China for more than twenty-five years. Kronick is a Senior Advisor of Ogilvy Public Relations, Asia Pacific, and was formerly President and CEO of the firm in the Asia-Pacific region. He is also an Adjunct Professor at Beijing University's Guanghua School of Management. He said, 'A brand is not successful until the local market tells you so. We've had Chinese companies go to the U.S. or elsewhere and try to impose their views and their ways of doing things and it doesn't work. If you want to be successful, you need to understand the local environments and adjust your business to that way. In the early days, one of the earliest multinationals that was very successful here was IBM, led by Henry Chow, who became like the tech godfather in China. I used to say to the Chinese companies, take a page out of the multinationals that are doing well in China and replicate that in other markets. If IBM is successful because they hired a Chinese guy to lead the business and to localize the business, then maybe in the U.S. look at building some trust and confidence by hiring an American. You cannot just send people out into other markets and operate a business like you did in China. You have got to be much more open and flexible.'

Through another lens, customers in China will view an American company negatively if it makes a contentious remark in the eyes of local consumers, while its American customers are oblivious to the same issue (more on this later). Kronick said, 'I think companies can be true to their values and operate in both the United States and in China and be successful; but you need to be very sensitive. And I really don't think companies can be global if they do not have a China business.'

The principle of multiple reputations even applies to stakeholders within a company. Jonathan Adashek, IBM's Chief Communications Officer and SVP, Marketing and Communications, observed that 'A lot of places talk about the culture of IBM or the culture of Starbucks or the culture of pick your organization, and I would argue while there is an overarching umbrella that the leadership is trying to drive from a cultural perspective, there are in fact microcultures within any company. The culture that I have on my team in communications and marketing is similar but not identical to the culture that my colleague who runs our cloud business has, and if you go even deeper the culture that my leaders create on their teams is another microculture. You need to make sure you're respectful of those microcultures, including geographic ones. What works in India, versus what works in Austin, is going to be very different.'

Just as different stakeholders have varied perceptions of a particular company's strengths and failings, they also use their perceptions to inform the actions they take in relation to the company. Basil Towers is Principal of Tie-Stone. For forty years, he has advised organizations on how to become worthy of trust. He suggested that 'Reputations have varying degrees of value. In other words, they are not all as valuable as each other, or they are valuable at different times. Business leaders need to make decisions around which reputations are most important in the short term, the medium term, and the long term, and how would they know if they are getting it right or not, using business measures.' This is about priorities, choices, and trade-offs. In practice, it means addressing the difficult grey areas and managing the risks.

This idea of multiple stakeholders having multiple views of a company's reputation makes earning reputations all the more challenging. David Gallagher is Managing Partner of Next Practices Group and co-author of *Truth Be Told: How Authentic Marketing and Communications Wins in the Purposeful Age* (2021), a book that examines marketing and communications in the age of purpose. Gallagher noted, 'I think companies face a multitude of paradoxes, but the sharpest seems to be how to deliver profits to shareholders today while protecting value for all stakeholders tomorrow. The value of a business has different metrics for different stakeholders—say, investors, who might want a quick return; and suppliers, who may need a reliable long-term buyer— and while these needs don't have to be mutually exclusive, it can be difficult to find the right balance between the two.'

At this point, it is worth stating that the term 'reputation management' needs to be treated with caution and even scepticism. Companies are often tempted to employ consultants who make promises about improving their reputation, however the external (and internal) landscape is complicated and shifting and does not allow for a simplistic or singular approach to be taken. Too often, a CEO will call in their head of Corporate Affairs and suggest (or complain) that the company does not have the reputation it deserves. That is a false assumption, given that the responsibility for reputation does not solely lie with the Corporate Affairs department. More on this subject will be covered in chapter three. The other problem is that there is no single reputation. The business needs to understand that it has multiple reputations and that this in turn will impact decision-making at the business level, as well as its communications and stakeholder engagement.

Trade-Offs

Viewed from the outside, most companies project a position of certainty and clarity about their position, priorities, and strategic focus. And rightly so, no one wants to be confused or underwhelmed by how a corporation talks about itself. On those occasions when it does happen, and a lack of confidence in the minds of that company's stakeholders takes hold, negative developments are likely to follow.

There is no argument that the company must layout a coherent vision for its place in the world. Behind the scenes, however, the reality is that all companies must prioritize and make trade-offs, and these trade-offs often, if not always, have reputational consequences. There is only ever a finite amount of time, money, and people, and there are often competing priorities or goals that need to be balanced. A considered effort must be made regarding these options before a decision is made regarding the action that will be taken.

Often the trade-off process does not explicitly involve reputational considerations. The impact of extending hours of operation on one stakeholder group might be considered, for example on customers, but the impact on other audiences, for example on employees, might be neglected. An article by McKinsey, 'The Real Business of Business',[2] provides another example. It states, 'Consider employee stakeholders. A company that tries to boost profits by providing a shabby work environment relative to competitors, underpaying employees, or skimping on benefits will have trouble attracting and retaining high-quality employees. Lower-quality employees can mean lower-quality products, reducing demand and hurting reputation. More injury and illness can invite regulatory scrutiny and more union pressure. More turnover will inevitably increase training costs. With today's more mobile and more educated workforce, such a company would struggle in the long term against competitors offering more attractive environments.'

With that said, there are few business decisions made where reputational considerations is the paramount factor. Such considerations will be *a* factor, but not the only one. The leadership team might also choose to allow reputational damage because it either thinks it won't result in any meaningful damage to

---

[2] Marc Goedhart, Tim Koller, and David Wessels, 'The Real Business of Business' (McKinsey, 2015).

the business or there is a belief that the damage can be mitigated. For example, the company needs to close a line of business that may have considerable customer support but is not aligned with the long-term direction of the company. Customers may be displeased. Employees working in the business might be laid off. Both outcomes may damage reputation, however the company may decide its future will be brighter at the end of it. Assessing possible reputational damage in connection to a potential decision being made requires the Corporate Affairs function to paint a picture to senior leaders without just been seen as naysayers. They need to introduce informed insight to the table. Furthermore, Corporate Affairs should be around the table early enough to have an influence on the decision-making process.

Given that trade-offs are an unavoidable part of doing business, which in turn impact corporate reputations, those making the decisions must be asking the right questions. These boil down to:

- Is my reputation for [subject] important to this stakeholder group? If it's not, then it is a non-issue. If it is important, then what level of value should the company place on it?
- What do we want our reputation to be in this context? What is our desired reputation in order to influence how those stakeholders behave?
- If it is not there now, how do we change it or what might change it? Does a policy need to be changed? Or a process? Or do changes to the product need to be made? Do we have the right mix of people involved?

Towers illustrated this process using the example of regulatory affairs when he said, 'In a particular area of regulation, if the policy moves in a particular direction that will help or hurt the business; who are the specific stakeholders? Does their perception of us impact how they will behave and the decisions they make? What impact will this/they have on our business? Do we understand how we could move them from point A to point B to achieve the impact we need?'

The Need for Insight

Companies need to take an informed and clear view of the realities of people's lives with whom they are trying to influence behaviour. To properly understand the impact of decisions on stakeholder perceptions, an investment in intelligence is required.

In practice, this investment is rarely made properly. What do most companies do to help them understand their stakeholders? They use media monitoring to understand what is said about them and their competitors. They use social media analytics to gain an insight into online sentiment about the company. Customer research is commonly taken to support marketing decisions. Firms may also use reputation models offered by various firms in the marketplace. While all these actions have varying degrees of value, none of them provide a tailored, real-time look into stakeholder realities, needs, and expectations in a way that informs the decision-making process. There is no business case made that considers whether reputation is a factor for success.

The ability to generate foresight is relevant—building a picture and then working out whether what the company wants to achieve will lead a particular group of stakeholders to support them or not. Foresight is also about how society/contexts are likely to change and at what pace. Depending on the possible outcomes, this may mean different stakeholder behaviours, beliefs, and expectations.

Bernadette Murdoch, who leads the global Reputation Management Center of Excellence at CSL, a global biotechnology company, suggested that 'Reputation management is an iterative process that starts with understanding people's perceptions of the company. The best type of research is where you can look at a trend. For example, doing reputation tracking research monthly to understand how likely people are likely to trust the company and advocate (or criticize) the company without being asked. This can be done on a 5-point scale to understand how the company's reputation is changing based on what the company does or does not do. It can be conducted among the general public, government, and other stakeholders important to the business.'

In contrast to this approach, most research undertaken by companies tends to be backward looking in nature, rather than giving a sense of what might happen in the future. Reputation by its nature is intangible. In this respect, the effort should not just be on finding data but rather on generating intelligence and insight that helps the business interpret the data and make decisions. What are the indicators this stakeholder group is beginning to change how they interact with the company or perceive the company and what can we do about it? Furthermore, what is happening in the business? How are the business indicators—whatever they might be—being impacted by how people see us and therefore behave?

Alan Sexton is Managing Director, Head of Corporate Communications, at Balyasny Asset Management, and, prior to this role, was Chief Communications Officer at Prudential Financial. Sexton made the point that 'One of the things that successful political campaign managers understand is how to really listen to constituents, and how to blend quantitative and qualitative research to create messaging that sticks. The best pollsters have a genius for latching onto what's happening in the zeitgeist, and for discovering what's driving audience sentiment—the beliefs and emotions that shape opinion and behaviour.' Sexton went on to say (in reference to his time at Prudential Financial), 'We have built a custom listening programme for the company that combines analysis of earned media coverage, social media, and, to the extent permissible, conversations happening within the company. We use a slew of platforms and tools to gauge tone and sentiment, levels of engagement, audience reach, and so on.'

This is not just about using technology platforms, although clearly, they have a valuable role to play. In the view of Adam Wyldeck, Head of Communications & Public Affairs, Australia and New Zealand, at The Janssen Pharmaceutical Companies of Johnson & Johnson, 'There are various technologies that give us deep insights into how different stakeholders are perceiving us, what they're talking about, general sentiment, and so on. However, experienced communications professionals should have their finger on the pulse, and should be out there in the world connecting with our most important stakeholders on a regular basis. You can get all the data in the world, but sometimes looking a stakeholder in the eye and having a conversation with them is the best way to understand what they really think about you.'

IBM's Adashek said something along similar lines, 'Simply put, what is paramount is what do our clients and partners think? To understand their mindset requires a multi-pronged approach, including surveys, client advisory boards, information that comes in from the business, from sellers, and I am also spending a lot of time with clients.'

Many existing reputation models or studies simply do not capture the nuances of the real world and are too rigid to shed insight into who perceives whom and for what. Murdoch makes the point that 'Off-the-shelf reputation tracking services may not be as relevant to certain business models because of who they target (e.g., they may engage with retail consumers who are not actually users of the company's service. There also can be issues associated with the specificity of the questions such services ask).'

Towers, on the topic of reputation models, stated that, 'For decades, business leaders have been presented with reputation data that they cannot relate to specific reputation or specific value. This type of reputation data aggregates reputation rather than drilling down to which stakeholders who are critical to the business and what do they believe now, what influences their perceptions, and therefore what do we need to do about it?

The data that generates insight—and certainly foresight—has been missing. It has been far too rigid in the past and very crude, based on *a* model of reputation not *the* model of reputation for specific parts of the business.'

Putting Insight into Action

If a company knows what it wants to stand for, has captured insights into how its stakeholders perceive it, and then behaves accordingly, then it should be all set in having the reputation it desires. Correct? Not quite. It also must understand the ways in which it interacts with its various stakeholders and the narrative it wants to tell to accompany its actions. As David Waller and Rupert Younger state in their book, *The Reputation Game*, 'Your choice of which networks to invest time in, coupled with how you engage, make a huge difference.'[3] The authors go on to note: 'If you are not part of the right networks, it makes it harder for your actions to be appreciated and your reputation to take the shape it deserves.' On the importance of narratives, the authors observe that, 'How you speak about yourself, and particularly how you persuade others to speak about you on your behalf, is a vital element of the reputation game.'

Armed with how it wishes to be perceived, committed to behave in a way that is consistent with that objective, and understanding its different stakeholder groups, the company must then engage with those stakeholder groups in a way that helps it earn reputations over time. This requires constant engagement across a range of constituencies—the company needs to find the most effective platforms and tools to reach its stakeholders, both to give and receive information; to act and respond.

---

[3] David Waller and Rupert Younger, *The Reputation Game: The Art of Changing How People See You* (Oneworld, 2017).

Summary of Principles

- A company has more than one reputation and not all of its reputations are equal. Different reputations can be more valuable at different times. A company's leaders need to understand and agree which reputations matter to them most, when and to what end.
- Trade-offs are part of corporate decision-making. In the context of reputations, it is essential to ask the right questions when deciding to prioritize one action over another. Three questions to ask are:
  - Is my reputation for [*subject*] important to this stakeholder group in this situation?
  - What do we want our reputation to be in this context?
  - If it is not there now, how do we change it or what might change it?
- Having an informed understanding about what lies ahead necessitates data but also intelligence and insight.
- In addition to using technology, it is also important for Corporate Affairs professionals to be connecting with the company's stakeholders in person on a regular basis to understand how different stakeholders feel about the company at different times.
- To earn its reputations, the company must know how it wishes to be perceived, commit to behave in a way that is consistent with that objective, have a clear understanding of how its different stakeholder groups perceive it, and then proactively engage with those stakeholders.

2

The Value of Corporate Reputations

Why should anyone devote time to think about corporate reputations as they go about running a business? The commercial world is hard-edged, struggling against constant and arduous competitive forces to generate profitable growth year-after-year. The development of strategic plans and the subsequent assessment of progress is based on a wide range of quantitative factors—technology platforms, supply chains, cost of production, pricing strategy, product innovation, operating models, headcount, and so on. The subject of reputation, while implicitly ever-present, has been less overtly considered by business leaders (except during times of crisis). This, however, is changing. Corporate reputations will continue to become an ever-larger element of discussion in the boardroom and among the senior leadership team. To win in business requires nothing less.

Business leaders tend to only have a visceral experience of the value of reputation when things go wrong. It is then that the realization comes to the fore that having strong reputations is fundamental to a company's ability to effectively conduct its business. Achieving positive and trustworthy reputations is the basis for any company to enjoy customer loyalty, employee engagement, as well as a general permission by wider society to operate. This translates into a range of strategic and practical benefits.

Strategic benefits include things like the ability to:

- Make decisions designed to boost growth.
- Improve timeframes in which to deliver on objectives.
- Enhance opportunities to test and innovate.

On a practical level, a stronger reputation can deliver a range of valued outcomes, such as:

- The ability to attract high quality employees and keep them
- Repeat business with customers
- Attracting optimal partners
- Quicker time to market

Global Trends Impacting Corporate Reputations

The necessity of earning and keeping strong reputations has been further heightened by the emergence of a number of global trends. These trends have accelerated the evolution of how companies must think about the value of their reputations. There are many forces at play, but three are of particular note: rampant social media use, changing public expectations toward the private sector, and the impact of the COVID-19 pandemic.

First, and well documented, the ubiquitous presence of social media around the world has dramatically increased the stakes for all companies. The internet, the smart phone, the immense popularity of social media platforms (in both international and local markets) have given everyone a voice and an effective means to engage. The unrestricted flow of information means that reactions to bad news can be amplified, the retelling of news and information gives rise to distortions, fake news can be spread quickly, and activism instigated with blinding speed. Grievances can be aired without any filter by customers, but also a range of other stakeholders, including employees. On the flip side, social media continues to provide a potent means for corporations to be visible (to the level that suits their needs), to get their messages out to their constituencies, to engage with stakeholders and to express what they stand for. Whether creating value or causing damage, social media plays a crucial role when thinking about corporate reputations.

This is the case as much in Asia as it is in the West. In 2021, a major Hong Kong beverage company known as Vitasoy, was to find out the reputational impact of social media in brutal fashion. An employee of the company had circulated a memo offering condolences to the family of a worker who had stabbed a police officer the day before and who subsequently had committed suicide. The attack on the police officer took place on the day of the anniversary of the city's handover from British to Chinese rule and also around the first anniversary of the introduction of the National Security Law to Hong Kong. Authorities described the attacker as a 'lone-wolf domestic terrorist' and the leaking of the condolence memo resulted in an avalanche of angry online calls in China for a boycott of Vitasoy. The hashtag #Vitasoygetoutofthemainland quickly reached around 100 million views.[1] Given that Vitasoy generated somewhere in the vicinity of two-thirds of its revenue from mainland China, the business impact was acute. In the immediate aftermath, the company's share price 'fell by as much as 14.6%, the biggest single-day drop since its listing in 1994.'[2]

This episode could be seen as a unique situation that could never have been predicted. Yet, it exemplifies the colossal power of social media to shape perceptions of corporate reputations and influence behaviour accordingly. There are numerous other

---

[1] https://www.reuters.com/world/asia-pacific/hong-kong-drinks-company-vitasoy-faces-china-netizen-calls-boycott-2021-07-04/.

[2] *BBC News*, 'Vitasoy: Beverage maker's shares plunge after China calls for boycott', July 5, 2021, https://www.bbc.com/news/business-57717141.

examples of social media commentary and activism impacting corporate reputations for good or bad the world over.

The second macro factor that has heightened the importance of corporate reputations is the drop, even collapse, in trust levels that the general public has in government institutions[3] (although there are exceptions to this around the world) and a rising expectation that the private sector contribute to society beyond a focus on providing a profit-making product or service. Some critics have complained that a reliance on corporations to be involved in social issues is intertwined with 'woke' culture. Woke can be defined as those who are aware, especially of social problems such as racism and inequality.[4] The term is used derisively among right-wing conservatives for actions that they see as insincere or overzealous, including in relation to corporate ESG programmes. The fact remains that when thinking about the reputations of a particular company, customers, employees, investors, and other stakeholders will consider a wider array of factors relating to how that company runs its business than was the case in the past. Ramiro Prudencio, Partner and Global Director of Communications at McKinsey & Company, said, 'Broadly across many societies, many citizens are saying, "if my government cannot provide me with solutions, I'm going to shift up those expectations to the private sector." This presents a significant opportunity for companies to show how they build societal and stakeholder value. But it is also a serious challenge. Private sector organizations are not set up to address all societal challenges, and there are many challenges that must be addressed

---

[3] 2023 Edelman Global Trust Barometer, 'Institutions Out of Balance: Government Far Less Trusted than Business', p. 9. https://www.edelman. com/sites/g/files/aatuss191/files/2023-01/2023%20Edelman%20 Trust%20Barometer%20Global%20Report.pdf.

[4] https://dictionary.cambridge.org/dictionary/english/woke.

by the government. Leaders responsible for managing reputation must recognize and understand how to navigate these pressures.'

Prudencio went on to elaborate that, 'Historically, McKinsey made limited efforts to explain our mission and what we do to broader audiences. However, as society demands greater transparency and accountability, organizations must engage stakeholders proactively and tell their story. Today, our website provides extensive detail on our leadership, governance, social impact, and sustainability commitments. Our leaders are engaging the broader public regularly. And we have an important story to tell about how we help clients across the private, public, and social sectors. For example, during the pandemic, organizations in the private, public, and social sectors had to evolve and scale capabilities at an unprecedented pace. Governments were building supply and logistics chains to vaccinate entire countries. Vaccine manufacturers were scaling research, production, and distribution at an unprecedented speed. Companies were working to assure their teams adapted to remote work and could sustain business outcomes. Our decades of experience in production, supply chain management, organizational performance, and healthcare allowed us to bring insight and capability building to our clients. We also created sections on our website where we shared insights broadly for any organization to access. In recent years, our institutional communication has become much more proactive. We have embraced building a compelling and authentic narrative for the firm, which now drives our communication. Our aspiration, to accelerate sustainable and inclusive growth, underpins our communication and engagement broadly. With clients, we aim to be impact partners, bringing a wealth of expertise and capability building, and working alongside them on their greatest challenges and opportunities.' This evolution in stakeholder communications and engagement that Prudencio describes is taking place in many other companies across the world. While debate will continue regarding the degree to which the private sector is responsible for societal issues, it seems clear that companies will remain under pressure to contribute to issues where they can make a difference and also to communicate the reasoning behind those actions. An inability or unwillingness to do one or both has very real implications for the reputations of the company.

The third macro factor is the COVID-19 pandemic, which has increased the imperative for companies to be clear—in actions and words—about what they stand for when interacting with their stakeholders. During the height of the pandemic, we saw many companies take a range of actions to help their employees and their communities. These included work-from-home arrangements, provision of masks and disinfectant, promotion of health and wellness activities, support for colleagues in quarantine, financial donations to organizations on the front line of fighting the virus, and in certain cases altering manufacturing operations to produce Personal Protective Equipment for healthcare workers. The pandemic also placed a spotlight on the ability of corporations to be nimble in how they adapt to a sudden change to how people interacted with them. How smoothly the corporate could continue to offer its services had an impact on how its stakeholders perceived it. The pandemic further raised the bar in relation to social responsibility, with a closer focus placed on which companies were authentically contributing to fight the virus in the community, and which were lagging behind. Employees needed to be reassured and motivated, customers wanted to be engaged, suppliers needed to be accommodated. Regardless of their vantage point, people have taken more notice about what companies do when times get tough.

The Business Case for Reputations

Given the connection between reputation and value seems tightly bound, why do business leaders tend to remain focused on a raft of other operational and strategic matters that do not explicitly reference the subject of reputation itself? Basil Towers noted that 'All CEOs understand the value of reputation. But what they are not being helped to look at is how to prioritize what is the materiality of reputation on different elements of the business and what decisions do we need to make?' This is a useful insight. Too many CEOs are not seeing a business case being made that shows the specific impact that could result from a stakeholder group changing its behaviour because of its altered perception of the company.

Earning positive reputations provides the foundation for competitive advantage. And the risk of damage to corporate reputations threatens any firm's ability to operate and even exist. Alan Sexton eloquently summed it up: 'Reputation is linked to everything that's important these days; it's about responsible, ethical behaviour; it's about good products and services; it's caring for your employees and customers; it's about innovation and whether you're investing in building products for the future, how you engage with the world around you, whether your practices are sustainable, and whether you pay enough attention to the components of ESG.'

This is not a clear-cut mission with a definite end point. There are numerous variables that contribute to corporate reputations. The company's products and services, its ability to be nimble and innovate, its corporate governance, its people, its track record of community involvement are just a few examples. Further, the factors that influence perceptions will vary given the stakeholder group and the relationship they have or want with the company. They will also change over time given changing stakeholder contexts and agendas.

Reputation Risk

Just as a healthy reputation provides essential benefits, damage to that reputation poses critical risks. HSBC defines reputation risk as: 'Reputational risk is the risk of failure to meet stakeholder expectations as a result of any event, behaviour, action or inaction, either by HSBC itself, our employees or those with whom we are associated, that may cause stakeholders to form a negative view of the Group.'[5]

Most reputation risks are the outcome of *other* risks materializing. As such, they should already appear on company risk register, a database that proactively identifies, ranks, and gauges likely risks that could have a negative impact on the business. The risk register ensures there is oversight of risk prioritization and the effectiveness of risk mitigation and management strategies. In the past, a corporate risk register would be heavily weighted towards aspects of financial risk—credit risk, liquidity risk, interest rate risk, currency risk, and so on. Today, the number of risk categories has broadened, including to encompass environmental risk and social risk. There are a limited number of reputation risks that would not appear on the risk register. For example, it is unlikely that McDonald's had the behaviour of the CEO on its risk register prior to 2019. And yet that was the cause of his departure in that year, which in turn raised numerous questions regarding governance at the company. The board was forced to take legal action against the ousted CEO and the lengthy episode cast a long shadow over McDonald's reputation.[6] Or take the case of Tyson Foods Inc., whose CFO, John R. Tyson, the son of the chairman of the company's board of directors, was arrested for public intoxication and criminal trespassing one month into

---

[5] HSBC Website: https://www.hsbc.com/who-we-are/esg-and-responsible-business/managing-risk/reputational-risk.

[6] Andrew Ross Sorkin, Ravi Mattu, et al., 'McDonald's Former C.E.O. Pays for a Workplace Scandal', *The New York Times*, January 10, 2023, https://www.nytimes.com/2023/01/10/business/dealbook/mcdonalds-ceo-sec-firing.html.

his appointment. Tyson Foods is a family-founded company, but it's also a public company, and the arrest of Mr. Tyson created serious issues and heightened stakeholder interest in the governance of that company.[7] There are plenty of other examples of CEOs or senior executives behaving badly. While this book will argue the CEO has a key role to play in earning corporate reputations, a focus by the company on amplifying the personality of the CEO through the media can make a bad issue even worse.

The impact of reputational damage can be severe and long lasting. A hit to corporate reputation can mean dramatic declines in share price, less profitability, loss of sales, and higher employee turnover. The importance of reputation risk necessitates a systematic approach to its management. This should not be confused with crisis management or issues management. Simply put, crisis management involves dealing with a risk that has become reality. In contrast, reputation risk management is a continuous effort to identify, discuss, and act upon those risks that have the ability to cause reputational harm to the business.

McKinsey's Prudencio said, 'We take on potential reputational upside or downside with every engagement. Our risk waterfront is quite broad, especially as the firm grows. And the risk environment is very dynamic given shifts in the regulatory, political, economics, and societal expectations. To manage this risk, we have invested extensively in a cross-functional approach that includes the legal, compliance, client service, technology, and communications teams. From 2018 to 2022, we have invested over $700 million

---

[7] Sheryl Estrada, 'Tyson Foods CFO's arrest is a "critical moment" for corporate governance at the company', *Fortune*, November 8, 2022, https://fortune.com/2022/11/08/tyson-foods-cfo-arrest-critical-moment-corporate-governance-at-the-company/.

in risk management across the firm,[8] and will continue to invest
as we move forward. The goal is to have a full appreciation
of potential risk and reputational risk, and assure our work is
consistent with our values, applicable regulations, and societal
expectations.' Interestingly, Prudencio went on to explain that 'We
have a specific team, within the communications and marketing
function, that looks at reputational risk and they participate in
these reviews. Even if we're working within our protocols and
policies, there is a level of perceptual or reputational risk which
may sit outside the policies themselves. Given McKinsey's brand
recognition and leadership, and our commitment to our values,
requires we apply a very high bar and multidimensional lens to
assure we are protecting the firm.'

IBM's Adashek said, 'The executive leadership team, which
are the CEO's direct reports, meet on a regular basis and often
there is the expectation in the room that we're going to have a
reputational issue discussion on the decision we might make.'
Adashek also said, 'A big piece of this is trying to be proactively
reactive so that even if we don't have something 100% how do
we make sure we've got something that's 90% on things that we
see are potentially larger issues? How do we get in front of that
and how do we make sure we're managing those and we're ready
to answer those questions? With help from our Issues Preparation
and Response Team, we anticipate issues, map out potential
scenarios and sometimes even stop things from happening before
they happen.'

Brian Lott is Chief Communications Officer of Mubadala
Investment Company and also Chair of the Page Society. Lott
noted, 'At Mubadala, we have a management committee that is
focused on those corporate activities of which reputation is one,
and I sit on the management committee along with our Chief

---

[8] https://www.mckinsey.com/about-us/social-responsibility/esg-report-
overview.

Risk and Strategy Officer. Reputational issues are discussed every week and it's chaired by our deputy CEO.'

A *Harvard Business Review* paper[9] provides a useful analysis of corporate reputation risk. The paper suggests that three factors can affect the amount of reputation risk a company faces. These are as follows:

1. **Whether the company's reputation exceeds its true character.** The process of managing reputational risk should reflect the reality that reputation is a matter of perception—how people think of the company. This in turn means that while behaviour, for example, helps shape reputation, somewhat paradoxically, reputation can be distinct from the behaviour of the company. In other words, once a certain perception has been established, it can take time to change that perception (good or bad) despite what is actually happening at the company. If the reality of the situation facing a company is more negative than the reputation it enjoys, this represents a threat that must be mitigated. The reverse can be true also—that a company is doing great things or has changed its model, but its reputation does not reflect the reality. At AIA, it took some time after the company spun off from AIG via an IPO for its stakeholders to stop thinking of it as an American company. Regardless of its direction, this gap in perceptions can create major issues if it is not identified and managed appropriately.

2. **The degree to which external beliefs and expectations change.** In other words, if the expectations of a company's stakeholders shift, but the company does not realize or react to the shift, then it can be exposed to greater reputation risk. An obvious example is how

---

[9] Robert G. Eccles, Scott C. Newquist, and Roland Schatz, 'Reputation and Its Risks', *Harvard Business Review*, February 2007.

consumers and employees increasingly expect companies to contribute to a more sustainable society. This is an ongoing shift compared to expectations from past eras. Having said that, we live in a noisy world. There is a constant drone of noise, which does not necessarily equate to material impact on reputation. 'There can be a lot of noise for a few days or weeks, but it makes no difference to the people whose respect you need,' Towers noted. The reputational impact on stakeholders, and how material that is for the business, is what matters.

3. **The quality of internal coordination between different departments or functions.** If there are internal breakdowns in communication and collaboration, then it becomes possible for one part of the company to create expectations that another group fails to meet. The authors of the paper cite the classic example of the marketing department of a software company launching 'a large advertising campaign for a new product before developers have identified and ironed out all the bugs: The company is forced to choose between selling a flawed product and introducing it later than promised.'

The existence of reputation risk should be an inherent motivator for companies earning reputations. Having a track record of good behaviour and of building enduring relationships with key stakeholders provides a potent platform for not only mitigating reputational damage, but for emerging from the other side of the risk materializing with your corporate reputations in stronger shape than ever.

Summary of Principles

- Having positive and accurate reputations underpins any company's ability to operate successfully on a sustainable basis. This reality will continue to become a larger element of explicit discussion in the boardroom.

- The imperative to earn and protect corporate reputations has been further heightened by several macro factors including: social media, evolving societal expectations of business, and the Covid-19 pandemic.

- There are many variables that contribute to corporate reputations. The factors that influence perceptions vary depending on the specific stakeholder and the relationship they have or want to have with the company. They will also vary over time given changing stakeholder contexts and agendas.

- The ability to proactively manage risk is key to business performance—as these risks are examined, their reputational impact should be clearly addressed. Generally speaking, a number of factors contribute to the possibility for reputation risk:

  - Once a certain perception of a company has been established, it can take time to change that perception (good or bad) despite what is actually happening at the company.

  - The expectations of a company's stakeholders shift, but the company does not realize or react to the shift.

  - Internal breakdowns in communication and collaboration.

3

Who Is Responsible for Corporate Reputations?

If this question was asked to a cross section of people at any sizeable company, a common response would be the PR department. It's not unreasonable to think that some colleagues have that expectation. They would say Corporate Affairs has the responsibility to tell the story of the company, to make sure the company has the appropriate share of voice and to position the company in the best possible light.

And yet, many drivers of reputation—product, customer service, pricing, partnerships, etc.—are *not* directly related to communications. As Basil Towers stated, '80 per cent of reputation is not about communications. It is the products, the policies, the delivery of customer service and so on. However, with that said, communications is incredibly important, and there is a role for communications in every stage of the process of earning and protecting reputation.'

Corporate Affairs has a vital role as the guardian of corporate reputation, but the act of earning reputations is a business-wide responsibility and the firm's leadership is accountable for that.

The Role of the Board

In its report Boardroom Best Practice, Spencer Stuart, a global executive search and leadership consulting firm, stated that

'Regardless of governance structure, the key responsibility of all boards is to balance the interests of the company, shareholders and other stakeholders by ensuring long-term growth that is sustainable and profitable. This involves oversight of the executive through ongoing active questioning, constructive challenge and support.'[1]

It is safe to assume that in past eras the subject of reputation was not an explicit agenda item for the board of directors. Board meeting agendas are traditionally focused on items such as business performance, financial reporting, compliance issues, regulatory matters, renumeration, and so on. Of course, these items remain at the heart of good governance and as such will always be embedded on the board's agenda. Today, however, through executing its responsibility to supervise the management and good governance of the company, the board has an essential role to play in ensuring that the leadership team recognizes and acts upon the impact of reputations on the business. Strong boards will both prompt and assist their executive teams to incorporate a reputation-focused perspective into the formulation of corporate strategy, major decision-making, and resource allocation.

In his excellent 2022 study[2] into the board's trust role, Basil Towers proposed that the board should oversee the process of answering four questions regarding corporate trustworthiness:

1. Whose trust does the company need?
2. What is the value of that trust to your business?
3. Where is the company prioritizing its efforts, deciding what action to take today, what tomorrow, and what you might choose not to do at all?
4. How, exactly, will the business earn the trust of those who matter most to you?

---

[1] https://www.spencerstuart.com/research-and-insight/boardroom-best-practice-chapter-1.

[2] https://www.tie-stone.com/download-reports.

Towers went on to note that boards, as they have explicit discussions on the role of trustworthiness, must advise the Chief Executive throughout, help the Chief Executive keep their focus firmly on the long-term, where the worth of trust will be realized, and pose the question: is our Chief Executive making our company more, or less, trustworthy? and act accordingly. While Towers study is focused specifically on perceptions and beliefs of trustworthiness (including the reputation for being worthy of specific trust), in the context of a discussion about reputations these questions remain valid for any board to consider.

Ian Stone has been an independent non-executive director of the Chinese technology giant, Tencent, since 2004. Among other business lines, Tencent developed and launched WeChat, the Chinese super app that combines instant messaging, social media, e-commerce, and mobile payments. The app today has more than one billion users. Stone agrees corporate reputations must be considered at board level. He said, 'At Tencent, which is now twenty-four years old, what might have enhanced its reputation at the beginning may not be the same as today. Things change as you grow and become bigger. In China, public sentiment can very quickly turn against any company. If everything works, then you can get some very positive support. If you take that for granted, you can run into problems.'

In relation to the need for a whole-of-company approach to reputation, Stone, who sits on the Audit Committee of the Tencent board, offered a specific observation. He noted, 'At any large company, internal control and auditing is critical, and this is separate and independent from external financial auditors and from internal management structure. Tencent has developed a state-of-the-art internal audit system. This allows the board of directors to see what's happening on the front line. Internal audit has access to every part of the business. They do fifty to sixty big projects a year and many follow-up ones. They present to the Audit Committee every quarter and show where things have not been done properly or rules are not in place or not being complied with, or simply that mistakes can be made. As a board director, this enables me to see whether things are being done the way that management says they are being done and that things are working properly. This audit team themselves have "right or wrong" in their mind, rather than explicitly thinking about reputational implications, but from the board perspective, their work enables us to see issues quickly and know they are being managed in a way that will mitigate any reputational damage.'

The Role of the CEO

Mark Tucker was Group Chief Executive and President of AIA Group Limited from 2010 to 2017, after which he was appointed Group Chairman of HSBC Holdings plc. Tucker is well renowned for his sharp commercial acumen, his clear view for how to manage and grow large companies, his eye for detail, and the unrelenting pace he sets. At AIA, Tucker devoted significant time to not only overseeing and advancing the Group's business agenda, but also to ensuring its stakeholders had an accurate understanding of AIA's vision and strategy as well as the progress it was making. It was inspiring to work with such a successful CEO who inherently understood the power of reputations to enable business growth.

The CEO is integral to the overall reputation of the firm, making decisions that set the tone for how the entire company interacts with its stakeholders. Put another way, the role of the CEO when thinking about corporate reputations is broadly two-fold: (1) to understand and prioritize the reputations that matter to short- and long-term performance (and in doing so, to set an agreed degree of appetite for reputation risk), and (2) to represent the company to best effect in the interactions the company has with all its stakeholders and, in doing so, to set an example for the rest of the organization to follow.

The first responsibility relates to the concept of trade-offs discussed in chapter one. Is the CEO mindful about the trade-offs that needs to be made when making decisions about where the company is going to focus, how it is going to go about its business, and what steps need to be taken to operate successfully in the short, medium, and long term? Those decisions will help determine the company's various reputations among its ecosystem of stakeholders. The CEO sits at the centre of the enterprise that must engage with this ecosystem in a way that creates the desired reputations, which in turn deliver business value. The degree to which a CEO is actively interested and concerned about the impact of business decisions on all stakeholders who matter for success will in turn impact the trajectory, up or down, of the company's reputations.

How a CEO represents the company varies greatly depending upon the person in the seat. Contrary to popular belief, CEOs are also human beings! They have different personalities and varying levels of comfort for putting themselves 'out there' in the public domain. Some will have a more visible presence inside the company. Regardless of personality type, the CEO has an unquestionable responsibility to embody the purpose, values, and vision of his or her company. With that said, it is also worth making the point that the responsibility for the reputation of the company cannot be left at the feet of the CEO alone. IBM's Adashek summed it up well when he said, 'I think it's instrumental (the CEO's impact on corporate reputation) because it goes back to that point of creating the culture and through leading from the top, but it can't be a one-person show. It's got to take everybody together to tackle these challenges and to make it a priority.'

Sexton provided a similar view: 'It's now more generally understood that reputation is the sum of the actions and behaviours that you exhibit as an organization and that, as a result,

managing reputation truly has become an integral part of overall
business management, as well as a team sport.'

The Role of Frontline Managers

Far away from boardrooms, strategy presentations, and whiteboards
full of charts and numbers, those at the coal face of the organization
have a tremendous impact on how the customer views the company.
There is little point in touting the company as being committed to
providing outstanding customer service if the customer service team
is not willing or able to bring that to life.

Adashek said, 'One of the ways we empower our sales
colleagues is through a product-first approach. We organised both
our sales structure and communications structure to lean in on
key products and invest time in a two-way relationship between
Marketing/Comms and Sales: 1) teaching them how to best talk
about our products, and 2) listening to what they are hearing from
clients so we can adapt our strategy and messaging.'

Frontline managers have a crucial role to play in the reputations
of any company. They are a visible employee segment that will
have a sizable impact on how things get done in the company
and in reinforcing the messages set at the top of the firm to the
employee base.

The Role of Employees

The attitudes, behaviour, and commitment of the employee base
has an enormous influence on the reputations of any company.
They make decisions daily that affect how it's seen by those inside
and outside of the firm. Adashek reinforced this when he said,
'IBMers are our best brand ambassadors. We've got roughly
275,000 IBMers around the world and if we're not starting with
them when we tell our stories, we're failing.'

This is very wise. At AIA, the launch of a new brand
promise (Healthier, Longer, Better Lives) started with employee

communications. We wanted them to understand the meaning behind it, to be actively involved in the programme and to be passionate advocates of it. We created new content that allowed employees to understand what Healthier, Longer, Better Lives was all about, and we also produced new experiences founded on health and well-being for employees to participate in. We knew if we could allow our people to become familiar with the new brand promise, to embrace it and help activate it, then the foundation for its enduring success would be strong.

On the flip side of the coin, employees can become among a company's most vocal critics even to the point of organized activism. Among many examples, in 2019, a group of Amazon employees formed a group they called Amazon Employees for Climate Justice. The group instigated a number of protests, including walkouts, as it lobbied Amazon to take more action on climate change.[3]

The quality of the work produced by employees, how staff members conduct themselves as they carry out their duties, their willingness to collaborate to get things done are some of the ways by which employees impact the reputations of the company. Just as employees have a key role in earning a positive reputation for their company, those colleagues that do not have a good experience will deter others from seeing the company as an attractive employment destination.

The Role of Corporate Affairs

The Corporate Affairs function has an increasingly vital opportunity to help organizations navigate their futures. Although earning and protecting reputations requires a whole of company effort, the corporate affairs function has a particularly critical role

---

[3] Sareen Habeshian, 'Hundreds of Amazon workers stage climate protest walkout', *Axios*, May 2023, https://www.axios.com/2023/06/01/amazon-workers-protest-climate.

to play. The function has moved well beyond the responsibility for issuing one directional communication to become stewards that help the company navigate uncertain and volatile landscapes. One of the biggest challenges to corporate reputation is the lack of understanding by the leadership of the organization of the interplay between issues, stakeholders, and business interests, and the need to manage that on a multilateral basis.

As Towers noted, 'A good Corporate Affairs function gives a business that broader view, bringing the outside world in. It is the voice of challenge and change, monitoring the ever fluid context, and divining how an organisation is perceived by all of those whose trust it depends on. In doing so, Corporate Affairs becomes a crucial part of the machinery of a business. It sees and addresses blind spots, divides what matters in the world around you from what doesn't and holds a business to the standards set by the outside world and to its own promises.'

Unpacking Tower's assessment, Corporate Affairs delivers value in a range of ways:

- It, among all corporate functions, should have the most holistic view of the external and internal landscape— to understand and present back the mindsets of the company's stakeholders—and be able to synthesize what that means for the corporate agenda.
- It uses informed insight to enable the company to move forward in a way that considers the expectations of its multiple stakeholders.
- It consistently and carefully looks at the strategic and operational decision-making process to consider reputational implications and what this might mean for the company.
- It is an adviser regarding the company's decisions, actions, and behaviour as well as how it communicates and engages with its stakeholders, to enable specific outcomes towards optimum reputations.

Sexton described the role of Corporate Affairs as follows: 'I see Corporate Affairs functions acting as something of a diplomatic corps within large organisations. Let's consider what a diplomatic service does. Its members must be excellent at listening, intelligence gathering, and real-time analysis. They must constantly be aware of their surroundings and be able to provide insights about what's happening on the ground, why it's happening, and how the dynamics are changing in real time. They must be experts in synthesizing those insights and conveying them to decision-makers. They must be able to participate in difficult discussions where there is disagreement because of a conflict of interests or conflicting priorities or agendas. They also need to be able to constantly evaluate their environment, preserving relationships but not compromising principles, because they also need to be seen as honest brokers by the people with whom they interact. And, of course, they need to be excellent communicators and be able to execute flawlessly when needed. If you think about that in a business context, Corporate Affairs teams must possess similar skills and perform similar work. They need to be able to understand and traverse a complex and constantly evolving ecosystem of stakeholders, issues, and business interests, both within their organizations and in the outside world. They must be excellent at connecting dots, gaining and maintaining trust among a variety of audiences, and navigating the trickiest of issues. And they must be skilled at influencing, persuading, and communicating. I believe the most sophisticated Corporate Affairs functions will increasingly resemble diplomatic services in years to come.'

We live in a time where the value of Corporate Affairs is not only clear but a pressing necessity. The Corporate Affairs function does not only have a seat at the table—it has the most volatile seat and whomever is sitting in it must be well prepared. The remaining chapters of the book are geared towards some of the dimensions through which Corporate Affairs can advise, act, and guard in pursuit of helping achieve optimum corporate reputations.

Summary of Principles

- Corporate Affairs has a vital role as the guardian of corporate reputations; however, the act of earning/protecting reputations is a business-wide responsibility.
- The CEO is integral to the overall reputation of the firm, but that person cannot do it alone.
- Boards increasingly want to understand how the executive team is incorporating reputation issues/risks into the strategic decision-making process.
- Frontline managers have a sizable impact on how things get done in the company and in reinforcing the messages set at the top of the firm to the wider employee base.
- The attitudes, behaviour, and commitment of employees has an enormous influence on the reputations of any company.
- The Corporate Affairs function has moved well beyond the responsibility for issuing one directional communications to become valued advisors that help the company navigate uncertain and volatile landscapes.

Part Two

Earning Corporate Reputations

4

The Role of Purpose in Defining Corporate Reputations

All companies have their history, their track record of achievement, and, in some ways, even their own mythology. More than ever, their stated purpose is also at the core of their reputations. The concept of corporate purpose has passionate advocates and vocal sceptics. Is 'purpose' truly a concept of substance when thinking about corporate performance and progress? Is being purpose-driven really a driver of profitability?

In the book *Putting Purpose Into Practice: The Economics of Mutuality*, the authors argue that 'most successful organizations are those that choose to be driven by a sense of purpose that transcends self-interest—a sense of purpose that seeks to develop reciprocally beneficial obligations amongst a wide variety of relevant stakeholders—a sense of purpose that can transform business performance for the benefit of people, planet and profit (in that order)—in other words, mutuality.'[1]

A point of contention here is the issue of purpose versus profits. Ranjay Gulati is the Paul R. Lawrence MBA Class of 1942 Professor of Business Administration at Harvard Business

---

[1] Colin Mayer and Bruno Roche, *Putting Purpose Into Practice, The Economics of Mutuality* (Oxford University Press, 2021).

School. He wrote that, 'as powerful as purpose is when fully mobilized inside a company, it remains fragile. Operating in a world where commercial logic reigns, leaders can find it difficult to run businesses according to both commercial and social logics. Confronted with the constant need to make painful short- and long-term trade-offs, many leaders can't sustain it, and commercial logic wins.'[2] In the same article, Professor Gulati went on to explain, 'The leaders who go deepest on purpose aren't those who push the social logic at all costs. They attend at all times to both the social and commercial logics.'

This book contends that, as outlined in chapter one, businesses will always need to make trade-offs in their course of business. Companies have a duty to their investors and shareholders to provide a return on investment, and they also have a duty to their other stakeholders, including their local communities, to act in a purposeful way that results in value beyond net income. The principles of purpose and profit can be concurrently adopted, with a degree of practicality applied to both along the way. A simple definition of corporate purpose, that is consistent with this position, is 'why the business exists, contributing something positive to people, and/or the planet.'[3]

The overlay of purpose with corporate activity is here to stay in some form or another. Having a basic yet informed amount of knowledge in this area is required for anyone who is interested in earning and protecting corporate reputations.

---

[2] Ranjay Gulati, 'The 'Do-Gooder's Dilemma': Why purpose-driven companies can't lose focus on profits', *Fast Company*, 2022, https://www.fastcompany.com/90698467/the-do-gooders-dilemma-why-purpose-driven-companies-cant-lose-focus-on-profits.

[3] John O'Brien and David Gallagher, *Truth Be Told* (Kogan Page, 2021).

How Did We Arrive at This Point?

The focus on corporate purpose has been steadily growing for much of the last twenty years. In 2009, Simon Sinek published *Start with Why: How Great Leaders Inspire Everyone to Take Action*, a bestselling book that (among other things) argued that great companies understand why they are in business—that their purpose, or their WHY, is what guides their path forward. The discussion around corporate purpose has markedly accelerated in the last five years. In 2019, Business Roundtable, the leading U.S. business group, issued a statement that encapsulated a major shift away from the conventional view that maximizing shareholder value is at the core of the corporate identity towards a definition that encompasses other stakeholders.[4] In his 2019 annual letter to CEOs, Larry Fink, CEO of BlackRock, wrote that 'Purpose is not a mere tagline or marketing campaign; it is a company's fundamental reason for being—what it does every day to create value for its stakeholders. Purpose is not the sole pursuit of profits but the animating force for achieving them.'[5] A 2022 Deloitte survey found that 'over half of employees (62%) consider an organisation's purpose before deciding to join, with over a third (36%) saying that an organisation's purpose was just as important as their salary and benefits package.'[6]

---

[4] 'Business Roundtable Redefines the Purpose of a Corporation to Promote 'An Economy That Serves All Americans'', *Business Roundtable*, 2019, https://www.businessroundtable.org/business-roundtable-redefines-the-purpose-of-a-corporation-to-promote-an-economy-that-serves-all-americans.

[5] https://www.blackrock.com/corporate/investor-relations/2019-larry-fink-ceo-letter.

[6] https://www2.deloitte.com/uk/en/pages/press-releases/articles/majority-of-employees-consider-an-organisations-purpose-before-choosing-to-join.html.

Mark Kennedy is senior partner at Kantar, a data, insights, and consulting company. He suggested that 'Once upon a time large corporates didn't need a purpose because their purpose was for the benefit of the nation—so for example, Ford made cars and helped to build Detroit.' While that might be true, as companies over the last century in particular have expanded across the world, and as there have been negative impacts on local communities and the environment, many people have looked beyond the product and service being offered to question the nature of corporations. In short, companies are being held to a higher standard. Kennedy went on to say, 'In addition, as governments have failed to deliver around social cause, then people have looked to large-scale companies, who are seen as having more muscle and expertise to get things done. Once, contributing to economic growth was enough. Then, people started to question the real cost of the growth to society, and more importantly, different factions of society. Today, people have enough choice to completely abandon a previously loved brand if it does not align with their personal values and has a negative impact on society. Now, people ask what the cost of the activity is to society?'

Around the world, climate change, income and gender inequalities, as well as the increase in both communicable and non-communicable diseases are some of the major factors giving rise to a new social awareness. This in turn has seen multiple stakeholders to ask (and expect) many companies to demonstrate and be accountable for their social impact. As stated by John O'Brien and David Gallagher in their book *Truth Be Told*, we have 'entered a new purpose-driven business era because new voices, not least some powerful investors and ever more consumers, are demanding much greater emphasis on determining why a business exists and the values and ethics through which the business is led. The assessment of whether a business is a good business to work for, invest in or purchase from is now as much determined by its impact on society and the environment, as a return of value of all stakeholders, rather than shareholders alone.'[7]

The Validity of Corporate Purpose

In fact, corporate purpose has become so popular that it has been accused by some critics of being, to speak plainly, a load of rubbish. The term 'purpose-washing' speaks to those companies who talk in platitudes about their purpose for being but take actions with no real connection to said purpose. Coca-Cola's corporate purpose is to 'Refresh the world. Make a difference'[8]. Critics of the company argue that Coke has played a role in contributing to global health issues such as obesity and diabetes. Coca-Cola has also long been under fire for its handling of plastic waste and its use of water resources in different parts of the world. While Coca-Cola will defend its practices and impact in these areas, the fact remains that its purpose is open to being critiqued as glib or generic by certain stakeholder groups. And if the corporate purpose is too generic, it becomes meaningless.

On the other hand, done well, the articulation of corporate purpose is a very meaningful action. Gallagher suggested that 'A defined purpose gives organizations a "north star" for making decisions on how it operates, focuses resources, relates to stakeholders and ultimately how it performs, which in turn defines its reputation in the marketplace.' If everyone in the business is clear about the purpose of the business, and that purpose is one that resonates, it will dictate the decisions the company makes, the actions it takes and the behaviour of employees of the company.

Stuart A. Spencer is Group Chief Marketing Officer at AIA Group. Spencer noted that 'We know that now, more than ever,

---

[7] John O'Brien and David Gallagher, *Truth Be Told* (Kogan Page, 2021), Page 66.

[8] https://www.coca-colacompany.com/about-us/purpose-and-vision.

consumers make choices based not only on their needs but also their affinity or connection to the organisation. Companies that clearly articulate what they stand for—what their purpose is—provide greater levels of transparency, authenticity and legitimacy. I think that is a powerful force in the market and it's a powerful marketing force as well. Those organisations that aren't clear will make it more difficult for consumers to choose and make decisions concerning why should you buy from me? I think consumers are seeking clarity on values, not just value.'

AIA's Purpose is to help people live Healthier, Longer, Better Lives.[9] The decision to adopt 'Healthier, Longer, Better Lives' as AIA's Purpose was driven by several foundational benefits:

- The concept of living a healthier, longer, better life is inherently relevant: the rise of non-communicable diseases (and subsequently communicable disease with the Pandemic) made the underlying idea 'how to be healthier' very topical.

- The concept is attractive: giving people services, insights, education, and inspiration about how to live healthier is a concept that everyone can get behind.

- The purpose helps drive the strategic direction of the company: for example, in 2022, AIA established a new pan-Asian Health InsurTech business, which it calls 'Amplify Health', as a joint venture with Discovery Group. The joint venture aspires to be a leading digital health business that improves the health and wellness outcomes of patients across Asia.[10] Spencer said, 'Amplify Health is just one example of our purpose driving the Group's strategic direction. If our purpose is to enable Healthier,

---

[9] https://www.aia.com/en/about-aia/our-purpose#:~:text=Our%20 Purpose%20is%20to%20help,what%20AIA%20has%20to%20offer.

[10] https://www.aia.com/en/media-centre/press-releases/2022/aia-group-press-release-20220215.

Longer, Better Lives, AIA's public declaration that it is going to be investing in health insurance expansion as well as beyond insurance into provision, administration and technology is a powerful illustration of how we are trying to enable consumers to embark on a journey of health and wellness.'

- It is a potent platform for activation, rather than only words: having a purpose to help people live healthier, longer, better lives enables the company to demonstrate its purpose through potent and differentiating actions. As Spencer noted, 'It is not merely an articulation of purpose; there must be an authentic demonstration of purpose in everything the organisation does, so the statement of purpose needs to be embedded throughout the organisation. Everyone needs to be clear within the organisation about what the organisation's purpose is and how they as individuals can play a role to deliver on that purpose. The organisation has to have proof points that it does business in such a way that it delivers on its purpose otherwise it's entirely hollow and illegitimate and merely a ploy is to generate business. Purpose driven companies are clear about how their purpose must be applied day-in-day-out to the activity of the company.'

Innovation is at the heart of a purpose-driven company, because without being innovative, it is very hard to continue to have a positive impact, while making a profit. Kennedy said, 'People want to buy from companies that make a positive impact. There is however an aspiration-action gap, in other words, people are aspiring to live a more sustainable life, but it is not necessarily showing up in their actions. One of the failings of corporates is that they can blame consumers for it. But in fact, it is caused by a lack of innovation on the part of the company—the ability of companies to deliver new offerings that work for consumers. It is a supply side problem. This is where purpose becomes very important—a socially orientated purpose becomes a driver of innovation, rather than waiting for consumer to tell you what to do.'

A Case Example: 'Helping Britain Prosper'

Llyods Banking Group has a history spanning more than three hundred years. It is the largest UK retail and commercial financial services provider and incorporates a number of brands, including Lloyds Bank, Halifax, Bank of Scotland, and Scottish Widows. Its stated purpose is Helping Britain Prosper. Andrew Walton is Chief Sustainability Officer & Chief Corporate Affairs Officer for Lloyds Banking Group. Walton shared a number of insights into the Group's purpose. The following passages are in Walton's own words.

How Lloyds Thinks about Purpose

We are careful about how we talk about things like purpose and values, because in the C-Suite and Corporate Affairs they tend to be used as hard nouns, almost as tangible objects. But you go into the outside world and tell someone like your mother that you're launching a purpose, and they have no idea what you're talking about.

We don't use 'Helping Britain Prosper' with anyone other than our corporate audiences. 'Helping Britain Prosper' is also not a strap line underneath the name, Lloyds Banking Group. We are a multi-brand business. Our customers see and know our brands such as Lloyds Bank or Halifax or Bank of Scotland. Our corporate purpose statement is used in association with the Group brand to talk primarily to licence-to-operate focused audiences—investors, politicians, and, to some extent, opinion formers and broader public. We are mindfully working with our marketing colleagues to make sure we don't create any confusion because each of our brands have their own marketing strap line, and I think it makes sense that they do so.

It's an expression of our social utility—what are we here for? I think that banks have a strong social utility, at a fundamental sense they are a social good.

How Purpose Drives Strategy

It's absolutely at the heart of our strategic planning. We do not have a separate department of purpose. It is not Environmental, Social and Governance (ESG). It is not any sort of offset against the ability to operate profitably in a separate part of the business. Clearly sustainability in the transition to net zero is critical to our strategy because we finance some of the highest-emitting areas in the UK. The areas that are most problematic to emissions in the UK are houses, cars, and agriculture, and we are the biggest bank funding all three of them. So, transition to net zero is at the heart of our sustainability and that's inherent to helping Britain prosper.

When Charlie Nunn, our CEO, arrived in 2021, he did not start with a strategic review—he started with a review of our purpose, and it was a retest. It was established as an expression in 2014 and accompanied the repayment to the taxpayer after the earlier rescue of the bank in 2009. Charlie looked at it, and we gauged whether it needed to be adjusted or amplified in any sense. That was step one, and then the business strategy came after that. We do not believe in 'aligning strategy to purpose'—they should not merely be aligned, they should be the same thing. We have a purpose-centred strategy where everything we do links back to our purpose—is this helping Britain prosper or not? If it isn't, then we shouldn't be doing it.

Purpose and Reputation

When I am rehearsing with the CEO or the board, I will make the challenge, how is that helping Britain prosper? Interestingly, when our external audiences talk to us, or are not happy about something, they very rarely raise this question in this way. They usually benchmark us against one of our retail brands. For example, Lloyds Bank talks about 'Being By Your Side'. This brand positioning has more profile and so tends to be more focused on by our customers, which is completely understandable. But 'Helping Britain Prosper' helps us with engagement and advocacy, it is not in many senses a public benchmark. We are helped by the fact that it is not a corporate portmanteau—it is easy to understand and doesn't raise the cynical hackles. And it is hugely important internally and reawakened pride in the organization when it was launched coming out of the financial crisis.

Measurement

We measure a lot of data to get insight into what our audiences think about us. One of those is an association metric: which bank do you most associate with Helping Britain Prosper? It is actually a very important one because it's a test of whether that mental linkage is being made. My team is measured on this, and we do it with all our audiences including political stakeholders and also the media. We ask a lot of other questions of course, but this one is an important jumping off point.

We have a variety of internal metrics against which senior leaders are held to account. At various points we have had published public targets for lending or societal impact, as part of what we called the Prosper Plans, and these have been successful that ran alongside our Strategic Reviews. These included things like gender balance hiring targets, lending targets for first-time buyers, supporting social house building. Our view is now that they lie at the heart of our strategy and that the separate plans looked like they ran alongside it, which is why we now have them as scorecard targets for leaders.

How to Articulate Corporate Purpose?

Deciding how to articulate the company's corporate purpose and bringing it to life is not easy. The process to do so can often give rise to a certain level of pushback and scepticism within the organization. This is understandable—the process of forming an explicit purpose statement should be a rigorous one. It is healthy for the company to ask itself to satisfy a wide range of questions as part of its internal debate. These include: is this moving our focus away from what makes us a viable business in the first place? Are we in danger of lessening our ability to achieve optimum profitability? Are we opening ourselves up to future criticism when times get tough? The path towards achieving certainty and confidence in a newly defined corporate purpose will always entail a degree of tension.

For those companies struggling to land on a purpose that works for them, key considerations to think about include:

1. **What do people need (and don't have) on a human level that your company can help address?** This speaks to the relevance of the corporate purpose to stakeholders. Is it too esoteric? Is it too generic? Is it too hollow? Finding a good answer to the question of 'need' necessitates the active involvement of a range of stakeholders, both within and outside of the company. Capturing a wide range of views will help to test assumptions, identify areas of potential weakness and encourage buy-in to the process being undertaken. As this process unfolds, the company should remain laser-focused on ensuring that its purpose is inseparably linked to the core of what makes that company successful in the first place.

2. **Is the purpose something that people at your company would feel genuinely energized by?** Done well, a corporate purpose galvanizes employees. People want to be part of an organization that is making a positive impact. The corporate purpose should capture the imagination of colleagues, injecting momentum and energy into the workforce. If employees do not connect with the company's purpose on a personal level, it is hard to see how that purpose can be effective. Spencer observed, 'Our ability to attract and retain younger talent is heavily dependent on their affinity with our purpose. Younger people want to want to work for a purpose-led organisation; they care about working for an organisation that's doing good, that's making a difference, that stands

for something. Perhaps in the past young people wanted to work for any place where they could make the most amount of money as soon as possible, but I don't think that's the case any more. What I am learning consistently is that the new generation of employees are much more concerned about agility, flexibility, purpose, and lifestyle. Can I look at my face in the mirror in the morning and say I am working for a good company that cares? This is something that I am hearing more and more.'

3. **How does the purpose enable your company to generate profitable growth?** This speaks to the mindset that being purpose-driven is not a marketing or feel-good exercise. It should represent a strategic advantage that underpins growth. Spencer made the point, 'There's ample research that indicates that corporate purpose is most important to younger people and so then you really learn that new customer acquisition is very dependent on purpose; growing the customer base where people choose you versus somebody else means what the company stands for is the critical point of differentiation that drives the purchasing decision. The fact is that we work in a very commodified marketplace and AIA can stand out because of the brand and what we stand for as an organisation.'

4. **Is your purpose timeless?** There is little point having a corporate purpose that is finite in nature. A balance needs to be struck between finding a purpose that endures while also being able to credibly demonstrate progress and impact over time.

5. **Can your purpose lead to credible actions rather than just words?** Companies need to ensure that their purpose is specifically aligned with their business strategy and that their actions are consistent with their purpose. Corporate purpose must be integrated throughout the

entire breadth and depth of the company—it's culture, its operations, its marketing programme, the people it hires, and so forth. The impact of any stated purpose needs to be consequential in real life. Gallagher observed, 'A compelling, meaningful purpose has two essential qualities: it must speak to people—human beings—in a way that is authentic and aligned with their needs (think of Maslow's hierarchy) and it must be true to how the company actually operates, inside and out. Otherwise it's an empty slogan.'

Keeping Purpose Alive

Producing a meaningful corporate purpose is hard. Ensuring that your stakeholders care about it over time is the real challenge. The commitment of the CEO and the senior leadership team is crucial. Gallagher said, 'I actually believe the CEO and senior leadership have no greater responsibility than to ensure the company "walks the talk" and minds the "say-do" gap in its operations. You can't commission a management consultancy to come up with a purpose statement and then go back to business as usual.'

Corporate Affairs must help to both keep purpose top of mind for internal stakeholders, as well as finding ways to communicate the impact of actions being taken as the company pursues its purpose. Chapter five looks at employee communications, and this critical stakeholder group is key if the company's purpose is to be a success. In practice, this means a range of actions, including:

- Achieving and maintaining a nuanced understanding of what employees care about in their lives and careers.
- Taking every effort to demonstrate the connection between individual purpose and organizational purpose.

In part, this means listening to the employee base and being willing to act accordingly. It also means the provision of training to help employees better appreciate how their role contributes to the company's purpose.

- Working closely with Human Resources to create and maintain incentives and recognition initiatives that reward employees who demonstrably contribute to the company's purpose.
- Having an effective communications programme that celebrates progress being made and that generates pride in being part of a purpose-led company.
- Monitoring the external environment to identify shifting trends and issues that are applicable to the company's purpose.

Setting Purpose-Led Targets: AIA One Billion

In 2022, AIA announced the launch of AIA One Billion,[11] an ambition to engage a billion people to live Healthier, Longer, Better Lives by 2030. Spencer noted, 'Our AIA One Billion initiative is a strong message of commitment to engaging a billion people across Asia, which is well beyond our base of customers, to catalyse and inspire individual wellness journeys that otherwise wouldn't have happened. Part of the reason behind doing it is leadership in our category; part of it is the demonstration of our commitment to our purpose and how we provide proof points in evidence of our commitment to our purpose; and, third, as the largest life and health insurer in the region we have a very strong financial vested interest in having healthy lives on our books and attracting younger, healthier people and holding on to them for the long term.

---

[11] https://www.aia.com/en/about-aia/aia-one-billion.

'It's a multi-year endeavour and it looks at every online and offline touchpoint that triggers a positive action. It must trigger a positive action whether that is somebody embarking on a relationship with AIA, or doing something they haven't done before that makes them believe they are on a pathway to health and wellness they otherwise wouldn't have been inspired to do. The effort now is to be able to trace and to demonstrate and track and attribute engagement to impact of that engagement. It is not even enough to engage billion people; I want to understand what that engagement of all those people is actually doing for them individually and collectively. I don't want to just measure and count engagements—I want to know what changes happened in the person's life after he/she said I'm in.'

Measuring Impact

Metrics are a must if the company is to demonstrate it is serious about its purpose. The ability to measure the impact of being purpose-led opens up a raft of considerations that go beyond the scope of this particular book. Suffice to say, it is vital to be able to demonstrate the value of corporate purpose in multiple ways—how it is benefiting your customers, how it is helping attract and retain the best people, how it is delivering returns to investors, how it is driving product innovation, how it is nurturing greater levels of trust with the local community, and so on.

If corporate purpose cannot be tracked through everything it does, then it becomes just an 'add on' that is optional for the company to take up or discard as circumstances change. As will be covered in the chapter nineteen, a focus on outcomes and impacts is required, rather than only actions and outputs.

Questions to keep in mind:

1. What data is necessary to monitor and demonstrate the impact your company is having as a result of its purpose?

2. Where are there gaps in your measurement efforts and how can you address them?
3. Is your leadership team aligned in regard to how progress will be measured?
4. Are you investing in research to understand how your purpose is being perceived by customers and other stakeholders over time?
5. How is your purpose helping to drive performance relative to your competitors?

A company's stated purpose will have an indelible impact on its reputation, for better or worse. A company that is guided by a meaningful and credible purpose over a sustained period is well placed to strengthen its reputations. A company that pays lip service to purpose, that acts in ways contrary to its purpose, will be punished reputationally. On the connection between purpose and reputation, Spencer said, 'Healthier, Longer, Better Lives is so publicly visible as a statement of AIA's existence and our promise to the market that it is inextricably bound with our reputation. If we do not live up to the enabling of Healthier, Longer, Better Lives that will be fundamentally detrimental to our reputation. The inextricable connection has been made and we must therefore rise to the occasion and be conscious and mindful and institutionally governed by doing everything we can to achieve our purpose.'

Summary of Principles

- Companies that meaningfully articulate what they stand for—what their purpose is—can use that knowledge to guide both their strategic direction and behaviour to create value over time.

- Considerations when developing a purpose statement include asking:
  - What do people need (and don't have) on a human level that your company can help address?
  - Is the purpose something that people at your company would feel genuinely energized by?
  - Does the purpose enable your company to generate profitable growth?
  - Is the purpose timeless?
  - Can the purpose lead to credible actions rather than just words?

- Keeping purpose alive within the organization requires an ongoing commitment:
  - Understanding what employees care about in their lives and careers.
  - Demonstrating the connection between individual purpose and organizational purpose.
  - Creating incentives and recognition initiatives that reward employees who demonstrably contribute to the company's purpose.
  - Celebrate progress being made and generating pride in being part of a purpose-led company.
  - Identifying shifting trends and issues of relevance to the company's purpose.

- Measuring impact is crucial:
  - Is there a clear understanding of what data is needed to gauge the impact of the corporate purpose?

o   How can gaps in the measurement process be closed?

o   Is there alignment and support among the leadership team in regard to how progress will be measured?

o   Has there been an investment in research to understand how the company's purpose is being perceived by customers over time?

o   Can you accurately discern how your company's purpose is driving performance relative to your competitors?

5

The Imperative of Employee Communications

It's March 2007. We are conducting an employee townhall in China with Charles "Chuck" Prince, Citi's CEO at the time. As well as several hundred people in the room, colleagues are joining via telephone conference from around the Asia-Pacific region. The townhall is about to start, but with one problem: no one dialling in can hear properly. I stand by helplessly as a small army of technicians confer in Chinese and twiddle buttons on a large control panel. Eventually a solution! We need to switch from lapel microphones to handheld microphones. Chuck and his entourage arrive, and he wastes no time hitting the stage. Everything starts well enough, but just as he talks about the need for the bank to continue to invest in technology, his microphone lets out an ear-piercing shriek. Chuck makes a reference to 'case in point' and looks in my direction, agitated. The mic emits another wild shriek for good measure. This is employee communications on the front line. There are high stakes tactically—and today more than ever, strategically.

There is a reason this chapter is located so high up in the section of earning reputations. Good-quality people are essential to the success of any organization. To find and keep those colleagues requires a robust employee communications capability. No one should be a more passionate advocate for the company than its employees. No number of strategic initiatives, product launches, or marketing programmes will be effective if a company's people are not engaged and motivated. They, after all, are the ones who must put planning into practice and engage with customers, suppliers, and other stakeholders to drive results. Done well, employee communications and engagement nurture an employee base that powerfully embodies the desired reputation of the company. Done poorly, the same employees can become potent adversaries that eviscerate the reputation the company is striving to earn. There is a deeply intertwined meshing between employee communications and the company's external reputations.

The COVID-19 pandemic was the catalyst for renewed corporate attention on the need for superior employee communication. Specifically, it resulted in a number of outcomes in this context, including the rise of remote working (heightening the need for frequent, reliable, and compelling information); the heightened use of mobile platforms to receive company news and alerts; a heightened focus on listening and sharing to better support employee needs; and the increased engagement of senior leadership to reassure employees during a very uncertain period of time.

Employees want to be appreciated and feel empowered. The lines between work and home have blurred. The imperative to engage with all employees, but particularly younger ones, will only continue to grow. McKinsey's Prudencio said, 'Today, younger employees demand more of their employer. They want to know what their employer stands for, what the institution's values are, are those values reflected in the organization's behaviour. They want to understand what the role of the organization is in broader society. And there's real interest in transparency and understanding how the organization makes decisions.'

Internal Communications vs Employee Communications

It is worth spending a moment talking about terminology. For many companies, this topic fits under the title 'internal communications.'

The term is traditionally used to describe a process of communication that takes place within any particular organization. Despite some industry debate, it remains worth distinguishing between internal communications and external communications. However, the term 'internal communications' is not particularly helpful. In the digital age, the bubble that surrounds an organization is permeable in nature, allowing information to move quickly and easily through it (in both directions).

Shel Holtz is Senior Director of Communications for Webcor, a commercial builder in California. Holtz is also the co-host of 'For Immediate Release', a long-running, popular podcast focusing on the intersection of communications, business, and technology. Holtz observed, 'Employees can do a Google alert for the company, they can do a search and read all kinds of commentary and news about the firm, they can go to Glassdoor and see what other employees are saying, so that line between internal and external has become very fuzzy. My team is also responsible for social media, and we produce social media content with a full understanding that about half of our employees follow the company on social media—primarily LinkedIn and Instagram—so we are targeting employees as much as anybody else with that content.'

Some companies also think about their communications with employees in connection to the 'paid, earned, shared, owned' media framework, and, worryingly, place their people in the 'owned' category. Ethan McCarty is the CEO of Integral, a leading authority in helping companies harness the power of their people. McCarty noted that while the 'PEO' or 'PESO' media models are fine in their own right, the problem arises when people or entire organizations misapprehend employees as 'paid' or 'owned'. McCarty said that such a framework implies that 'we're communicating to you that you're this audience we could disrupt whenever we wish. I think that that construct is just completely out of sync with the current reality of the work that we all do and that of our expectations for relationships at work.'

On the contrary, employees need to be—and deserve to be—persuaded. The assumption they can just be interrupted with an email or a message and be expected to see that communication and act upon it without question is deeply flawed. McCarty noted that 'One of the first principles I would say of my work is that employees are a public—they are a group of people who are defined by a relationship with an entity in the same way you would say the public in Australia or the public in New York are defined by their relationship with an entity, in that case a country or a city.' He went on to say that, 'I find the term employee activation very helpful because there is a relationship in the word employee. You can say okay, somebody is working for someone else so that's an identifiable group of people. And activation focuses the attention and energy and downstream activity and funding, resources, and skills around an action.'

Holtz recalled, 'I was talking to the two consultants once who were doing employee communications work despite the fact that they had never worked in internal comms. They argued that employees are just another audience. That is completely wrong. Roger D'Aprix, whom I consider to be the father of modern employee communications, calls employees 'informed insiders,' and that is distinctly different than any other stakeholder audience out there.'

The terminology used is relevant because it reflects how a company thinks about its people. The old cliché that 'our people are our most important asset' happens to be true. Whatever the role of a particular employee or group of employees, whether they are highly technical or working on an assembly line, treating them as actual people with their own priorities and concerns is not only the right thing to do, but it makes good business sense too.

The Foundation for a Successful Approach

Connecting with employees and listening to them necessitates multiple ways for employees to hear from the company's leadership and to share their experiences. When I asked about the ingredients for successful employee communications, Holtz said, 'Broadly speaking, first you need executive commitment to communicating strategically with employees, which means executive understanding of what employee communications is, and agreement that it is not a department that does something discreet and apart from the rest of the organisation; it is a management function. It also must be two-way communication defined as an exchange of knowledge or information. Just publishing stuff and distributing it is not communication; it's messaging. There must be a lot of listening to what employees are interested in and accommodating that with your messaging or even making changes to the organisation, whether it's processes or programs, based on what you're hearing from employees. It also must be multidirectional, across organisational functions.'

Mubadala's Brian Lott provided a good analogy when he said, 'I always use the airport analogy when you're at the gate and the screen is blank, you're looking at your watch and your flight should have taken off 10 minutes ago and there's nothing on the screen. That causes anxiety and confusion and distress. Whereas if the screen says the flight is delayed and they will update you in 15 minutes, and then you get another update then, at least it alleviates that sense of anxiety. So, when we have issues that come up within the company where people are looking for an answer even as a short-term balm if you will it helps to say something. I don't think it's ever helpful to just stay silent and so my ethos is over-communication, especially as we saw during COVID. It is really appreciated by employees.'

To keep colleagues informed, engaged, motivated, and to mitigate issues that arise on the minds of employees, communications is key. Attaining a strong programme necessitates understanding what you are trying to achieve in the first place. Done well, employee communications delivers a range of lasting benefits:

- It finds a way to ensure that every individual employee feels engaged with how they are contributing to the company's purpose (which itself cannot be meaningful if employees don't believe in it). Effective employee communications brings purpose to life in creative and consistent ways over time.

- It helps employees have an informed understanding of corporate strategy and what is required of them to help execute it. As with purpose, the best corporate strategy in the world doesn't mean much if employees don't understand it or are not enthused about executing it.
- It instils a sense of belief in the direction of the company through delivering a consistent set of messages and stories. A regular drumbeat of updates that reflect the values, progress, and impact of the firm is the basis for reinforcing confidence among the employee base.
- It provides the basis for employees to work together in team towards a unified vision.
- It allows the company to properly listen to employee sentiment, and to reassure and respond accordingly.

Having clarity about these benefits enables the formation of an employee communications programme that is unequivocal about what it is trying to achieve. This provides the basis for a strategic overlay to the programme that elevates actions beyond the tactical and generates value accordingly.

A Multi-Channel Approach

The ability to disseminate information through a company—in a manner that ensures relevant messages are reaching employees (or a segment of employees) in a timely manner—requires a sophisticated effort. This can mean both transferring information from one point to another and also allowing information to move in multiple directions around the organization.

IBM's Adashek noted, 'If I look at how we do that, there's minimal push of information to them (employees) because we've taken the time to figure out how they want to receive it. There is minimal push with once-a-week newsletters and then the CEO does an office hours live Q&A session once a month. Beyond that it takes a lot to get to them and a lot of it is pull. We have an internal news website and we're curating for what they want so they can get it easily. The last data I saw said 61% of IBMers are looking at that news and understanding where our reputation is and issues that impact our reputation at least once a day. Around 85% of IBMers say that the newsletter they get once a week is the number one trusted source for news and they read it every week.'

This is useful insight. All companies should aim for a balance between push and pull mechanisms to inject flexibility into their employee communications. Holtz echoed the need to be flexible with how information is communicated. He noted, 'Among your employee population, you have people with different preferences about how they receive information, and you need to accommodate these preferences with your channel strategy. To understand these preferences, and to produce content that employees want, research is necessary. We are in the midst of our second internal communications audit since I have been here, which includes a survey but also executive interviews, focus groups, and a channel review. It's understanding what channels employees pay the most attention to, but you cut through the noise with the messages that everybody needs to see by employing virtually all of your channels so that they don't miss it. I also believe that people do pay attention when executives speak, so using them is important. We have a quarterly all-hands meeting on Zoom, which was annual in-person before the pandemic. Then, when the pandemic hit, we started doing them weekly then we backed off to monthly.'

It makes sense that employee communications requires more than an online strategy. In-person gatherings of varying types allow for important interactions to occur. These can be large-scale townhall meetings with the senior leadership team, but they do not always need to be this format. For major milestones and announcements in particular, it is important to empower line managers to help get the word out, and to this end, equipping them with talking points, question and answer documents and presentation slides is required.

Employees as Brand Advocates

Employees can be potent advocates for the company and their company's reputations. Their voice is immensely valid and formidable. If someone wants to really understand what it is like to work at a company, they will look at the corporate website or talk to a head-hunter, but what they will really heed is anecdotes from people who have worked, or are working at, that firm.

McCarty said, 'The same thing goes for goods and services; if you know somebody who's at a company and they are like, wow you have really got to try this new soda that I'm making over here, my boss has a secret recipe and it's really amazing, there's 100% chance I'm going to try that, and I am going to be positively inclined to it. By comparison to somebody who's at some company and I ask them where they work and they say, "you don't want to know." If I push them and they say, "well I work at this soda company." Then, even if they say we have this new recipe, just from that person's tone I am going to stay away from that product.'

Given that the employees are a key advocate, the question then is how to properly amplify the voice of the employee? There was a time where companies seized upon the idea of using their people to disseminate content on social media, with the intent of blowing up the visibility of corporate messages. It did not last for long given the moves made by technology firms to monetize that type of activity. McCarty added that 'Unless you have like Beyoncé show up, your content is never going to go viral—even the presence of hundreds or even thousands of employees sharing something isn't enough to catch virality. And besides, employees on balance do not want to do it anyway.'

McCarty explained the need to design employee advocacy programmes that are as valuable to the advocate as they are to the brand: 'What has to happen is a really intentional value exchange, which I have identified and advocate for as the individual being able to bring his or her authentic voice, where that authenticity cannot be replicated.' This means finding employees who are either subject matter experts or who have an interesting career path to share or are making a special contribution to the company. These people are the ones that have very genuine stories to tell. On the other hand, what the company brings to the table is the inherent authority of being large or having been around for a century or having state-of-the-art facilities and so on. As McCarty explained, 'There is a fair amount of value exchange that can happen when you get that authenticity of the individual and the authority or reach of the brand. Then it becomes very beneficial to those individuals because most people who end up enrolled in these programs are at the high end of skills and labour. To be more known for what they love to do and they're good at is an appreciable benefit. Putting the brand behind them is a motivator. They want training on how to optimize their presence on LinkedIn or whatever platform they are on.'

IBM has a programme it calls 'The Social League', which is designed for influential employees who are hand-selected and empowered to talk about IBM in their own words, using their own social media channels. It is completely up to them when and how they post—these are employees who are already organically helping build IBM's reputation. The Social League equips the most socially networked IBMers with content and assets for sharing, while the company offers training support as to how this segment of employees can better build their personal brands.

Major benefits can accrue to the company through identifying and enlisting this group of employees to be advocates. It won't be for all employees, but if the company can identify the right segment of its people, the benefits for all involved can be material. Employees feel good about taking part in these kinds of programmes, which builds further goodwill towards the company. Those employees that are active advocates for their company tend to also be stronger believers in the direction the company is heading, will devote more time to their role, and be committed to stay at the firm for longer.

Change Communications

All companies operate in a world where change is constant. Emerging opportunities, challenges, and even crises mean that the corporation is never allowed to stand still. Strategic change, personnel change, operational change, and cultural change are part of corporate life. The ability to communicate in a way that reaches and resonates with employees is critical to the success and sustainability of these changes. And employees should be regarded as the highest priority audience—they should never hear about the news from an external source first.

The change communications process is about more than just issuing communications to coincide with the implementation of a given change. In fact, good change communications is about an ongoing initiative to socialize the factors that could produce change. In this way, your people are ready, rather than shocked or surprised, when the change is announced. Holtz explained, 'Employees should be prepared for change based on ongoing communication designed to keep them connected to the marketplace (that is, the economic conditions that affect the industry and the organization, the competition, customers, etc.). If communicators do a good job of this, not only will employees not be surprised by change, but they will also anticipate it and perhaps even recommend action to address it before a major shake-up becomes necessary.'

Of course, one of the toughest changes to communicate are those which result in job losses. How companies approach communicating lay-offs will have a notable effect on corporate reputation and on the morale of those employees remaining at the firm. When handled badly, the fallout can be both swift and serious. What is the ideal way to approach such announcements? When asked about this, Holtz said, 'The primary consideration is to remember that employees are adults who can take bad news, especially if the reasons for it are explained (as with change, employees who understand the forces at work on the organization should not be surprised by most bad news companies may share with them). Candour and transparency are critical. Equally important is letting employees know what to expect in the days and weeks ahead, and how the bad news will affect them.'

For larger firms, the announcement of lay-offs may often commence with an email from the CEO. There are some clear guidelines when constructing such messages. These include:

- Be clear and get to the point quickly. Avoid using jargon in an attempt to mask the real story being conveyed.
- Ensure the rationale(s) for the lay-offs is clearly explained, and in doing so, do not be inconsistent with what has been said in the past.
- Be as specific as possible about things like timing of layoffs and measures to support those employees affected.
- Be sensitive and empathetic. Showing respect and sincerity will go a long way to helping people deal with the news.

While an email might be required to commence the process, it cannot be the entirety of the process. Holtz said, 'For both change and bad news, it is important that people managers have a strategized part to play, interpreting broader information in order to explain to team members what the change or bad news means to members of the team.'

Dealing with Employee Discontent

Employees can be advocates, but they can also be ardent detractors on any number of fronts. Employee empowerment, and in some cases activism, is on the rise. Return-to-office policies, organizational changes, DEI challenges, environmental sustainability, and business partnerships, among other areas, can all spark commentary from the employee base. CEOs for the most part are not particularly well equipped to respond to these scenarios, which have the potential to cause substantial damage to corporate reputations.

One problem is that the senior leadership team tends to downplay how a particular issue might be regarded by the employee base while also misunderstanding the degree to which employees feel comfortable raising their true feelings. This is particularly pronounced in Asia. Often at a Town Hall, or on a conference call, the CEO will ask for questions, only to be met with silence. If questions are asked, they are usually gentle in nature. And if a mildly sensitive topic is raised on stage, it might be met with nervous laughter. Afterwards, the executive team feels great about how things went, while strong disgruntlement lurks beneath the surface. This can become dangerous if not addressed and requires the management team to be acutely aware of the need to listen and to find a variety of ways to capture feedback.

Holtz suggested, 'Listening is the key to it. While you can usually detect backlash, it is harder to identify what's driving that backlash, and I think it's too easy especially in the leadership ranks to make assumptions about what's driving the backlash. If [employees] are resisting a particular change, you have to find out why. It could be that they don't think they'll succeed in the model that has been adopted in the organisation as a result of a change; it could be that they disagree with it on a moral or ethical basis; it could be that they just think it's the wrong thing to do. There's lots of reasons and you have to ask. This is why I think focus groups and even one-on-ones that our managers are required to hold on a regular basis with employees are tremendous opportunities to dig into that. There needs to be a process where you collect that information and then raise it up to the executive team so that they understand what is driving that and then have the conversations. You cannot be prescriptive around these things; you can't just tell employees you're wrong to be upset about this or we understand why you're upset but . . . I think there has to be empathy, there has to be transparency, and there has to be candour around these things.'

Employees and Politics

What is the balance between balancing the company's interests with employees' rights to express themselves? In the end, employees, in their personal lives, should not be restricted from expressing their opinions and views, including those on political subjects. At the same time, it is not a contradiction to remind employees that they should not conduct themselves in a way that brings the company into disrepute. And, while at the office, to refrain from pushing a particular political agenda with colleagues. Like much of the material throughout these chapters, these concepts are more easily understood on the page than applied in the heat of the moment. As discussed in chapter one, companies operate according to an ongoing series of trade-offs. Enhancing reputation with one stakeholder group may come at the expense of losing favour with another. There are no perfect solutions, just actions that reflect why the company operates in the first place and how it is committed to conducting itself, especially when things get difficult.

Summary of Principles

- The term employee communications is preferable to internal communications, in recognition of the fact that employees are a distinct and critical stakeholder group.
- Having clarity about the benefits the company wishes to generate from its employee communications enables the formation of an effective programme.
- Employees have different preferences about how they receive information, and the company's channel strategy should accommodate these preferences through a mix of push and pull communications.
- Employee advocacy programmes should be as valuable to the advocate as they are to the company.
- Change communications is about an ongoing effort to socialise the factors that could produce change. In this way, employees are ready, rather than shocked or surprised, when the change is announced.
- Corporate leaders should always be careful about underestimating how a particular issue might be regarded by the employee base and also misjudging the degree to which employees feel comfortable raising their true feelings, especially in a public forum.
- Employees, in their personal lives, should not be restricted from expressing their opinions and views, including those on political subjects. They also should not conduct themselves in a way that brings the company into disrepute.

6

The Impact of ESG on Corporate Reputations

Environmental, social, and governance (ESG): a collection of corporate performance evaluation criteria that assess the robustness of a company's governance mechanisms and its ability to effectively manage its environmental and social impacts.[1]

The subject of ESG is a technical one that can be examined through a variety of dimensions—there are realms of information about ESG from an investment perspective, as a risk management issue, the impact of ESG on business strategy, and of course as part of the wider sustainability discussion. This chapter seeks to layout the implications of ESG for corporate reputations and how companies can think about the subject in this context.

ESG represents expectations on the part of certain stakeholders regarding how the company is impacting environmental, social, and governance issues. Historically, these stakeholders were typically NGOs and regulators, but today the spectrum of stakeholders has widened to include major investment funds, employees, and customers. In turn, the company must determine how to meet these expectations and manage the risk associated with them. The pursuit of an ESG programme can deliver points of difference

---

[1] https://www.gartner.com/en/finance/glossary/environmental-social-and-governance-esg-.

to the corporate reputation as positive impacts are optimized and negative ones are eliminated.

Many sources of risk that companies face today can be connected back to factors within the ESG framework. Mark Harper is Group Head of Sustainability for Swire. Harper, who is based in Hong Kong, noted, 'The World Economic Forum produces a risk report every year, highlighting the key risks facing the global economy and business. For the past five years the majority of the risks identified have all been ESG risks. Issues that you wouldn't have expected a few years ago to appear as a significant risk for business—such as the impact of biodiversity loss on supply chains and commodity prices, the impacts of extreme weather events, the increase of cyber security issues, and the issue of rising income inequality and the social and economic disruption that this can create. Historically you wouldn't have seen these issues appearing on an organisations risk register [but they] are now starting to appear as significant risks to the ability of a business to operate and create value in the future.'

Whether the actual term 'ESG' will continue to be as prominent as it has been in recent years is hard to predict (the next section touches upon the debate in the U.S. regarding the subject of ESG, with many companies veering away from using this term). What is more certain is that no matter what it is called, the need for companies to address the issues, risks, and opportunities under the ESG umbrella are not going away. Stakeholders across the board are actively engaged in how companies are addressing matters related to the environment, how they are committed to diversity, equality, and inclusion matters and the way in which they are governing themselves. On top of this, regulations around the world will continue to put in place to require companies to act, whether they wish to or not. The influence of ESG *factors* on the assessment of companies—and corporate reputations—is here to stay.

Global Differences

The adoption of, and views regarding, ESG, differ in different regions of the world. Although this chapter will not look in great detail at the nuances of these differences, it is worth acknowledging the variations that exist around the world.

In general terms, Europe leads the world in adopting ESG practices. According to a report by RBC Asset Management, investors in the United States lag well behind their global counterparts in ESG adoption—65% compared with 94% of respondents in Europe, 89% in Canada, and 72% in Asia.[2] The same study found that 94% of European investors said they use ESG factors in their investment approach and decision-making, compared to 72% of investors in Asia and 65% of the U.S. investors. A report co-produced by The Diligent Institute and Spencer Stuart in 2023 stated that 56% of European directors are more likely to focus on the opportunity of ESG, compared to 30% of their U.S. counterparts. The report found that U.S. directors are more likely to indicate that their organizations view ESG issues in terms of risk compared with their European counterparts (34% compared to 13%).[3]

In the United States, there have been vocal detractors of ESG investing. Questions have been asked about ESG metrics lacking standardization. Accusations have been levelled at investment firms that their ESG focus represents an effort to impose a 'woke' political agenda on the corporate world. In 2023, Larry Fink, CEO of BlackRock, said that he's no longer using the term 'ESG' in his communications because it is being politically 'weaponized' by the

---

[2] https://institutional.rbcgam.com/documents/en/esg-executive-summary.pdf.

[3] https://www.spencerstuart.com/-/media/2023/june/diligentesg2023/2023-sustainability-in-the-spotlight.pdf.

far left and the far right.[4] The explicit use of the term 'ESG' has been used less during the U.S. earnings calls than in the past.[5] In August 2023, it was reported that McDonald's had been dropping the use of the term 'ESG' from some of its communications.[6] It is not alone in taking such steps.

At the risk of generalization, companies in Asia remain at a relatively early stage in adopting ESG practices and disclosures, although much activity continues to take place that is making ESG a priority. Asia is forecast to be a driver of the global growth in ESG Assets Under Management (AUM) with ESG AUM in Asia projected to quintuple from $90B in 2021Q3 to more than $500B by 2025.[7] Asian markets are highly diverse, covering highly developed markets like Hong Kong and Singapore, emerging markets like Indonesia and Thailand, and frontier markets such as Bangladesh. A 'lift and shift' of ESG regulations and standards from the West may not be fit for purpose across the region. At the same time, there is a focus by regulators, investors, employees, and other stakeholders on achieving higher standards of rigour when it comes to corporate ESG reporting and disclosures in the region.

---

[4] https://www.axios.com/2023/06/26/larry-fink-ashamed-esg-weaponized-desantis.

[5] Ben Maiden, 'The week in GRC: ESG mentions in earnings calls have declined and EU lawmakers back tougher AI rules', *Governance Intelligence*, June 2023, https://www.corporatesecretary.com/articles/technology-social-media/33477/week-grc-esg-mentions-earnings-calls-have-declined-and-eu.

[6] Daniela Sirtori-Cortina And Bloomberg, 'McDonald's is removing 'ESG' from parts of its website amid a conservative backlash against 'woke capitalism'', *Fortune*, August 2023, https://fortune.com/2023/08/11/mcdonalds-removes-esg-from-parts-of-website/.

[7] https://www.invesco.com/apac/en/institutional/insights/esg/esg-opportunities-and-challenges-in-asia.html.

In 2023, the International Sustainability Standards Board (ISSB) released standards designed to provide greater levels of consistency and verification by companies undertaking ESG reporting.[8] Many jurisdictions in Asia are expected to adopt ISSB standards and make them mandatory in the years to come. Hong Kong in particular has been quick (on a global scale) to do so. In April 2023, the Stock Exchange of Hong Kong (HKEX) issued a consultation paper with a view to aligning the reporting practices of its issuers to the new standards. The Singapore Exchange (SGX) introduced a phased approach to mandatory climate reporting based on the recommendations of the Task Force on Climate-related Financial Disclosures ('TCFD') following a public consultation in 2021.[9] Other jurisdictions in the region, including Australia, Mainland China, and India, are delivering regulations to introduce more stringent ESG reporting requirements.

It is not just regulators that are pushing for change. A 2022 survey by Bain & Company found that 75% of employees in the Asia-Pacific region now expect their companies to follow sustainable business practices.[10]

Which components of ESG are most concentrated on by business leaders also changes with geography. McKinsey, in a report entitled 'ESG momentum: Seven reported traits that set organizations apart', stated that 'While environmental issues are increasingly being featured in headlines globally, responses suggest that Europe is the only region where environmental

[8] https://www.ifrs.org/projects/completed-projects/2023/general-sustainability-related-disclosures/#:~:text=In%20June%202023%20the%20International,IFRS%20S2%20Climate%2Drelated%20Disclosures.

[9] https://www.sgx.com/sustainable-finance/sustainability-reporting.

[10] Zara Lightowler, Gerry Mattios, et al., 'Unpacking Asia-Pacific Consumers' New Love Affair with Sustainability', Bain & Company, June 2022, https://www.bain.com/insights/unpacking-asia-pacific-consumers-new-love-affair-with-sustainability/.

topics tend to outrank governance on leaders' agendas. According to respondents, social topics are of outsize concern among organizations based in North America, where diversity, equity, and inclusion (DEI) issues have come to the forefront in recent years. On the other hand, respondents working for organizations with headquarters in Asia-Pacific and developing markets tend to rank governance topics as their organizations' most important ESG priorities.'[11]

Lapman Lee is a Professor of Practice at the Polytechnic University of Hong Kong as well as Willis Towers Watson's Asia climate and ESG insurance value proposition leader. Lee noted a Willis Towers Watson survey conducted with more than three hundred board members on the subject of ESG.[12] The study found that in Western Europe the primary ESG focus relates to the 'E', whereas North America focuses more on the 'S', with social issues such as diversity, equity, and inclusion likely to continue this momentum. In Asia-Pacific and Latin America, where there tends to be a wider range of corporate governance maturity levels, the focus revolves more around the 'G'.

Lee also suggested that in Asia—being a region exposed to acute and chronic physical climate risk—there is also an increasing focus on environmental matters. He said, 'Especially in the financial services industry, climate scenario analysis and stress testing is [are] being fuelled by banking and insurance regulators in Hong Kong and Singapore, and also Malaysia, New Zealand and Taiwan.'

Adam Harper (no relation to Mark) is founder of Ashbury Communications, a strategic communications consultancy

---

[11] https://www.mckinsey.com/capabilities/strategy-and-corporate-finance/our-insights/esg-momentum-seven-reported-traits-that-set-organizations-apart#/.

[12] 'ESG and Executive Compensation: Hearing from board members globally', Willis Towers Watson, page 32.

headquartered in Singapore. In reference to the 'S' in ESG in Asia, he said, 'I think the tendency has been to focus on inclusion, livelihood, and education. These types of social issues are not controversial. In this mosaic of countries in Asia with completely different systems and cultures, I think that regional firms have made a big shift in the last five- or ten-years [in] terms of gender, and I think LGBTQ equality has momentum as well. But I don't think you see to the same extent in Asia what you would see in the U.S. or Europe, where companies are entering into the debate and becoming participants in the public forum.'

More broadly, talking about the changing mindset needed by many Asian corporates, A. Harper said, 'It goes well beyond staff volunteering and charitable donations to fundamentally addressing what your environmental social governance risks are and what your strategy is for addressing them. That means things like having a lot of information, being able to collect and disclose a lot of information about your carbon use, your water use, and so on. That is operationally challenging, and I would say until recently many of these companies felt ESG was an obligation they had to respond to and was in some ways a cost of doing business or a compliance burden. However, I think this is changing fast and that the U.S. Inflation Reduction Act has been a catalyst. Banks have been trying to communicate to corporates for years that sustainability is a business opportunity, but I don't think that has really gained traction until what we've seen happening with the IRA in the U.S., where there are economic incentives to invest in renewable energy, electrification, sustainable technology, and so on. That has changed the conversation in the U.S. about sustainability and the energy transition for corporates and the EU is following suit. Companies in this region can see that this is the shape of things to come. There is a growing realization that this is an opportunity and the question that follows from that is how do we take it—how can we go about the energy transition in particular in a way that boosts our business?'

Speaking of regulations in one part of the world that trigger changes to how companies operate in other parts, the European Parliament in 2023 introduced the Carbon Border Adjustment Mechanism (CBAM), which will be rolled out in phases from 2026 to 2034. This will see the EU impose a Carbon Border Tax on certain imports, such as steel, fertilizers, cement, and hydrogen. The CBAM incentivizes non-EU countries to increase their climate ambition and to ensure that EU and global climate efforts are not undermined by production being relocated from the EU to countries with less ambitious policies. Regulatory developments such as the IRA and CBAM will continue to have an international impact on how companies operate, how they evolve their ESG programs and how they communicate these changes to their stakeholders.

Catherine Chan is Head of ESG Coordination Office for Tencent. Chan said, 'From the very early days, our founders thought of using technologies for good, and a decade later, this was elevated to become our vision, which is Value for Users, Tech for Good. Everyone inside the company knows that when you say tech for good, it means using technology in an innovative way to identify and resolve pain points faced by users or society.' Reflecting this sentiment, Tencent's CEO, Pony Ma, has talked about a concept he terms the 'CBS Trinity', which speaks to the company's intent to serve customers, businesses, and society.[13] Here, customers are retail consumers and businesses are Tencent's enterprise clients as well as the broader technology industry. Chan said, 'The "S" speaks to the convergence of the digital economy and the real economy; we are interested in how we can help solve pain points faced by users or communities with special needs. Investing in social value creation is as important to Tencent as our

---

[13] 'Pony Ma: Tencent is an Enabler and Connector for Tech for Good', Tencent, March 2023, https://www.tencent.com/en-us/articles/2201535.html.

investment in research and development. For example, a major pain point in China has been the issue of queuing and waiting to see doctors. Patients or their families used to stand in queues at hospitals for hours to book and pay for their medical appointments. We have worked with hospitals in China to help digitalize their 'book and pay' systems since several years ago. Users can now use this special function within Wexin to make medical appointments conveniently and efficiently, saving waiting times.'

Reference to Tencent in this context raises a principle put forward in chapter one, that companies have multiple reputations and will be perceived differently by different stakeholders. In 2022, Sustainalytics, ESG ratings arm of the U.S. financial services group Morningstar, announced a downgrade of Tencent—along with several other Chinese tech companies—because of what Sustainalytics viewed as their role in internet censorship in China.[14] Despite this action from a U.S. firm, Tencent argues with conviction that it has a long-standing commitment to upholding ESG-related practices.

ESG Governance

The establishment of a governance structure to oversee the ESG programme is a crucial step towards the success of the effort. Meeting the rising expectations of regulators and investors in particular makes crucial the process of identifying a strategy, setting objectives, and capturing ESG data. The executive leadership team therefore needs to be involved in the development and execution of the ESG programme. Board level involvement is also a necessity.

---

[14]   Edward White and Leo Lewis, 'China ESG reckoning looms for investors', *Financial Times*, 4 January 2023, https://www.ft.com/content/55058f28-8c47-40c8-9919-8ded9daa53e9.

A steering committee is one such means of governance. Members could include the chief financial officer, chief legal officer, chief investment officer, chief marketing/communications officer, and chief human resources officer. Once established, the committee can play a number of roles including discussing and assessing feedback from the organization's stakeholders, overseeing the integration of ESG into the business and reporting to the board on ESG matters (in some jurisdictions, board involvement is mandatory for listed companies. For instance, Appendix 27 of the Hong Kong Stock Exchange Listing Rules states that the board has overall responsibility for an issuer's ESG strategy and reporting.[15])

Chan explained the structure at Tencent as follows: 'Our ESG Working Group has a three-tier structure. The first is the ESG Steering Team, comprised of senior executives from the company. The next is the ESG Coordination Office, which is my team managing priorities and performances across ESG topics in collaboration with ESG Champions. The ESG Coordination Office also serves as the secretariat of ESG Working Group and reports to the Corporate Governance Committee of the board regularly. We have more than 90 ESG champions across business and functional teams. The working group holds a conference annually to share progress or new projects and get updates on global trends from external specialists.'

Developing an ESG Strategy

A comprehensive approach is needed that reflects the company's values and purpose. It should also embed a commitment to *actions* the business itself can take in the spirit of embracing an effective ESG programme. Turning this principle into practice is not easy.

---

[15] https://en-rules.hkex.com.hk/rulebook/environmental-social-and-governance-reporting-guide-0.

By its nature, ESG is wide ranging, encompassing many different aspects of corporate existence.

Building an ESG strategy should, in large part, be directed by the firm's stakeholders. Identifying who they are, how they are affected by your operations, and who you should prioritize, will inform the entire strategy. More specifically, conducting a materiality assessment provides a means by which to create a blueprint for any organization's ESG strategy. A materiality assessment will help to identify those topics that can be considered material to the performance of your business as well as to the impact of your business on the economy, the environment, and to society. The materiality assessment provides a summarized view of ESG topics from external and internal stakeholders. It also is helpful to enable clarity as to what the business will not commit to do and providing a clear rationale for why certain topics are prioritized over others.

M. Harper said, 'An interesting development largely driven by international reporting frameworks like GRI and the EU's Corporate Sustainability Reporting Directive (CSRD) is a shift towards "double materiality". The double materiality concept requires companies to disclose information on how sustainability risks and opportunities may impact the company's value in the future. The business evaluates the impact it has on the outside world as well as the impact of the outside world on the company's ability to generate value. Essentially adopting an inside out and outside in view of sustainability. In relation to the impact of the company on the outside world that's where you'd want to engage with your external stakeholders – the NGOs, members of the public, customers to get an idea around how they view those issues and how they view the impact that the company has on those challenges whether that is climate change or whether that is the availability of clean drinking water, etc. On the other side, you generally would do more with internal stakeholders or maybe your investors regarding their views around how those outside influences can impact on your value creation approach. This then creates your 4x4 grid – your materiality matrix.'

Identifying these topics will in turn enable the firm to produce an ESG strategy that shows how the topics are being addressed by the firm.

The ESG Narrative

A systematic approach is required to presenting corporate ESG credentials to a range of stakeholders, including investors, customers, employees, and governments. Rather than being viewed as a burden, this should be seen as an opportunity to enhance trust between a company and its various stakeholders. M. Harper noted, 'The best companies have already realised that this can be a big competitive advantage, that rather than being at odds with business growth, in fact it's an enabler of business growth and they're beginning to tell that story. But it is an emerging story, a story that is still coalescing. That's the key challenge now, for Corporate Affairs professionals to be able to advise the company and explain this not as an obligation or even only the right thing to do, but also as a big competitive advantage and differentiator for the firm.'

Companies in general and in Asia in particular have not only fully appreciated both the risks but also the massive upside regarding communications of an organization's sustainability standards and performance. There is an opportunity for Asian businesses to get out their sustainability message more effectively. Tencent's Chan said, 'Under our working group, we have a special committee on ESG communications. It comprises internal and external communications teams catering to different stakeholder groups. The internal communications team are [is] responsible to help elevate awareness of our Tech for Good culture within the company and as an extension, our ESG program. They love this, as it enables us to demonstrate our Tech for Good culture in a more tangible way. External communications includes investor communications, our China PR team and our international PR team.'

The development of an effective ESG narrative includes taking steps to secure third-party validation of the company's programme and progress. Rating agencies provide independent research and commentary on corporate ESG performance. ESG rankings and scores by rating agencies are often seen as proxies for how effectively the company can deliver its ESG agenda. Rating agencies such as MSCI, ISS-Oekom, and Sustainalytics are therefore relevant stakeholders in relation to running an ESG programme. To arrive at an ESG assessment, rating agencies consider all publicly available material. They then provide feedback to investors via an ESG score and feedback report. It is essential that any company seeking to be recognized for its ESG achievements disclose its ESG practices to meet these rating agencies' requirements.

It is also useful for companies to be involved in wider discussions on a variety of ESG topics. Joining ESG memberships is a simple but effective step in this direction. Examples of note include United Nations Global Compact[16] (a principle-based framework that promotes responsible business practices across sectors with a goal of achieving the SDGs); Task Force on Climate-related Financial Disclosures[17] (a global initiative that seeks to develop voluntary and consistent disclosure of climate-change impacts), and Principles for Responsible Investment[18] (a United Nations–supported international network of investors working together to implement its six aspirational principles for responsible investment).

---

[16] https://unglobalcompact.org/.

[17] https://www.fsb-tcfd.org/.

[18] https://www.unpri.org/.

A. Harper said, 'Joining organizations like TCFD is in itself a statement of ambition but it requires you then to have targets, which in turn gives you direction – it's a common goal that everyone in the organization can get behind. The challenge for companies everywhere is explaining that to their stakeholders whether it's the employees, the investors or the clients and telling a story about why that's what they've decided to do. Targets and strategies generally, not just in ESG, can be rather abstract, but it is a story that management must be able to tell. It is great to have targets, and they should be ambitious, but it is the narrative about why and where it is going is what we all retain. People do not retain numbers unless they are woven into a narrative.'

Investor Communications

Companies are receiving an increasing flow of investor queries about how they integrate ESG criteria in their business operations, and how they measure, monitor, and address ESG risks and impacts. Investors will seek this information both directly from the company, or indirectly through rating agencies. Chan said, 'Tencent has a very international investor base, and we do a lot of ESG engagement calls with fund managers and stewardship teams. On average, we meet over 3,000 investors a year in one-on-one meetings, roadshows and investor conferences. ESG topics were discussed in more than half of these meetings.'

Investors will not only have enquiries but will also demand action in certain instances. For example, they may ask for more details into a company's position regarding the risks of climate change, setting emissions reduction targets, and reporting on the carbon footprint of the company. Ramifications for non-compliance can include the investor divesting from the company, publicly naming the company for not taking action, or voting against the board directors at shareholder meetings.

The team overseeing ESG should work in close collaboration with Corporate Affairs and Investor Relations to field and manage enquiries from institutional investors.

Here are three means by which corporates are engaging with investors on the subject of ESG:

1. Interacting with ESG Ratings Agencies

The role of ESG ratings agencies was referenced earlier in the chapter. A lot of investors might not necessarily have the internal resources for their own ESG analysts and so will use third-party proxy data from these agencies. The ratings agencies will often contact the company in question to check if there is any additional information that is not in the public domain that needs to be incorporated and/or to give the company a chance to confirm the agency's analysis is accurate. Others will send a questionnaire and ask the company to submit answers to those questions and provide either publicly or non-publicly available documents as evidence to support its answers.

A concern in this area has been a tendency for inconsistency across ESG indexes and ratings. Lee said, 'There is some divergence in ESG ratings compared to debt ratings, where you typically have less than one or two notches between the major ratings agencies. In the context of ESG, there tends to be divergence in scope, weighting and measurement of ratings between agencies. Having said that, a deterioration of an individual ESG rating does send a signal to investors and may trigger uncomfortable questions at the annual general meeting and investor relations meetings.'

2. ESG Reports

The production of ESG reports is another means by which the company explains its ESG progress and impact to investors. Well run companies will engage with investors as part of their materiality assessment process and also use the questions being asked by ratings agencies as an indication of market interest.

ESG reporting is becoming more essential—and even mandatory as part of the regulatory requirements of listed companies. In Hong Kong, from the 2022 financial year, companies must release their ESG report simultaneously with the annual financial report.[19] M. Harper said, 'When investors are analysing companies based on their financial performance, they are increasingly incorporating sustainability into that assessment. Investors, therefore, need the most up-to-date ESG data to analyse alongside the company's financials. They don't want to wait six months for six months old data; they want to be looking at the most up-to-date data that's available.'

The intensity of noise surrounding ESG means there is a challenge for the company in cutting through that noise to reach its stakeholders. The company needs to explain how it is approaching all aspects of ESG, as well as its end goal, in a way that's authentic and distinctive to the company. A. Harper noted, 'I would always encourage any company to think about what is the insight that your business gives you into ESG, whether that's the energy transition, biodiversity or any aspect of sustainability more broadly. If you're a manufacturing company, for example, you know a lot about supply chains. What can you say about how supply chains are decarbonising? If you're an energy company, you're in a really strong position to speak about the future of energy. You already see global energy firms doing that very effectively but more companies in more sectors in Asia could be leading with insight as well as talking about their own businesses.'

3. *Engaging with Investors Directly*

One means of investor engagement on this subject is through interim and annual results announcements. There is an opportunity

---

[19] https://www.hkex.com.hk/-/media/HKEX-Market/News/Market-Consultations/2016-Present/April-2021-Review-of-CG-Code-and-LR/Conclusions-(Dec-2021)/cp202104cc.pdf?la=en.

to include more information at earnings announcements about the company's sustainability performance and achievements. M. Harper also noted, 'Our operating company Swire Properties organise annual ESG investor roadshows to engage investors directly on their ESG performance and strategy and plans. Engaging investors on both financial and non-financial performance is, ultimately, where the market is moving.'

Public companies of a certain size will receive ad hoc enquiries from big institutional investors. The key is for the company to have a considered view internally as to which enquiries it will respond to, otherwise it can find itself all consumed with responding to incoming questions. Such a threshold can consider the level of shareholding or debt the investor holds and also if they have been active buying a lot of shares or selling a lot of shares. M. Harper said that, 'Ultimately the primary role of a sustainability team should be to manage the environmental and social impacts of the business and help identify associated opportunities. However, with the rising level of interest in a company's ESG performance, you run the risk of spending more time than necessary answering the same questions from different ESG ratings and indices. It is important, therefore, for businesses to produce clear, comprehensive, and navigable sustainability reports so investors and analysts can access the information directly, as well as establishing a set of internal criteria to help determine which questionnaire there is value in responding.'

Greenwashing

Greenwashing refers to behaviour or activities that make people believe that a company is doing more to protect the environment than it really is in reality.[20] It is not hard to find instances of companies that are taking risks in relation to their

---

[20] https://dictionary.cambridge.org/dictionary/english/greenwashing.

external communications because they are attempting to lead with headlines rather than the story.

Consumers in particular are subjected to a regular flow of sustainability-related messaging from companies seeking to sell them products and services. And consumers *are* interested in the subject. At the same time, general levels of understanding among consumers on the subject of sustainability remains quite low. A 2022 study by Morning Consult found that although eight in ten U.S. adults said they were familiar with the term 'renewable resources', only 58% could accurately identify a renewable resource from a list of renewable and non-renewable ones. And a vast majority of respondents did not know what 'ESG' stands for, with many misidentifying the 'S' as representing 'sustainability' instead.[21] The same issues apply in Asia, where generally speaking, consumers tend not to have a strong understanding of sustainability. A Bain and Company Asia-Pacific survey more than sixteen thousand consumers across eleven countries found that about 70% of those surveyed failed a simple sustainability quiz.[22]

The practice of greenwashing has captured the attention of regulators. Among many examples, in January 2024, the European Union passed a new law banning greenwashing and misleading product information. In the UK, the Financial Conduct Authority in 2022 announced plans to clamp down on greenwashing.[23] In June 2023, the FCA also sent a letter to banks to warn them about

---

[21] 'What Sustainability Means to Consumers', Morning Consult, September 2022.

[22] Zara Lightowler, Gerry Mattios, et al., 'Unpacking Asia-Pacific Consumers' New Love Affair with Sustainability', Bain & Company, June 2022, https://www.bain.com/insights/unpacking-asia-pacific-consumers-new-love-affair-with-sustainability/.

[23] https://www.fca.org.uk/news/press-releases/fca-proposes-new-rules-tackle-greenwashing.

greenwashing in the sustainable loans market.[24] M. Harper said, 'There is a rising trend for new regulations around corporate green claims, aimed at reducing the risk of corporate's making false or overblown claims about the "green" credentials of their business or product/service also known as "greenwashing". This is, unfortunately, leading to many businesses choosing not to communicate their commitments and performance – "green hushing", for fear of opening themselves up to criticism. This is regrettable, as the act of big businesses communicating regularly around their sustainability performance and strategies also sends a strong signal out to other companies that they need to be taking these issues seriously and they need to be stepping up their efforts. Corporate affairs and communication teams play a significant role by ensuring that all sustainability communications are genuine, fact-based and linked to real on the ground action.'

In the face of reputational risk around greenwashing, companies must educate themselves to understand the science, the relevant regulatory frameworks, and to ensure they have an accurate picture of all relevant components of their operation before using sustainability phrases and terms in a public setting. As M. Harper notes, green hushing is not desirable, but companies should take a cautious approach to laying out their green credentials. Any claims made need to be verifiable if challenged. It is notable that in 2023, the Asia chapter of the Public Relations and Communications Association (PRCA) issued a set of guidelines on environmental sustainability claims, providing an example of steps being taken to encourage accurate and trustworthy reporting of sustainability actions by companies in the region.[25]

---

[24] https://www.fca.org.uk/publication/correspondence/sll-letter-june-2023.pdf.

[25] https://apac.prca.global/wp-content/uploads/2023/09/Sustainability-Communications-Guidelines.pdf.

Greenwashing will remain an issue as the world continues to attempt to address the enormous challenges involved with climate transition. In September 2023, the U.S. Department of the Treasury released its Principles for Net-Zero Financing & Investment.[26] It noted that 'Climate change is a shared, global, and existential challenge that poses a severe risk to the productive capacity of the economy and requires an economywide response to safeguard U.S. economic growth and energy security.' The Treasury outlined nine principles in relation to net-zero pledges by financial institutions. While this is U.S. focused and targeted at financial institutions, it is indicative of the ongoing global effort to get the economy to net zero. Regardless of what happens to the 'ESG' acronym in the future, pressure will continue to rise on companies to show and explain how they are transitioning to a low carbon economy as part of their overall growth narrative. While there is a strong vein of trepidation out there among companies that are concerned about making statements that could be construed as greenwashing, in the end, they will have to speak up. The transition process is bringing much change with it—change that affects a cross section of the company's stakeholders, including employees, supply chain partners, customers, and local communities. The process of large-scale change in this context entails reputational risk if businesses get it wrong. Stakeholders will be watching closely with the expectation that companies are doing the right thing and making a positive contribution to the transition process while showing care for their constituencies as they do so.

---

[26] https://home.treasury.gov/system/files/136/NetZeroPrinciples.pdf.

Summary of Principles

- Many sources of risk to the company are those related to ESG factors.

- The future of the term 'ESG' is open to debate, however no matter what it is called, the need for companies to address the issues, risks, and opportunities under the ESG umbrella are not going away.

- It is important to recognize that corporate priorities regarding ESG differ in different regions of the world.

- The executive leadership team needs to be involved in the development and execution of the ESG programme. Board level involvement is also a necessity.

- Building an ESG strategy should to a large degree be directed by the firm's stakeholders. Identifying who they are, how they are affected by your operations, and who you should prioritize, will inform the entire strategy.

- The company needs to explain how it is approaching all aspects of ESG, as well as its end goal, in a way that's authentic and distinctive to the company.

- Joining ESG memberships can be valuable as part of a wider intent to contribute to discussions around best practice across a range of areas.

- Inclusion on key sustainability indices and benchmarks enables further recognition for the company's ESG efforts.

- Reporting on ESG matters to investors should be done systematically. Liaison with ratings agencies, ESG reports, and direct engagement with investors are three ways by which the company can keep investors informed about their ESG progress.

- Greenwashing—and green hushing—are both to be guarded against at every step of the ESG communications programme.

7

When and How to Speak Up
on Social Issues

Inherent in the rise of the stakeholder society is growing expectations on the part of many people that companies take a stand on societal issues. In the United States in particular, pressure on companies to join the conversation on a wide range of emotive subjects such as Black Lives Matter, #metoo, gun rights, and LGBTQ inclusion has been well documented. More broadly, and certainly in Asia, issues such as poverty, access to education and climate action, are ones that companies must consider and, to varying degrees, take a stance on. The ability to decide what issues to speak up about and how to do so is a high-stakes game that has profound ramifications for corporate reputations.

What Constitutes a Social Issue?

What is a social issue anyway? One definition is as follows: a social issue, also called a social problem, is a state of affairs that negatively affects the personal or social lives of individuals or the well-being of communities or larger groups within a society and about which there is usually public disagreement as to its nature, causes, or solution.[1]

---

[1] https://www.britannica.com/topic/social-issue.

Alison DaSilva is Global Managing Director, Purpose & Impact at Zeno Group. She said, 'I think of social issues in a construct of societal issues – what are the issues that are top of mind and impacting society at large on a human level? This would include issues that are more traditional in nature, like education, health, social services, community development, and housing.' DaSilva went on to note that 'What we've seen is an expansion of this spectrum of issues over the last few decades. We're seeing environmental, health and climate issues change impacting people in society in new ways. And then, there are also people-issues that connect to all thing's equity. So that's around gender equity, racial equity, sexual orientation, environmental justice equity.'

DaSilva's approach is a useful way for companies to think about social issues—a spectrum of concerns with more traditional topics around the well-being of people and communities in general at one end, and more recent topics (in the context of corporations) regarding equity-related subjects at the other end. All have relevance to a discussion on companies being vocal on social issues.

The Need for Companies to Speak Up

Is it becoming mandatory for companies to take public positions on social issues? David Gallagher said, 'It's impossible for companies to speak up on every social issue, and probably not helpful. But it's also impossible for companies to pretend to operate in some sequestered space in which social issues aren't their concern at all. The key is to identify those issues that intersect most prominently with the interests and concerns of their most important stakeholders, and to take a course of action accordingly. And the benefit of a clear sense of purpose is that it helps discern which issues are material and which actions are relevant.'

Brian Lott said something similar, 'With my Page hat on, particularly in the U.S., companies are feeling compelled to speak out about issues that are more socially divisive. I think that really is an individual decision based on the company's values and its business and I still think it resonates most when companies take a position that is closely aligned with their brand. If you have gone out to your customers and said look, we're at the forefront of XYZ whether it's fashion or something else you want to speak to your consumers from a place of relevance rather than just feeling like you need to speak up on every issue.'

It's no secret that most companies prefer not to talk publicly about controversial subjects. Why? Because their stakeholders—customers and employees in particular—are comprised of very diverse group of people. Taking a stand on any political issue is not going to please everyone and indeed might disenfranchise a decent portion of those who interact with the company. And yet, certainly in the U.S., it seems that the one thing many people do have in common is an expectation that companies need to speak up. Andy Whitehouse is Senior Partner, Managing Partner, Strategy at Penta Group. He said, 'I think consumers expect companies to be engaged, employees expect companies to be engaged and to some degree investors do too. It's just not an option for a company to choose not to play, particularly on those public issues that are directly connected to the business that they're in.'

DaSilva, talking about employee expectations, said, 'The pressure is predominantly coming from the Gen Z and millennial generation, which have higher expectations of companies to address these issues than the older generations. I think it's fair to say the power of employees is real. The lines are blurred for employees between work and home, and they want to bring their values to work. They want to see companies who are supporting issues that are important to them. But it's also being driven by the communities themselves that are being impacted by a lot of these issues.'

Global Differences

Is the need to speak up on social issues primarily a U.S. phenomenon or does it have global relevance? Paul Holmes, founder and chair of PRovoke Media, has covered this area extensively. On the question of geography, Holmes observed, 'I think American companies have been in the forefront on social justice issues. Some have chosen to make issues and causes a central part of their brand positioning. Others have been galvanized by Black Lives Matter or other social movements. But it's more and more a global phenomenon. First, consumers and (especially) employees expect companies to stand for something beyond the products they make and sell. Strong relationships between companies and their stakeholders are rarely built on product alone (although Apple, for example, shows that it can be done). Customers and employees like to know that companies share their values, or at least that they have values. That they are interested in solving problems, being a force for good. And I think we are transitioning from this being a geographic issue—with the U.S. and Europe in the lead—to being a generational issue: Gen Z, all over the world, has higher expectations, and is more willing to hold companies accountable and punish those it sees as being part of the problem rather than part of the solution.'

Su Lin Yeo is Associate Professor of Communication Management (Practice) at the Lee Kong Chian School of Business, Singapore Management University. When I asked her about this trend in Asia, she said, 'Social advocacy has increasingly been more pronounced in Asia, but the types of social concerns are very different from those in the United States. More controversial ones are less visible and sometimes to a certain extent, even not considered as essential. In this respect, Asia is very different from the West.' Yeo went on to elaborate that 'There is no one Asian country that is democratic in exactly the same way as the United States, which means companies need to tread very carefully. And you cannot have one size fits all for Asian societies, where many Asian societies have a long history of cultural, religious, and different political concerns. The political landscape of Asia is a kaleidoscope constituting of absolute or constitutional monarchies, one-party states, self-defined democracies, military dictatorship, and various forms of independence movements.'

Yeo referenced the fact that in 2017, Starbucks faced calls for a boycott in Indonesia, the world's most populous Muslim country, for its support for the LGBTQ community. A Muslim group in Malaysia joined calls for a boycott of Starbucks in the same year. 'In Asia, there are Muslim countries whose populations are highly conservative, that may not only discriminate but also persecute those who support certain types of lifestyles.' She went on to note that 'When companies in Asia take a position, it is better to advocate on topics such as health, education, poverty, and environment. Asian societies are always very collectivistic and the mentality across many Asian countries has been how to benefit the whole of society and not individual segments of society.'

As in so many ways, China provides a stark contrast to the U.S. in this area. Scott Kronick said, 'If you want to be successful in China, you must be part of the social environment. The government regulates all industry, and you must be aligned with it.'

Multinational companies can have different reputations in different geographic markets and this is very relevant to a discussion about social issues. Swedish fashion company H&M experienced a challenging time in China after it spoke out in relation to Uyghur Muslims in China's Xinjiang province, which produces about a fifth of the world's cotton. When H&M pledged not to source cotton from Xinjiang, it may have been a well-received move by some Western stakeholders, however, it was subjected to pushback in China, with many online Chinese platforms and apps removing all references to the fashion brand.[2] What is considered a social concern in one country is not always

---

[2] 'H&M: Fashion giant sees China sales slump after Xinjiang boycott', *BBC News*, July 2021, https://www.bbc.com/news/business-57691415.

going to be seen in the same light in other parts of the world that have a markedly different viewpoint.

A number of American brands have apologized for making a stance/statement on the subject of Xinjiang or other subjects considered sensitive within China. In 2021, U.S. chip maker Intel apologized in China after the letter it had sent telling suppliers not to source products from the Xinjiang region triggered a backlash.[3] This underscores the necessity of conducting comprehensive stakeholder research and game planning the consequences of such public actions in order to traverse potential pitfalls as effectively as possible, albeit understanding the high degree of difficulty attaining perfect outcomes.

Companies need to be aware that different countries and cultures require a different approach be taken when talking about social issues. Companies cannot be overtly contradictory in their stances, but as Yeo notes, it's not a one size fits all approach.

Speaking Up versus Being Forced to Speak

Holmes noted, 'If a company is going to proactively engage on social issues, it needs to do so with a complete understanding of the likely response—positive and negative—and its own risk tolerance. Companies that have a strong, authentic history of leadership on social issues, companies like Patagonia and Ben & Jerry's, may choose to engage on controversial topics. More conservative companies should probably start with something safer. And of course, it's important to think about how the issue relates to the business, so for example a financial services

---

[3] 'Intel apologises in China over Xinjiang supplier statement', Reuters, December 2021, https://www.reuters.com/technology/intel-china-apologises-over-xinjiang-supplier-statement-2021-12-23/#:~:text=HONG%20KONG%2C%20Dec%2023%20(Reuters,rights%20issues%20in%20the%20country.

company has the "right" to engage on financial inclusion but may be out of its comfort zone talking about trans rights.'

Holmes agreed that companies can be forced into needing to respond to an issue because of where they operate or the industry sector in which they operate. He said, 'Think of companies in Texas after the State passed a draconian abortion ban. Texas-based companies were asked legitimate and important questions about whether they would pay for their female employees to access women's health resources—they were dragged into the abortion debate through no fault or action of their own and needed to have a position. In such cases, companies need to be guided by their values.'

This point about values is a considerable one. Companies do not need to weigh in on every social issue in the world, but if their values come under fire, then the corporate voice should be unequivocal. In a 2023 interview with CNBC, Nike CEO John Donahoe articulated this philosophy: 'If it's core to who you are and your values, then no, you stand up for your values,'[4] he said. 'If it's commenting on some political issue that's in someone else's backyard, then we may have that personal feeling, but we don't comment on it with our brand and publicly.' In the same interview, Donahoe went on to speak to three values that are integral to Nike's brand: racial and social justice; sustainability; and youth involvement in sports, particularly for young girls.

Not every company operates in the same vein as Nike, which is well known for its social advocacy. Nonetheless, a company may want to speak up on a particular issue, or it might be forced to do so. Either way, serious discussion must be devoted ahead of time to enable the company to achieve agreement internally about its level of risk tolerance in this area—and to be certain

---

[4] Gabrielle Fonrouge and Kevin Breuninger, 'Nike CEO John Donahoe says brands need to stand by their values amid DeSantis, Disney feud', *CNBC*, May 2023, https://www.cnbc.com/2023/05/23/nike-ceo-john-donahoe-weighs-in-on-desantis-disney-feud.html.

about the values that guide its existence, progress, and position in the world.

Deciding What Issues to Advocate

If it is reasonable to conclude that there's reputational upside attached to a company proactively supporting one or more social issues, the question then becomes, which issue or issues to support? Making public comment on a contentious issue is potentially perilous, so the company wants to be sure of what it is doing ahead of time. Whitehouse said, 'Is it an acceptable thing for a senior leader to be devoting the company's time and energy and effort to a topic if it isn't squarely at the centre of the company's interests? I think it depends. I think if you're an insurance company, not spending some time thinking about climate change would be a mistake. Executives or employees can be passionate about issues that don't directly affect the business, and I think as long as your view is that you are intervening to make the economy stronger, or to help society work more effectively, then I think that is fine. The risk always with issues that aren't directly related to the business is that it becomes a distraction from running a great business. But for every company, there are going to be three or four issues that they've just got to have a point of view on.'

DaSilva reinforced this point of view, 'What issues are critical to your stakeholders, your employees, your consumers, understanding the values of those different stakeholders, understanding how those issues relate back to your business operations? And are those issues integrated into what you do every day? And if so, those are the issues you should get behind and have the authenticity and the proof points to say yes, this is why we are taking this action.' She further elaborated that 'Companies can't support all issues that are important to their stakeholders. Having the framework of, the purpose, the values, the mission of the organization allows companies to think about not only what they will support, but also be able to explain why they don't support other issues.'

Adashek said, 'We don't practice politics at IBM, we practice policy. Getting involved in social issues has got to be at a time when it's going to impact the company – it's important for the business, to our employees, our partners and communities in which we live and work. We can't comment on every issue otherwise we'll do nothing but comment and get involved in every issue. So, if there is an issue that might be rightfully important, but it is focused on a single city, for example, that is a localized topic, we would not take a corporate position on it.' IBM uses a series of 'guidepost questions' to help the company decide what issues it should engage in. This approach helps to ensure a level of consistency and objectivity over time.

The types of questions IBM uses are:

1. Is the issue directly linked to the business?
2. Does the company have a history of engaging with it?
3. What are the stakeholders (employees, clients, and shareholders) saying?
4. What are competitors doing?
5. Could the company make a meaningful difference by engaging?

This is an excellent example of how a set of simple questions can help the company to be objective and consistent about its engagement with social issues. Without unpacking IBM's questions specifically, the following are some relevant principles (which overlap with IBM's approach):

- Alignment with corporate purpose and values: If the company has defined its purpose and values in a manner that is sufficiently prescriptive, then it will be well placed to understand those issues on which it should be taking a stand. Having such clarity will provide a solid basis upon which to define a strategic approach that allows the company to demonstrate support for aligned issues.

- The connection between a social issue and the operations of the business: Establishing the direct relevance of a social issue to the business itself goes a long way to deciding whether to get involved or stay on the sidelines. For the most part, the company's customers do not expect it to have a public position on every social issue, but they are more likely to be interested in the company's view in relation to what that company does.

- The company's risk appetite: Not every company will want to adopt an activist pose in the vein of say, a Ben & Jerry's. Rather, companies need to agree internally how much risk they are willing to take, and to feel comfortable with that.

- Stakeholder views: Social topics generate divergent and strong opinions. What one stakeholder group is saying doesn't necessarily represent the views of other stakeholders. Employees are particularly important to consider, as those who feel alienated by the company's actions can inflict serious reputational damage on the company. Make the proper investment to ensure the company has an accurate read of how different stakeholders think about the issue in question.

- The Potential for impact: Companies should not expect to get tonnes of credit because they are committed to working on an issue that no one agrees is necessary or it is not a big problem—if you take on easy problems don't expect to get much kudos from your stakeholders.

What Advocacy Means in Practice

Words matter, of course. But so do actions. Unless the corporate can demonstrate its commitment to a chosen cause, then it leaves itself exposed to accusations, it is only making superficial gestures. DaSilva made an interesting point when she said, 'It's not just about saying something, but what are you actually doing as a business and making sure your business practices are aligned with what you're saying? And now it's not even what you're doing – it's, how far will you go in order to advance progress? What role are you going to play? Are you driving awareness and understanding? Are you a mobilizer? Are you an advocate, are you an activist?'

On the question of credibility, Holmes said, 'I think consumers today—and employees even more so—have pretty good bullshit detectors, and their tolerance for insincerity and a lack of authenticity is almost zero. That means that companies need to do more than talk. Anyone can denounce racism, for example, but stakeholders today want to see companies taking action that has an impact in the real world.'

This does not mean every company has to make grand commitments. Not every company by any means is in the mould of Patagonia, the outdoor clothing and gear company, which among many other actions, donates 1% of their total sales to support environmental organizations around the world.[5] There are a wide array of smaller, practical actions a company can consider, spanning things like lobbying pressure, philanthropy, participation in industry-wide initiatives, employee volunteering and consumer education to improve understanding and awareness of the issues in question by those consumers that

---

[5] https://www.patagonia.com/one-percent-for-the-planet.html#:~:text=Since%201985%2C%20Patagonia%20has%20pledged,difference%20in%20their%20local%20communities.

interact with the company. Whatever the action, the timeframe should be a long-term one. Short-lived campaigns do not move the needle in any meaningful way, and a consistent and sustained commitment is required for the company to be seen as a credible advocate for change.

When Criticism Arises about the Company's Position

Returning to the theme of values, Whitehouse said, 'Figure out what you believe as a business. And if you're then going to make a public stance about it, you had better be willing to stand up for it because otherwise people will question your company values. A lot of people are quite sceptical about corporate values, but I'm the biggest advocate for well-reasoned corporate values, because if you get them right, and then a crisis occurs, the values should help you through it. I think if you start with your values, defining what you believe on public issues, knowing how you should cope with tough political conversations, knowing how to deal with crisis, it all just gets a lot easier if you've done that hard thinking about what you really believe in advance.'

DaSilva said that, 'When a company apologizes for offending one group of consumers or stakeholders over the other, they unequivocally will alienate everyone. So apologizing is not the answer and retracting is not the answer. It's about acknowledging the situation. It's about recognizing there are multiple opinions and it's about going back to why you did it in the first place. Why did you support that issue? And I think there are some companies that didn't think about that question prior to engaging on the issue.'

On the topic of backlash, DaSilva also made an interesting observation about a practical or structural source that can lead to discord. She suggested, 'Another trend that we're seeing is sometimes Marketing is not aligned with Corporate. And those organizations that are approaching these issues exclusively from a marketing perspective, are going to be the ones that aren't prepared for the backlash. That's because marketing's "why" is not always aligned with the that of the wider enterprise. It might be just that they want to expand their consumer base by reaching a particular audience. As you look at content creators and influencers and marketing campaigns, we need to bring marketing and corporate closer together.'

Significance for Reputations

Speaking up on social issues may well be a necessity but, consistent with the thesis of this book, multiple factors contribute to reputation. Being vocal in support of a social issue will not in itself be a means of achieving success if the company's product or service proposition is not up to scratch, or if it has governance issues, and so on. However, all things being equal, then taking a considered and strategic approach to talking about relevant social issues can not only help meet stakeholder expectations but in doing so, become a source of competitive advantage.

Summary of Principles

- Social issues can be represented along a spectrum of concerns. More traditional topics around the well-being of people and communities are at one end. Issues regarding equity-related subjects are towards the other end.

- There is no single answer to if and how companies need to speak up on social issues, but there are rising expectations that they do so (especially in certain parts of the world and among certain demographic audiences).

- Multinational companies face difficult challenges standing up for social issues of concern in Western markets when their stakeholders in other parts of the world have a different viewpoint. It's not a one size sort of fits all approach.

- Companies do not need to weigh in on every social issue, but if their values come under fire, then the corporate voice should be unequivocal.

- Developing a formal framework can help the company to assess what issues it will support and explain why it won't support others.

- Corporate advocacy for a social issue requires a demonstration of genuine actions to match words, including the alignment of the company's business practices to the position being taken by the company.

- The worst thing a company can do in the face of backlash to its stance on an issue is to waffle through it. Taking a stand should be based upon why the company supported the issue in the first instance.

8

The CEO as Chief Communicator

Chapter three references the responsibility of the CEO to earn and protect corporate reputations. The CEO sets the tone that cascades throughout the organization, is crucial to enabling a motivated workforce, and provides the basis upon which the company proactively engages its external stakeholders. The CEO needs to have the ability to connect with people—both inside and outside of the firm—in a way that unites them towards allowing the company to achieve its desired outcomes.

It's a challenging job and requires strong support. In his book *Tough Calls*, Dick Martin writes, 'Successful CEOs are like thoroughbred horses. They wear blinders to block out distractions and stay focused on the finish line. My job was to provide peripheral vision, even if it was occasionally at the price of being nipped.'[1] The provision of such peripheral vision is invaluable. This chapter turns to the practicalities associated with the CEO as communicator in chief, as he or she balances the need to address issues of the day with the long-term priorities of the business.

The most effective CEOs are able to communicate (through words and actions) with their various constituencies in a consistent

---

[1] Dick Martin, *Tough Calls: AT&T and the Hard Lessons Learned from the Telecom Wars* (American Management Association, 2005).

and transparent way that fosters trust and optimism, enabling the business agenda to be achieved.

Onboarding a New CEO

If you work in Corporate Affairs for long enough at a particular company, it is bound to happen sooner or later. The average CEO tenure continues to shorten.[2] The arrival of a new CEO usually is a moment of tension given the high stakes involved. Ascending to the top seat naturally represents a career highlight and the CEO will be anxious to ensure it goes well from day one. For many, it will be their first time as CEO, and they are stepping into the spotlight amid intense scrutiny. The board, who made the appointment, will also be watching with keen interest as they will be judged in time for the appointment they have made.

The first objective for any new CEO should be to make the best possible first impression with employees, recognizing that the circumstances surrounding a CEO's arrival will be different each time. Perhaps the previous CEO retired after twenty years of unblemished service. Perhaps the previous CEO was sacked for bad behaviour. Maybe they left quickly for a job with a rival. Or passed away. And so on and so forth. Regardless, the incoming CEO should be mindful of the imperative to engage with the company's employees, to provide reassurance that their contributions are respected and to reinforce the value of their dedication to the company. In doing so, the CEO can start to get employees familiar with their background, working style, and priorities. Many employees will wonder 'what does this all mean for me?' and CEO communications should be designed to

---

[2] 'CEO Tenure Rates', Harvard Law School Forum on Corporate Governance, February 2018, https://corpgov.law.harvard.edu/2018/02/12/ceo-tenure-rates/.

answer that question in a way that builds energy and support for their agenda.

During the initial phase of a CEO's tenure, there will be a level of pressure, including from journalists, for the CEO to go external with their communications as soon as possible. Only yield to this pressure when the time is right, and the CEO is ready to provide an informed view of their vision for the organization. Of course, the timing may not be able to be chosen. For example, earnings announcements may arrive soon after the new CEO is onboard, which necessitates media relations. Andrew Walton commenced his position as the Chief Corporate Affairs Officer at Lloyds Banking Group in 2018 (he has since been promoted to Chief Sustainability Officer & Chief Corporate Affairs Officer). In August 2021, Charlie Nunn joined Lloyds as its new Chief Executive Officer. Walton said, 'We spent the first year establishing our CEO with the right audiences and have been selective about his external engagements. The inbound requests are numerous, but we say no to most of them. This is not because we are trying to create any mystique but because he has been very focused on getting our strategy moving. You don't want very high visibility when you are still in the process of delivering what we said we will deliver. Charlie did an open and transparent interview in *The Sunday Times* two weeks ago (in April 2023).[3] That was his first big public interview done and we waited eighteen months to do that because we are building to a long-term place that we want to get to.'

Setting the Tone

The holder of the CEO role has a far-reaching impact on the culture, values, and behaviour of the organization. The personality

---

[3] Jill Treanor, 'Lloyds Bank boss Charlie Nunn: I know what it's like to be hard up', *The Sunday Times*, 15 April 2023, https://www.thetimes.co.uk/article/lloyds-bank-ceo-charlie-nunn-interview-9z7rvcbk6.

of the CEO flows throughout the company. A CEO who enjoys interacting with people, who likes being out 'in the field' talking with employees and customers, and who eschews formalities is more likely to create an open and relaxed culture. A CEO who is more intellectual, hierarchical, and who prefers to spend time on strategic planning and financial reviews may lead a more formal organization. How the CEO sets the tone for the company has a meaningful impact on that company's reputations, but this does not mean the effort to do so can rest entirely on the CEO's shoulders.

Gary Sheffer was the chief communications officer at General Electric for thirteen years and is the Sandra A. Frazier Professor of Public Relations at Boston University. When asked about the role of the CEO setting the tone within the company, he said, 'The role of the CEO is essential, but not exclusive. People look to the CEO on strategy and action, and to be the cultural North Star of the organization. In that context, the role of the CEO is important. That said, every study that you look at about employee culture, morale or engagement, shows that people look to their immediate managers more than they do to the CEO for direction.'

Another senior practitioner, Selim Bingol, who held chief communications officer roles at three major U.S. corporations—Duke Energy, General Motors, and AT&T—made a similar point. Bingol said, 'Being very visible and accessible is really important. And the company's ability to get the CEO's message spread throughout organisation, especially big organisations, I think is where the rubber meets the road. The CEO may know where he or she wants to go, and his or her direct reports know, and the next couple of layers down all get it. But as you get further away from the CEO office, it gets harder and harder. That's where I think the communications team really must flex its creativity.'

Sheffer, in a separate conversation, also raised this issue of the ability to convey information throughout the company. 'The CEO will set the strategy but must have a group of people throughout the organization who understand it and are able to engage with employees on those initiatives. In the old days, when you had hierarchical organizational charts, there was what we would call a concrete layer in the middle, where information would trickle down and just stop. You've got to break through that layer. That means training your senior managers, your middle managers, your frontline managers, on communication. That is a responsibility of the CEO.'

Walton, talking about the approach of Charlie Nunn, said, 'Charlie has a very modern, engaging CEO style. When he joined, we produced a video of him at home that showed him running, fixing his bike, and so on. His "nice guy energy" came across clearly. He is very visible and sets the tone for the organisation and we use that to our advantage. Our internal channels now use a more informal style that is less about a presidential address and more about engaging with colleagues directly. He is very accessible and visible.' Walton went on to note, 'The challenge is that you cannot then change course and have him not be visible. Once you have established such a transparent and open style, you cannot really modulate it down.'

Thinking about CEOs with open styles, one that comes to mind is Shayne Elliott, CEO of ANZ Bank in Australia. He is a charismatic presence and has a strong conviction of the importance of doing the right thing. The Royal Commission into Misconduct in the Banking, Superannuation and Financial Services Industry[4] was established in December 2017 and was covered extensively by the Australian media. Shayne Elliott sent a letter to ANZ staff, which was also made available on ANZ's website[5] (an example of the blurred line between internal and external audiences). Here is a short excerpt which gives a sense

---

[4] https://www.royalcommission.gov.au/banking.

[5] https://bluenotes.anz.com/posts/2018/01/Elliott-why-ANZ-backs-the-Royal-Commission.

of the tone of the message: 'For me, it's completely unacceptable that we have caused some of our customers financial harm and emotional stress. I'm ultimately accountable for this and once again apologise. I am also completely committed to the changes we are making – leadership, strategic, systems, people and cultural – to build an ANZ worthy of the community's trust and respect.'

Furthermore, Elliott also did a radio interview with the Australian Broadcasting Corporation where he not only apologized to customers, but also extended an invitation for them to contact him directly. He then gave out his email address on the air and promised a personal reply.[6] This is a brilliant example of the CEO setting the tone, leading from the front, showing accountability, and being customer focused.

The Significance of Language

Setting the tone is about a wide range of things—not just the actual tone in which things are said, but also the body language of an individual (in this case, the CEO), whether the person prefers casual or formal attire, the policies and actions that the CEO takes, and so on. Having said this, words matter and it is worth being clear about the significance of the words used by the CEO.

I versus We

Dr. Laura McHale is a business and leadership psychologist, and author of the book *Neuroscience for Organizational Communication: A Guide for Communicators and Leaders.*[7] McHale noted, 'Obviously,

---

[6] Peter Ryan, 'ANZ boss Shayne Elliott urges disgruntled customers to email him directly', *ABC News*, October 2018, https://www.abc.net.au/news/2018-10-12/anz-boss-shayne-elliott-fronts-parliament/10368460.

[7] Laura McHale, *Neuroscience for Organizational Communication: A Guide for Communicators and Leaders* (Palgrave Macmillan, 2022).

communicators have always known that words matter, but when we look specifically at some of the structure of language and also things like pronoun use, the use of "I" and "we" pronouns activate very different parts of the brain.'

McHale elaborated that, 'The concept of pronoun agility is really important, and leaders need to flip back and forth. "I" and "we" pronouns are connected to a concept in psychology we call self-construal. "I" pronouns can signal a high degree of personal involvement which can be very reassuring, but "we" pronouns give us a collective sense of being in things together. Not being a member of the collective – being socially excluded – is a stress producing event in the brain that is just as painful as if you broke your leg. Where organisations and executives get tripped up with "we" pronouns is that there are two types of "we" pronouns – an inclusive "we" and an exclusive "we." So, if a CEO is talking about the leadership team, they are using an exclusive "we", but the more inclusive "we" refers to, for example, everyone in the company, or it could be all of humanity if talking about something like climate change. The problem is that the executive sometimes does not know which "we" they are using or do it on purpose as an evasion tactic. Sometimes those exclusive "we" pronouns can subtly but potently signal that there are certain people in an organization that are perceived to have a more legitimate stake in the organization's success. We see this most commonly when talking about front office, client facing staff and then back-office support staff, who are not part of the "we".'

She further explained, 'The pronoun "I" can signal a very comforting sense of personal accountability, especially if you trust the leader. But overuse of it can signal narcissism, that causes massive stress in the brain. There are no hard rules, such as to use 50% "we" and 50% "I", but we just need to be more mindful and agile about how we use them.'

Do versus Feel Communications

McHale also noted, 'Research has found that analytical tasks (such as financial analysis and problem solving) activate regions of the brain known as the Task Positive Network (TPN). However, there is a different network—the Default Mode Network (DMN)—which is activated when an individual pays attention to understanding others, being fair, and openness to new ideas. But here's the kicker: these two networks have little overlap and actually suppress each other. Our brains can't do both at the same time. This has big implications for CEO communications and indeed, comms in general. Task oriented (what people need to "Do"), it activates the TPN, and consequently, suppressing the DMN, e.g., how to "Feel". As a result, "Do" communications might actually constrain our ability to emotionally integrate, build relationships, and be open to new perspectives. This means we need different comms for different objectives. If the CEO is sending a "Do" communication, it should aim to be cleaner, focus on technical skills and specific deliverables and outcomes. CEO "feel" communications should be separate and focus on how we work together, how we learn from mistakes and overcome them, and what kind of organization we are aspiring to be.'

External Engagement

The CEO of any large company, and by extension his/her Corporate Affairs team, will have to consider the degree to which they want to proactively engage with the media. Chapter nine is devoted to media relations, but at this point, it is relevant to examine media relations in the context of the CEO's stakeholder engagement programme.

The goal of media relations for the CEO should not be to make that person famous in their own right. Andrew Walton spoke to this principle when articulating Lloyds Banking Group's external communications work. 'We do not engage with external audiences without a clear reason. Which stakeholder group are we trying to move from point A to B, and if we think they are already at B, are we trying to reinforce it or take them to point C? Our CEO always wants to know why he is being asked to do something and expects a logical argument in support of it.'

Bingol said, 'The degree to which a CEO is comfortable with media relations puts different demands on the communications organization in terms of preparing that CEO for the interview. Some CEOs will know the reporters, they know what to say and they're very comfortable and don't need a lot of prep work. Others will need a lot of detail, a lot of information and a lot of reassurance.'

The extent to which a CEO agrees to the gamut of external engagements available—conferences, speaking on panels, visiting customers, media relations—is a balancing act. It is valuable—and essential—for the CEO to proactively represent the company externally, but there is such a thing as overexposure and the CEO also should not be distracted from the actual task of running the company.

Walton, talking about external commitments, noted, 'To take a systematic approach, first, you map it out against dates in the financial calendar which you know are pre-set. Then you set yourself a kind of campaign issue led line, where we agree this is the level of visibility we want on this issue and our plan for the year ahead. And then you engage around that to achieve the outcomes you want. We have a five-year strategy, so it takes some time to generate the returns from that strategy and you want to build external engagement accordingly. We have recently launched a new campaign on social and affordable housing, and we have established a partnership with Crisis, a homelessness charity, about building a million social homes in the next ten years. We are already the biggest funder of the housing association sector and Charlie will lead a convening role and work with government and others to see how we can unlock further funding. This means we will start to build his external engagements, he has started to write some opinion editorials and engage with opinion formers on social media, and so on.'

Building the CEO's Social Media Presence

Savvy CEOs, particularly at public companies, understand that social media offers them the means to amplify their personality, expertise and leadership. It also gives them the opportunity to be part of a larger conversation regarding topics relating to their company.

Marshall Manson is a former Partner at Brunswick where he advised C-suite and board level clients on how to utilize digital and other disruptive technologies in their communications. He observed, 'In the past, we had to twist the arms of CEOs to use social media, but that's not really the imperative any more. The imperative now is to get them to do it well. I think we're going to end up in a place where they are going to be some CEOs, not all from big name companies by the way, who are really credible and interesting and where their presence on LinkedIn makes a big difference for them and for their company. There will be a bunch of other CEOs who do things with limited effectiveness and limited impact and so that imperative to not just do it but do it well I think is the thing for us to focus on with CEO clients over the next 24 months or so.'

> ## Practical recommendations for CEO's use of social media
>
> - Have a clear strategy for the CEO's social media presence, including the types of content they will share, the platforms they will use, and the audience they want to reach.
> - Authenticity is vital. Audiences want to hear from the CEO about their own opinions, insights, and interests.
> - Set a regular cadence. Establish a posting rhythm that works for the CEO, which might be a couple of times a week—and then stick with it.
> - CEO should be willing to engage with their followers and respond to feedback and comments. This can help build relationships and demonstrate your commitment to your customers and employees.
> - The CEO is volunteering to put him or herself 'out there' and that comes with a degree of risk. There might be negative comments left on the CEO's platforms and the CEO should be prepared to handle such instances.

Delivering Bad News

By virtue of their position, CEOs have a responsibility to report on all aspects of company performance. Even the most successful CEOs will at some point in their career have had to be the bearer of bad news of some form, from earnings that don't meet expectations, to deals that fall through to the need to lay-off employees. True leaders take ownership of making tough announcements. How they go about it can make a big difference to the impact of what is being said. A common temptation is to try and put a spin on things or making promises that cannot be kept.

Sheffer was frank in his assessment of this topic. He said, 'Providing bad news to the organization I think is the central weakness of CEOs. Anyone can give good news, whether it's CEOs or just in your personal life, but giving bad news and doing it in an effective way is an art. It is a learned skill for people.' The CEO needs to be prepared to convey difficult news in a way that is clear, humble, and that provides the basis to resolve the situation in time. Here, as in all communications, the leader needs to lean into their individual strengths and character in order to be as authentic as possible. Empathy is key too—understanding what is on the minds of the audience in question, whether that be employees, investors, customers, and so on. Only by having a genuine sense of their mindset can the CEO address their concerns in a way that is productive.

McHale noted, 'In times of crisis clear language is especially important. Look at the remarkable Churchillian language – "We shall fight on the beaches, we shall fight on the landing grounds, we shall fight in the fields and in the streets, we shall fight in the hills; we shall never surrender." Churchill wasn't saying, "well maybe" or "possibly we might." It really doesn't matter where you sit on the political spectrum. Everybody in times of crisis prefers more robust leadership.'

Practical recommendations for delivering bad news

1. Wherever possible, avoid catching people off guard. In many cases, the company can predict where things may not be going well, or where problems could present themselves. If the CEO is communicating consistently in a way that keeps stakeholders informed and that conditions people for whatever is ahead, then this will ensure the company's stakeholders are more understanding than they might otherwise have been.

2. Be accountable and responsible. If the news is seriously bad, the CEO needs to be the one who addresses it rather than delegating it to someone further down the chain.

3. Don't use jargon or corporate speak. If the CEO regrets what has happened, then they need to express that regret in a humble and authentic manner. Sheffer put it well: 'It's a word that's overused, empathetic. That means just be a good human. Be a good person when you deliver bad news and I think that goes a long way to helping people to manage.'

4. Make your words credible by showing a commitment to act. Life is far from perfect, and mistakes happen, or difficulties arise all the time. Show that the company is serious about the issue at hand by spelling out the actions that will be taken to fix it and to ensure that it doesn't happen again.

5. Test your messages (if there is time), monitor the reaction to the news and be ready to correct misinformation if necessary.

Whether the news is good or bad, the CEO's ability (and for that matter, all leaders at a company) to adapt quickly and effectively to dynamic conditions has a crucial impact on the wider organization. McHale referred to Ronald Heifetz, a professor of leadership at Harvard University's John F. Kennedy School of Government. 'Heifetz's work focuses on the need for leaders to be able to adapt to changing circumstances. He talks about the five core functions of leadership: direction, protection, role orientation, conflict resolution and group norms. And leaders when they're setting the tone at the top, all of those are important to the degree that they're able to provide them. Fulfilling those leadership functions gives people a lot of faith and confidence in the integrity of the leader, in the competence of the leader, and in the caring of the leader.'

Summary of Principles

- The most effective CEOs are able to communicate (through words and actions) with their various constituencies in a consistent and transparent way that fosters trust and optimism.
- Onboarding a new CEO is a critical time to enable them to make a positive first impression with employees. External communications should be done selectively and only when the timing is right.
- How the CEO interacts with stakeholders has a huge impact on the tone of the entire organization but the CEO cannot do all the communications with the company themself. Support is required from managers throughout the company.
- The words used by CEOs in written and verbal communications matter. The CEO should be mindful of how pronouns such as 'I' and 'we' are used, and what types of messages are included in which communications.
- External engagements, including media relations, should be conducted only when there is a business reason for doing so.
- Savvy CEOs understand that social media offers them the means to personally amplify the values and progress of their company. It also gives them the opportunity to be part of a larger conversation regarding topics of relevance to their company.
- Delivering bad news is part of the job and must be done in a manner that is timely, authentic, and accountable.

9

The Art of Media Relations

It was 8.30 a.m. one morning in Shanghai and the office was still quiet. Nonetheless, I had just lost my cool. A Bloomberg journalist had rung me. She told me that she had seen an article in the *Financial Times* about the Chinese regulator being punished for violating currency control rules, and that she was under pressure from her editors to run something. I had explained to her on a background basis—meaning that I was not to be quoted—that Citigroup had not been punished and hence should be left out of any story to that end. I had been under the impression that the journalist agreed with what I had to say. I was taken aback, then, to see her article run shortly afterwards. The headline read: 'China Punishes Citigroup, HSBC, 8 Other Overseas Banks, FT Says'. Furthermore, I had been quoted inaccurately: 'Citigroup spokesman Stephen Thomas said the bank hasn't been told by the government that it's being punished.' I was outraged! To my shame, I rang the journalist with a head of steam and yelled at her not to call me again. She didn't back down and was shouting back before we abruptly ended the call. We later patched things up, but it was a classic example of the frustrations that can arise conducting media relations and of how to *not* react when things skid awry.

Traditional media relations remain highly influential on corporate reputations. Media coverage helps to shape public opinion; it can affect how consumers think and act and it can produce regulatory and/or political actions. Negative or inaccurate media coverage can cause reputational damage that generates serious problems. Yet, in large part due to the rise of owned media, the art of traditional media relations is often not as strong as could be within the corporate world.

The Importance of Media Coverage

Despite the rise of paid and owned media, the value of earned media coverage will always be important. Positive coverage delivers two things in particular—excitement and credibility. If a story can be placed in the right media outlet for the company's target audiences (including employees) then seeing that story up in lights creates a buzz that owned media cannot replicate. Gary Sheffer reinforced this view. He said, 'Traditional business media is still largely the driver of your public reputation. And it comes in many forms. *The Wall Street Journal*, the *Financial Times*, and so on, all have different platforms on which they disseminate information about your company. And then, of course, social media and other platforms pick it up.'

Johnson & Johnson's Wyldeck said something similar, 'Communications through your own channels is important, but also there is always going to be a sense of well, of course, you'd say that. If you own the content, then there's always going to be a vested interest in what you're communicating. It's like if you see an advertorial taken out in the newspaper, you always take it with a grain of salt.'

Traditional Media in Asia

The value of traditional media is global. Like other parts of the world, media outlets in Asia have suffered from declining advertising revenues and lower circulations amid the rise of social media (traditional media outlets have also transformed to digital versions, which has enabled them to stay viable). The health of traditional media platforms varies across Asian markets. Newspapers remain popular in markets such as India and Japan.[1] Print media in Singapore is dominated by Singapore Press Holdings (SPH), the main publisher of prominent newspapers and magazines in the country. Live television remains very popular across Asian markets.[2] Even in China, which has arguably led the world in adoption of digital platforms of all kinds, still retains a large number of traditional media platforms. CCTV, the state-run broadcaster, dominates television. The primary news agency in China is Xinhua News Agency. A raft of business newspapers operate in cities throughout the country.

In a number of markets in Asia, there are issues around press freedom. Without downplaying the seriousness of these issues, coverage of business news in the region, at least on many topics, is given more latitude. For companies operating in the region, interacting with both international and local market journalists is required. Being on CNBC Asia might have certain benefits in some markets, but less so somewhere like Japan, where everyone reads Nikkei in local language. The calibre of business journalists in the region is varied but tends to be stronger in those centres that are financial hubs, namely Hong Kong, Singapore, Tokyo, and Shanghai.

---

[1] https://wordsrated.com/asian-newspaper-publishing-statistics/.

[2] 'Leading through the Media Landscape in APAC', Page 8, https://commercial.yougov.com/rs/464-VHH-988/images/yougov-apac-Media-Report-APAC-v2.pdf?utm_medium=email&utm_source=whitepaper&utm_campaign=WP-2023-01-APAC-Media-Landscape-Report&mkt_tok=NDY0LVZISC05ODgAAAGNd75R8xCA9f3lX6zGiQF0E5k0_Qwg0Vvfk0pMHcSa7FMZ2KLQ-N0wiEpbsG6dMSJVrY-B5xqBp30DUhrUK1nYXwctmdpHQUo9ioo-Ve4l.

The Challenge of Share of Voice

We need more coverage! How come Company X is always in the news? We do so much but we are too quiet. These are mutterings that executives utter at points of time, and it can be frustrating for the Corporate Affairs team. Of course, companies of a certain size should expect to have a proactive and effective media relations programme that enables them to tell their stories via earned media. The frustration can creep in if the same companies are not willing to say anything newsworthy in nature. And it's the journalists and their editors who are the ones with the power to decide what constitutes a story. Serious journalists are not interested in being a glorified PR outlet for spruiking a product or service. They want *news*. More specifically, they are interested in subject matter that is topical, that will resonate with a particular audience and that has some acute insight as opposed to generalities.

Some announcements are news-breaking by nature. The delivery of an earnings report. The unveiling of an M&A deal. The appointment of a new CEO. Such topics are inherently interesting and thus sought after by media outlets. But what about in the normal course of business? Pitching and securing interviews then becomes more challenging, and this is where a thoughtful, focused, and creative approach is required. This translates to identifying 'hooks' that can be pitched to a journalist who wants to position your interview idea in the context of a topical trend or challenge. The company will also need to provide data and/or anecdotes to make the story idea credible. The reason that so many companies conduct thought leadership initiatives is to generate such data and insight that provide the basis for a media relations campaign.

Accepting the view that traditional media coverage remains valuable, and that achieving share of voice is not always straightforward, how then to approach the art of media relations? The remainder of this chapter touches upon some of the practices underlying effective media relations.

Interacting with Journalists

The best practitioners of media relations are the ones that embrace the process of getting to know the journalists who cover their industry sector. Selim Bingol emphasized, 'Media relations people need to have the kind of relationships with reporters where they can have frank and full conversations. I always bang a table on this, and I used to kid with all of my media people, telling them, I'll sign any expense report you submit to me if it's in the interest of building relationships with key reporters. We can do these jobs, by phone and by video and by email and text, but it's so much better if you've gotten the chance to go have lunch with these guys once in a while.'

Wyldeck said, 'Communications is a profession and there is a huge amount of inherent knowledge required to understand how you can work with the media. What makes a good story, how to communicate effectively with journalists, how to deal with journalists' questions, understanding and anticipating what they want to get out of a story. These are the things that you can't just pick up overnight.'

Despite this reality, often those representing companies in this capacity prefer to do media relations from behind a laptop. It doesn't work—whether pitching proactive stories or trying to manage a damaging story—having a good professional relationship with journalists necessitates personal, face-to-face interactions. Gary Sheffer summed it up when he said, 'Digital tools make it easier to, in a sense, protect yourself from the media, by issuing email statements and that kind of thing. If your strategy is to protect yourself from the media, that's okay. But imagine saying that investor relations isn't important any more. I can just send the investor a message about our company, but I don't have to know the people that work there. That would be suicidal from an investor relations standpoint. Building trust, understanding the kinds of stories that journalists are interested in, being a credible source on both good and bad information is essential to reputation.'

When time comes to pitch a story to a busy journalist, a proper approach is required. At the least, the executive pitching the story needs to know ahead of time that it's relevant to the reporter's areas of interest and worthy of their attention.

Media Interviews

The interview is not a normal conversation. A normal conversation can be wide ranging, skipping around from one topic to the next, without the need to stay focused or worry too much about the implications of each and every word you speak. There is less of a need to be repetitive. An interview is a very different situation. This is something that executives do not always understand. A media interview is a constructed situation between two parties with competing objectives. On the one side is the interviewee, the company executive. On the other side, the journalist. The executive wants to get his company's good news out— the expertise the company has, the quality of the company's products, the investment the company is making in technology, and so on. On the other side of the net is the journalist, who wants news. And what is news? It is a range of things. It could be a prediction about future performance. It could be a comment about the company's interest in an acquisition of another company. It could be about any number of things, including those subjects that are not necessarily positive in nature from the perspective of the company. The interview is a game of give and take.

This means knowing your objective prior to the interview commencing—what are the talking points and key messages that you wish to convey as part of the story being written? If the executive does not have a coherent view of what they want to communicate, then the prospect of a positive result for the company is not high. At best there will be a great conversation that leaves the journalist with no clear story to write. At worse, the article will contain references that the executive didn't mean to be published.

This chapter is not focused on media training techniques, but suffice to say, the executive giving the interview should be well prepared ahead of the interview. Doing so, will give that executive both the skills and the confidence to represent the company to optimal effect during the interview. A written brief should be provided that outlines the talking points and messages to be communicated during the interview, together with supporting proof points. The ideal headline that could possibly result from the interview should be articulated as well. This will help focus the spokesperson and also ensure that all relevant internal stakeholders are on the same page as well.

Knowing the messages is one thing. Knowing how to deliver them is another. Even executives who are experienced media performers benefit from a rehearsal ahead of time, and this is especially so in the case of a broadcast interview. The executive should be able to make their points succinctly. They should also be trained to navigate their way through the interview by having a framework and techniques that they can rely on. Even the most seasoned media performer should be encouraged to have refresher sessions on a semi-regular basis.

Finally, journalist's usually baulk at the idea of quote checking, but there is no downside in at least asking the journalist to check the quotes for factual accuracy. Often, they will agree, and it is very beneficial to be able to take a preview of the quotes and make sure there is nothing there that raises a red flag.

Making Announcements via a Press Conference

Media strategy is great but means little unless you have the tactics to carry it out. Pulling off a press conference puts the Corporate Affairs team on notice. The questions that need to be addressed at the outset include:

- Are you confident your announcement is sufficiently topical that journalists will show up? This is no joke.

Although senior executives might be in love with the topic being announced, this does not automatically mean high levels of media interest. There are never guarantees as to how many journalists will come to your press conference, so consider the question in a dispassionate way before launching into preparations.

- Who will represent the company as spokesperson for the event? Is it the CEO? Or is another senior executive, such as the CFO or Head of Technology, best placed to do it? Or a combination? This is a balancing act, as further down the food chain you go, the harder it will be to secure media interest.

- Will you be able to provide an opportunity for a memorable photo moment? This sounds elementary, but a good image can go a long way to boosting the end result. And lining a few executives together in front of a backdrop is not inspiring. The photo shouldn't be one that puts executives in an awkward position but there is room for some creativity.

- How will you run the Q&A session following the formalities? A good moderator adds a lot to the effectiveness of the session, and this ideally means someone who is familiar with the journalists in the room and who has the assertiveness to direct traffic.

No Comment

A debate that often arises within the company is how to respond to a media enquiry about a topic the company is not comfortable to discuss publicly. Many times, for instance in the case where the company is involved in merger or acquisition talks, the response will simply be 'no comment'. There is nothing to be gained from saying otherwise, and indeed, often this is a matter of law rather than a judgment call. So, it is wise to never say never.

However, there are also many times where the company can say something beyond 'no comment' that helps convey its position on a particular matter.

Bingol said, 'I think "no comment" is a default and that's fine. But you don't want to miss an opportunity to help shape something. I've been involved in stories where we will say for the record, we have no comment, but can we go off the record? And you can say, look here, here's what's happening. And this is why I cannot say this for you on the record, but I want you to have context here. You can also then marshal some of your third parties who may be experts in this area, and have them contact the reporter or vice versa, to give them additional colour that you wouldn't want to under the company's name.'

This makes sense. Sometimes, the reporter asking the question has a valid viewpoint, but the company spokesperson cannot be the one to confirm it. This is not to say that some guidance cannot be given on background that will help ensure any inaccuracies are addressed or that the focus of the story is aligned with the company's position. Even if the response is a 'decline to comment', the starting point should always be trying to be helpful in response to the media enquiry that's made.

Terminology

The following phrases are often used when talking about media relations. Some people have slightly different views of what such terms imply, so any use of the terms should be spelled out with the journalist in question to ensure everyone is on the same page.

- On the record: what is being said to the journalist can be attributed in the article to a specific person at the company.

- Off the record: the information provided to the journalist can be used in the story but cannot be attributed to any specific person (for example, it could be attributed to 'sources close to the company'.)
- On background: the information being imparted is done to help guide the journalist's thinking but should not be used at all in the resulting article.

Responding to Leaks

Typically, the company should have a policy in place that makes clear that the leaking of proprietary information is not permitted, and that action will be taken against employees who are found to have disclosed sensitive information without authorization.

The reality though is leaks to the media will happen and finding the source of the leak is a waste of time. Sheffer summed up, 'Anytime someone asks you to find who the leaker is, it's a bad idea. It really is a fool's errand. Because you end up alienating or insulting a lot of people who weren't leaking. In M&A, leaks happen all the time. Just make it part of your communication strategy and move on.'

Staying Out of the News

An interesting part of media relations is that an executive working in this space can be judged for not just making something happen, but also for preventing it from happening. When talking about the art of media relations, stopping a story from appearing, or getting your company's name left out, is part of that art.

This is a legitimate and valuable skill. In some instances, the company will be alerted to a story coming down the pipe that is simply factually incorrect. In this case, the journalist must be told, in no uncertain terms, that the story (or the inclusion of the company in the story) has no merit. On other occasions, and this can be a more ambiguous area, it can be argued that the piece being planned is not newsworthy and as such, it is not reasonable for the media outlet to publish it. For example, a journalist bumps into a CEO at a social gathering and listens to the CEO mention the cost of his kids' private school fees. This was said in an informal setting and it can be argued it's not in the public interest to report it.

Getting the desired result is not necessarily easy. It means, broadly, convincing the journalist in question of the company's position on the matter. One thing that can be hugely helpful is the degree to which you know the journalist in question. Again, this is where it is valuable to have media relations professionals who have invested time in building relationships with the journalists that cover their business. Having that foundation enables robust discussions to be had more constructively. It might also mean that some horse trading can be done. That is, if you do this for me, I can give you something else. This is not always a great outcome, being in debt to a journalist, and it can also implicitly feel like your initial argument wasn't sufficient in the first place. Finally, there is the threat of going over the journalist's head and speaking with their editor. This is unlikely to endear you to the journalist but in some cases, speaking to someone up the chain can help achieve the desired result.

Negative Media Coverage

The appearance of a negative article can create a white-hot degree of angst within the company. A bad headline or an article that is critical of the company can become a distraction internally as the leadership team either howls about the unfair nature of the piece or demands something is done about it, or both!

Bingol made an astute observation that, 'It's important to distinguish when we say "negative news", to distinguish from the case where your company has done something wrong or something bad has happened. People will tend to understand the negative coverage in this situation. And if you have had an incident or a self-inflicted wound, then you cannot just communicate your way out. The company needs to make change to address what has happened. In other situations, you may have, for example, somebody is saying something bad about the company, or the company is being criticized as part of a wider legal or legislative fight. Then it starts to become a little less about what the company has done and that can provoke a different reaction internally.'

Sheffer said, 'I would say, first off, don't let people inside the company view the media as the enemy. We need good journalism. I liked it when we had strong journalists covering my company. Of course, there will be negative stories from time to time. Companies are not perfect entities. And so those stories are going to come. But if you take the view, they are out to get us, they don't like us, why would I talk to that reporter, then that becomes sort of a cancer and an excuse inside a company to not engage. Good communicators knock that down.'

When the Corporate Affairs team knows media coverage is coming, they must keep colleagues informed and set expectations for what the story will look like. They must also build a plan while the story is being constructed to respond, including identifying all the stakeholders to reach out to about the coverage, whether it's customers, investors, regulators, or employees.

In closing, the demise of traditional media has long been predicted. Despite its challenges, there will remain a place for professional, independent, verifiable journalism long into the future. Amid an ocean of churning news, opinion, and content, the role of credible and trusted journalism will be as vital as ever, even as the formats in which it is delivered continue to change. The onus remains on companies to be savvy and proactive in how they engage with the press to tell their story.

Summary of Principles

- Earned media coverage remains a key driver of corporate reputations.
- Beyond major announcements, a thoughtful, focused, and creative approach is required to achieving share of voice in relevant media outlets.
- The best media relations professionals are ones who invest time in building personal relationships with the journalists and editors who cover their company.
- The interview is not a normal conversation and thorough preparation is required before putting any executive in front of a journalist.
- 'Declining to comment' is sometimes necessary but should not be done automatically. If it does have to be done, consideration should be given to providing background information to guide the story that is being published.
- Don't waste time looking for the source of leaks.
- Keeping the company out of the news can be as crucial as getting it in the news.
- Negative coverage is a fact of life. Don't let the company view the media as the enemy.

10

The Influence of Social Media

A social media presence represents an essential conduit between a company and its stakeholders. It provides the means to demonstrate corporate purpose and values, to listen to what people think and to engage in a dialogue on matters relevant to the business. Social media is so ubiquitous that everyone of course has some level of knowledge about it. Yet, many senior business executives typically do not have an informed view of what makes for an effective social media programme.

Alex Pearmain is co-founder of OneFifty, an independent digital consultancy. On the question of how companies should think about social media in the context of their reputation, Pearmain said, 'The two big strands for me that companies need to reflect on are first, connecting their role on the ground in communities – and this just happens to be digital communities. Digital or social communities have a wide-reaching impact on corporate reputation. Then strand two is thinking about it as a direct and tangible expression of the company's actions – you very rarely have a reputation crisis; you have a business crisis. Therefore, your digital reputation is probably the quickest, most tangible, most specific expression of how your business is in providing its services and interacting with the wider world.'

This chapter is not about social media marketing, which is a different animal, focused on sales, customer experience, promotions, advertising and so on. These activities do influence and impact the reputations of the company but at their core, they are focused on selling more products and finding more customers. That is the subject of a separate analysis. Rather, the chapter sets out some basic principles to help those at companies who might be still grappling with how to approach their corporate social media programmes in a consistent and effective manner.

Establishing a Corporate Social Media Presence

New companies need to build their social media footprint. Existing firms should be thinking about how to refine or expand their presence. But how to do so in a manner that produces the best results? In short, it depends on the type of company and the objective of the activity.

On the question of how companies should think about their social media footprint, Manson (ex-Brunswick) said, 'I like to look at this on a continuum, so there's some companies for whom their social media presence is about satisfying an audience demand. So, for example, a company has an investor relations page on its website because it has investors who are looking affirmatively, searching for information about the company and you need to give them a destination for it. Another example is around litigation communications where someone is looking for information about a certain case. So, there are scenarios in corporate reputation situations where your activity is very much limited to satisfying demand. I have a client at the moment that is not interested in having any type of public profile; it just requires a "serving demand" strategy that focuses on search. But that has social media elements because social media performs well for search, so for example, they have a LinkedIn profile in order to have the presence that they want when people go looking for them, but there's absolutely no effort being made to raise visibility. The world of marketing is all about raising visibility, raising awareness, raising affinity and ultimately driving conversion to sales. However, many corporate communication situations do not have the objective of raising visibility. If one end of the continuum is serving demand, the other end of the continuum is driving demand. I think most companies lie somewhere in the middle. The question is, where on that continuum do you fall broadly and what are the implications of that for how you establish your digital presence in order to manage your reputation in the right way?'

This makes sense and speaks to having a clear understanding about the company's overall objectives at the outset. That in turn enables a selection of channel choices and content decisions— how often you're producing, how often you're publishing, who's it going to, who you're targeting and so on.

A Model for Digital Corporate Reputation

Where specifically must companies focus their time, attention, and money on social media? If the company takes an ad hoc, tactical approach, the danger is that much money will be invested for little return. Manson provides an excellent way of thinking about this challenge in a more systematic way. He said, 'I talk about four legs of a stool: (1) Search; (2) Social; (3) Owned; (4) Wikipedia. Those are the four legs of the reputational stool for me and then the question becomes what kind of company it is and where does it fit on the continuum. That in turn will inform the platforms you want to be on.'

This model provides a useful point to dive into the effort of optimizing the corporate digital ecosystem. The subject of social media is so vast that focusing on four dimensions—how people find your company online; which platforms the company wants to be active on; how the company approaches owned content; and the power of Wikipedia in shaping reputations—provides a digestible means for the layman to think about the topic.

1. Search

This chapter does not provide a technical analysis of search engine optimisation (SEO). It will not go down the rabbit hole of keyword research, meta descriptions, backlinks, website structure, etc. However, from a helicopter view, it is obvious that search engines are many people's first port of call when it comes to finding out information. Yet many companies are not sufficiently focused on this aspect of their digital presence.

Manson said, 'Think about your Google search results as a piece of real estate and you're basically in a monopoly game and the game is to own as much of that real estate as you possibly can and to do so in the most forthright and ethical manner that you possibly can. You want to own as much real estate as you can on the first page. How do you go about doing that? The answer is pretty straight forward. You need a really good dynamic website that performs well in search, you need to make sure that you have got your social platforms up and optimised. But there is also some other things for corporates that come in here, for example, every corporate for example has a Bloomberg profile page. Is it accurate? Have you ever looked at it? There are three or four others like that which usually score well.'

There is another source of ammunition to achieve better search results that highlights the enduring value of earned media. Manson explained, 'There's usually one or two pieces of media coverage that score on a corporate's first page of results. This is one of the strong links between doing digital reputation well and good old doing fashion PR well. [I] often find myself saying to clients in order to solve this search problem, you just need a really good, dynamic interesting article in *The New York Times* or *The Wall Street Journal* or *The Straits Times* or whatever it is in your corner of the world.'

There is a large existing body of analysis that explores the best approach to the SEO effort, which the reader can research separately. It is worth noting though that SEO does require its own strategy, and that to achieve results usually requires a consistent undertaking over at least twelve months or more.

2. Social Platforms

Social media platforms encompass online platforms and communities that enable people to create, share, and swap information. Different social platforms serve different audiences. Being clear about which audiences are most crucial, the company can then segment its various platforms according to those that are critical; those that are optional; and those that are pointless. This approach allows a simple matrix to be constructed, with target audiences on one axis and platforms on the other. Suffice to say, LinkedIn, Instagram, X (formerly Twitter), TikTok, and Facebook are among the most popular platforms for companies to consider. McKinsey's Prudencio noted, 'We take a multi-channel approach to social platforms. Given the nature of LinkedIn, we focus extensively on that platform. We're also on Twitter, Instagram, Facebook, and YouTube. And in China, we will be on Weibo and other channels.' The choice of platforms will reflect knowing your target audience and understanding the local market. For example, in Japan, LinkedIn is used far less compared to other parts of the world and is thought of as a job seeking platform.[1] Rather, a platform like LINE would be in the mix, given it's the most popular and successful messaging app in that country.

Adam Wyldeck said, 'One of the considerations that businesses need to be making is where they are going to play, because everyone has limited bandwidth. Our company used to have Twitter page for Australia and New Zealand. But who are the audiences we are trying to reach on social channels? It's doctors,

---

[1] https://consulting-japan.com/strategic-consulting-japan-articles/why-linkedin-is-not-effective-in-japan.

patients and support networks including families, patient groups
and patient advocates. Plus, government and the general public.
Take patients as an example. I don't think that patients are on X
waiting to see what Janssen has to say about a certain treatment.
Rather, I think that person will be on Facebook and Instagram.
So, we took the decision to sunset our Twitter channel and launch
a Facebook page that would allow us to drive campaigns to reach
audiences that we wanted to reach.'

Company culture needs to be considered as part of the
process of deciding which platforms to be on. Pearmain noted,
'One of the many reasons for LinkedIn's success is how sanitized
it is it feels like a natural extension of being in a business
conference . . . no one says anything horrible; you use real identities
and most of us have shirts on in our pictures. It feels familiar and
safe. Tik Tok, which increasingly is relevant to stakeholder groups,
is terrifying to most corporate affairs cultures . . . the idea that you
might dance on a video.'

Of course, this landscape is constantly changing, making
it difficult to speak definitively about specific platforms. At the
time of writing, Gen Z and Gen Alpha are powering the growth
of Tik Tok, and this also has major implications for corporate
reputations—both in terms of reaching this demographic and also
in relation to issues management (as, for example, McDonald's has
contended with in the wake of employees giving their assessment
of working at the franchise via Tik Tok)[2]. The process of assessing
and agreeing which platforms a company will be on or leave (and
at what levels i.e., headquarters versus local market) is an ongoing
one that requires review at regular intervals.

---

[2] Margot Harris, '9 things customers should know about McDonald's,
according to a former cashier going viral on TikTok', *Business Insider*,
August 2020, https://www.insider.com/viral-tiktok-mcdonalds-former-
employee-2020-8.

3. Owned Media

Owned media are those sites and channels that the company has total control over. There is some debate over whether this extends to a company's social media pages, for example its LinkedIn or X page. The content that companies place on these platforms is owned by the company, but the platform itself is not. If LinkedIn or X or any other social media platform crashes for whatever reason, or experiences an issue or controversy, this is not in the company's control—the company is just a guest or part of the community of that platform. In contrast, company websites, blogs, and emails are completely within that company's control.

Manson said, 'One of the trends in corporate digital communications at the moment is a real concern that a lot of the assumptions we've made over the last 10 to 15 years are beginning to be eroded. This means that may be distributed content strategy doesn't work as well as it did five years ago and so there is a retrenching happening where we're all saying we've got to get back to first principles—we need to make sure the website works really hard, we need to get back to owning our own distribution channels, which means having a really good e-mail database, etc. I would say that over the next five years things will tilt in the direction of corporate ability to own and publish their own stories from their own channels will become more important than the distributed content strategies that we've been pursuing these last ten years or so.'

In the context of publishing content, Prudencio explained, 'We are innovating our formats to engage audiences in different ways. The *McKinsey Quarterly*, our flagship publication, now does what we call a 5-50 format, which provides a five-minute version and a 50-minute version of an article. The *Quarterly* has now gone digital as well.' He went on to say, 'We are doing more video. We are also doing live events which are open to all audiences.

McKinsey Live is such a platform, which is open to anyone. It features interviews with McKinsey partners or external experts on a variety of timely topics. We use our own platform for the live session, and then post a recording on LinkedIn.' These are great examples that reflect how leading firms are making smart use of their own platforms in a variety of mediums to engage directly with their stakeholders.

4. Wikipedia

Manson cited Wikipedia as the fourth stool because of its influence over the other aspects of being online—namely that is viewed as a trusted source and it's promoted widely in search. Whether Wikipedia is truly a trusted source of information remains open to debate, given it is crowd-sourced information. The reality though is that, today at least, there are few online sources more sought after for information than Wikipedia. What is less known is how Wikipedia works. Companies are not allowed to edit their own company page. Rather, Wikipedia is maintained by a community of volunteers through open collaboration and using an editing system called MediaWiki. Manson said, 'The first thing that I say to clients when we start talking about Wikipedia is you need to get through your head that your Wikipedia entry is not yours, it really isn't, it belongs to Wikipedia, and it belongs to the community. It is not for you to manage and your participation in editing your Wikipedia entry is against the rules and you cannot do it. The question is how do you influence that community, because it is a group of volunteer editors. We have had really good success over last few years helping our clients learn how to engage the community that looks after Wikipedia. The other strong linkage between digital reputation and traditional PR is Wikipedia. You'd be amazed how often we start talking to clients about Wikipedia and the problem is that they've got lots of things they want to say and have no citations for it and then that's a PR problem that's not a digital problem.'

Social Media Listening

Another simple need, but with no simple solution, is listening to what is being said about the company online—about its brand, products, and services, about its competitors and about announcements it makes. Prudencio observed, 'For communications professionals, separating signal from noise is the big challenge in social media listening. We use a suite of listening tools, and benchmarks against past issues to understand whether a new issue is gaining traction and merits attention.'

Manson said, 'As the web in general gets more atomized it's harder and harder to get a clear picture of what's happening and there are many reasons behind it, including the platforms explicitly and thoughtfully blocking the ability to know what's happening in those conversations taking place on the platform for privacy reasons. WhatsApp is basically a walled garden where the only way to know what's happening on WhatsApp is to have somebody in the group. We invest a lot on tools to help us understand what's going on out there, but I always say to clients that we should never ever feel like we're getting a comprehensive picture because we're not. There's also content being published that disappears, so what if one of those things goes viral, 14 million people have seen it, but the company has not. It's gone.'

Alan Sexton summed it up when he said, 'The world of media and public opinion has become so fragmented that no one listening tool can cover everything. To capture and make sense of all the disparate conversations, you need to assemble an interconnected series of monitoring tools. We are identifying which vendors should be part of the ecosystem we need. For example, if we have a vendor that measures social engagement and influencers, their data need to be connected to the data provided by the vendor that monitors earned media coverage. And we need to apply standardized approaches across tools so we're able to make apples to apples comparisons using different data sets. And that needs to be done on an international scale. This will enable us to understand what is happening on a day-to-day basis and gain a clearer sense of whether we're making progress over the long term.'

Advances in this field continue to be made. Companies need to work out the signals that matter most to them and monitor accordingly.

Dealing with Online Backlash

Companies must brace for times when customers and other stakeholders vent about them using social media. A backlash of any scale online can cross over into traditional media outlets, it can do immediate damage to your reputation and tear down the levels of trust your company has with its stakeholders. So how to respond to it?

1. Be Prepared

As with all crisis work, preparation is paramount. This includes having the right social media platform to enable the company to respond when circumstances require it to do so. Manson explained, 'Your company may not want to be on Instagram, but we know that lots of people are talking about your company on Instagram. If something were ever to happen and you wanted to try to address the problem, you don't have the ability to do that at the moment because you don't have a corporate presence there and none of your leadership has a presence there. You have made a conscious choice to limit your ability to engage with the problematic story, so the question of where do we need to be in the event that an issue ever comes up is important.' This is worth reinforcing—if your company isn't there, it can't respond to the backlash and defend itself.

2. Always Be Listening

As discussed above, listening is a challenge, but the company should monitor as much as it can in order to minimise any surprise.

Through listening, the company can capture shifting sentiment in order to determine if any changes to the overall strategy are required.

Pearmain said, 'I think social listening can often be overutilized in that people get very obsessed about what the sentiment shift is in that particular moment which lacks the nuance of understanding to find the thing that matters. I need to pick apart that noise to find the different groups and work out what's changed for them? Who is more or less prominent? What are the flows of information? Instead, we try and make it too reductively simple to we've moved from 50% neutrality to 42% . . . that doesn't help drive any meaningful action and often the time periods are too short, so you get sample size errors particularly when we're talking about specialized communities for reputation. Where there is much greater benefit to be had is using social listening to understand the flows of information on topics that matter to your business. Who instigates? Who accelerates and who distributes that sort of information?'

3. Be Thoughtful about Engagement

When backlash happens, the executive team must think about whether to respond, how quickly to respond, and what to say. Although the conventional wisdom is that the speed of making a response is paramount, it should not be a matter of speed at all costs. Manson said, 'I think this is probably different than how we were dealing with Twitter 10 years ago, where we probably would have advised clients to move quickly in a new cycle that is now measured in seconds rather than hours or days. I think now with more experience we recognise that actually you don't need to do [make an immediate response] – that it's much better to come back with something that is reasonably definitive.'

When the company does engage, great care must be taken with the style of language employed to do so. Manson explained, 'You do not want a statement put out that reads like something from ChatGPT. Writing for social media is not the same as writing for, say, journalists where there is a certain kind of language that is understood to convey certain things. That doesn't work in social media because you're not speaking to a certain segment of professionals. You need to deal with an issue in social media in a way that it sounds like it's coming from a human being.'

As this process unfolds, the company should be cautious about placing BAU posts on its social media platforms until the issue in question dies down to help minimize the occurrence of trolling. It should not delete negative posts made on company-owned social media channels. Removing the posts will be seen as underhanded by critics and even some supporters. And it should not try to 'flood' the company's pages with positive content to dilute the negative posts. Visitors to the pages will see through it and call it out for being inauthentic, and the company will risk generating further rounds of negative commentary.

The Noise of Online Backlash

In 2022, Halifax, a subsidiary of Lloyds Banking Group, posted a tweet noting that it would allow staff to display their pronouns on their name badges, in a post that read 'pronouns matter'. It showed a photo of a female staff member's name badge, which featured 'she/her/hers' in brackets under the name Gemma. When someone took issue with the post, a member of the Halifax social media team replied: 'If you disagree with our values, you're welcome to close your account.'[3] This led to the post going viral amid complaints about the bank's stance on the issue.

---

[3] Tom Espiner, Halifax says pronoun badge critics can close accounts, *BBC News*, 30 June 2022, https://www.bbc.com/news/business-61992057.

Andrew Walton said, 'This was a very standard piece of inclusion and diversity output, talking about gender pronouns on badges for Halifax staff. It was not the first time; we had posted about it before. On this occasion, we made two mistakes. First, we did not make it clear enough in our post that we weren't imposing gender pronouns on everyone's badge; it was purely optional – although that was clear to colleagues internally who were very supportive. And then the second mistake was at an online response level. We have a triaged approach which escalates depending on the severity of people's responses online. We do not like to ignore comments that are made that are overtly racist or sexist in nature for instance – we do not want our people or our customers seeing us ignoring things like that believe in being actively anti-racist. So, we respond and depending on how the dialogue goes, we start with a relatively mild response and then we have a stage two position and then, if necessary, there is a stage three position that advises the individual to take their business elsewhere if they do not like our values. Before stage three is implemented, there is an approval process to be followed. In this case, we went too quickly to the stage three response. Then it went viral, and we had to decide what to do. We chose to stand our ground and did not retreat from our position.'

Walton also raised an interesting point in relation to noise and impact. He noted, 'There was a lot of noise. One interesting learning was that despite the large amount of noise, we had fewer than 200 complaints but only 11 of those turned out to be customers. Because it was trending on Twitter (X), it jumped across in the mainstream media and was front page of the *Daily Mail*. We received a large volume of questions from the media to try and keep the story going and while we held firm on our position, we said nothing to avoid prolonging coverage. The marketing guys said it did no discernible brand harm.'

Employees and Social Media

Employees' use of social media can be a source of authentic and interesting content that helps to tell the corporate story. It can also represent a source of reputational risk. Manson said, 'I think there's some companies you need to worry about this, but for the vast majority you don't. I love British Airways, who were my client at one point, and they had this amazing group of pilots who were making fantastic films by sticking a GoPro in their cockpit and making total aeroplane geek content, but it had a big audience, and the pilots were known in the community and really beloved. However, British Airlines had a problem not too long ago where they rolled out some new uniforms and a bunch of employees went on Twitter and complained about the uniforms. As a result of that they rolled out a new social media policy banning employees from using social media during working hours, which probably wouldn't have helped with the uniform issue and stopped the pilots from posting their videos. I think you have to just let people be themselves and give them some security guidelines, give some behaviour guidelines but be permissive rather than prohibitive.'

While acknowledging the value of being permissive rather than prohibitive, there is a range of practical guidelines for any company to consider. These include:

- Avoiding the instance of employees having their personal social media platform(s) being mistaken as an official company social media platform. However, they should be able to identify themselves as being an employee for the company on those platforms that request users to identify their employer, the most obvious current example being LinkedIn.
- It is a good thing if employees wish to advocate on behalf of the company by sharing company-approved

content relating to specific announcements, events, news, and milestones. The nuance is that posts/comments that are personal opinions, for instance in relation to political issues, should not be confused as representing the position of company itself.

- If employees wish to establish a social media platform that officially represents company rather than the employee themself, then they should obtain prior approval from the company.

- Ensuring employees never disguise themselves as a customer or try to conceal their employment relationship with the company if promoting its products and services on any social media platforms.

A systematic training programme will help to ensure employees have a good understanding of the company's policies and guidelines and feel well-equipped to follow them.

What Does a Successful Social Media Programme Look Like?

The short answer to this question is that it depends upon the objectives for the social media programme. There isn't one metric for all. Manson said, 'In terms of metrics, I want to know (a) are we reaching the audience? What proportion are we reaching? (b) Are they reacting or responding the way that we hope? If not, why not? If yes, is that delivering the outcome that we need?'

Wyldeck said, 'For us, it's about educating patients and customers and our clinicians. In a market like Australia, where we rely on government to approve and then subsidize medicines, we feel it's our responsibility to ensure that patients and patient groups are aware of opportunities to advocate. We want to inform patients of their ability to share feedback with government on important deliberations. If you do that in a

sophisticated way, that grabs people's attention, and you can
drive powerful advocacy from the general public, from patients
and patient groups.'

Pearmain suggested, 'Share of voice on relevant topics
within relevant audiences. Why? It overlaps really well to other
reputation led metrics – you either don't want to be on an issue
or topic you want to be all over it that's a very simplistic way of
looking at it depending on what the issue is . . . and within your
category you generally want to be number one or nowhere
– again depending on the category: some companies want
to hide and some want the spotlight. This is (a) measurable
and it can be applied across all channels and (b) you can read
across to other places but the second thing is there's now
an increasingly strong body of evidence showing that there
is some proxy to purchase intent where share of search in
particular is a meaningful lead metric for what your share of
commercial market will be.'

The benefits of an effective social media programme
(whether surgical in nature or large-scale) are significant, but
there is no single playbook that applies to all companies in
relation to how they can show up on social media. A large array
of factors will always be at play—the nature of the company
itself, the stakeholders it wants to reach, the geographic markets
it operates in, and so on. These factors, among others, will
dictate how the company approaches social media and how it
invests in it (this chapter did not discuss 'paid media' which is
another consideration for companies who want to boost their
social media presence). While many executives feel uncertain
about how their company should build an online presence,
what is certain is the power it offers to enable companies
to earn (and protect) their reputations with a wide range of
stakeholders.

Summary of Principles

- Every company needs to understand where it sits on the continuum of serving demand by stakeholders versus driving demand by stakeholders. Knowing this will help the company to find the right balance in the context of its digital footprint.
- One way (among others) of thinking about a company's digital ecosystem in practice is through looking at four legs of the stool: (1) Search; (2) Social; (3) Owned; (4) Wikipedia.
- Despite the proliferation of listening tools, no company can safely assume it is capable of capturing every conversation about it. Separating what matters from what is just noise is a key challenge and a suite of listening tools is required to meet that challenge.
- Be prepared for the occurrence of a backlash online, always be listening and be thoughtful about when, where, and how to engage in response to it. Transparency demonstrates care for those invested in the issue at hand.
- A general stance of being permissive rather than prohibitive is better when it comes to employee use of social media, but training and guidelines are helpful to avoid issues arising.
- The success of a corporate social media programme should be gauged against the specific objectives that have been set for that particular programme, as these objectives will differ for different companies.

11

The Use of Sponsorships to Build Reputation

In 2018, preparations were underway for David Beckham, AIA's global Brand Ambassador (at the time), to take part in a health and wellness forum the company was running in Sydney. Beckham was headed to Australia to attend the Invictus Games, and we had secured his presence at our event in the lead up. Beckham had signed up for this role with AIA in 2017,[1] and had been a thoughtful, hardworking, and courteous presence when engaging with the company. In the lead up to the Sydney event, a journalist from 'The Project', an Australian television talk show, went to London to interview Beckham ahead of his visit. The segment would air on the eve of Beckham's visit to Australia. Unfortunately, things did not turn out well. The interview included questions relating to his family life, and Beckham made a point relating to the need to work hard in any marriage over time. The idea that any marriage requires hard work is hardly earth shattering, but it gave the global news media a clickable headline of the highest calibre. 'David Beckham calls 19-year marriage to

---

[1] 'AIA appoints David Beckham as its Global Ambassador', AIA, March 2017, https://www.aia.com/en/media-centre/press-releases/2017/aia-group-press-release-20170323.

Victoria Beckham 'hard work'' was the *USA Today* headline,[2] and similar headlines were splashed around the world. The end result—we had to cancel all of the media interviews we had planned to do with him in Australia. Beckham still spoke on a panel at our (closed-door) event, which was very well received. But the episode is illustrative of the unforeseen difficulties associated with sponsorships and partnerships. Done well, they can provide a basis for amplifying the company brand and for effective engagement with its stakeholders. But they are not without their challenges. This anecdote did not result in any harm to AIA's reputation but speaks to the difficulty of achieving media coverage for the sponsor via a huge celebrity. In other cases, however, should the sponsored entity run into controversy or scandal, the sponsorship can deliver a significant negative impact to the company itself.

Sponsorship and Reputation

Conventional wisdom is that sponsorship can help build brand awareness and resonance, support sales campaigns, and provide a means of engaging with customers through providing them with unique experiences associated with the rights holder.

There is also a deeper reputational element underpinning corporate interest in sponsorships. Andy Sutherden is an industry expert who spent sixteen years at Hill+Knowlton Strategies, including seven years as global head of sport & partnership marketing. He observed, 'The daylight between words and action is where reputational risk thrives. Where I've seen the sponsorship industry mature and become more impactful in the minds of

---

[2] Cydney Henderson, 'David Beckham calls 19-year marriage to Victoria Beckham 'hard work'', *USA Today*, October 2018, https://www.usatoday.com/story/life/people/2018/10/18/david-beckham-calls-marriage-victoria-beckham-hard-work/1688544002/.

C-suite is when companies understand that they must back up their words with credible proof points. Sponsorship can be a very effective channel to do exactly that.'

Well chosen, an effective sponsorship delivers fundamental benefits beyond marketing a product or service. It can enable the company to showcase its own purpose and values, or to demonstrate its commitment to the local community, or to create new thought leadership programmes, and so on. Sutherden noted, 'A sponsorship can provide powerful proof points for a company, including in areas such as climate change. SailGP (an international sailing competition that is actively involved in encouraging sustainability practices) is a good example of this, having a lot of success in recruiting companies that really want to be part of their sustainability narrative.'

Tim Collins is an independent consultant in London whose career has been immersed in sports and entertainment sponsorships, including as a managing director at Octagon and also United Entertainment Group. Collins shared an example of a successful sponsorship he'd been involved with, where he'd seen unequivocal reputational value for the company. He said, 'A past client of mine, AIG, were looking for a global sponsorship that reflected its new brand and company position post the 2008 financial crisis. It wanted a platform that reflected its new values to support and motivate employees globally. It wanted to be able to speak about teamwork, innovation and preparation through all its internal and external communications. After a lengthy identification, selection and negotiation process, AIG entered into a five-year partnership with the New Zealand All Blacks becoming the first brand to appear on the front of the famous All Blacks shirt. The partnership was later voted "Best Rugby Union Sponsorship of the Decade" at the prestigious Sports Industry Awards. Not only did it allow AIG to benefit from the values held by the team, but it also helped the All Blacks reach new global audiences outside of traditional rugby playing nations.'

Assessing a Sponsorship Opportunity

It's not uncommon for a company to end up sponsoring something that the CEO happens to be personally interested in. Sutherden said, 'You've heard the expression "Chairman's whim" and it is still alive, although less so than in the past. What I do most days is to mitigate against Chairman's whim. That is, when one of the higher ups in any organization just happens to love cycling or just happens to be obsessed with cricket. And suddenly, sponsoring cricket or sponsoring the Tour de France is the thing that we do, and the rest of the executive team privately or visibly rolls their eyes. Sometimes, it can end up working, but that is mainly through luck rather than strategic thinking.'

Chairman's whims aside, sponsorship is still largely seen as the responsibility of the marketing function, which is expected to coordinate and supervise a company's sponsorships, and also to assess new opportunities as they arise. However, more holistic thinking is needed. Sutherden offered this view: 'If sponsorship were an Olympic sport, what sport would it be? I coined the phrase *"corporate decathletes."* Normally, the front door for most rights holders is through marketing. Most sponsorships are negotiated and evaluated against the objectives of the CMO. And yet, I've been in organizations where I've seen sponsorship be unbelievably powerful for the employer brand. So, where's the HR director? I've seen sponsorships that are a brilliant testbed for R&D, such as Team Sky's professional cycling team working with Jaguar engineers on aerodynamic technologies. The symbiotic relationship between sponsor and sponsorship opens other parts of an organization. Sales, HR, R&D, corporate philanthropy, communications are all relevant stakeholders. A *"corporate decathlete"* needs to understand that it may be marketing's budget, but there should be internal stakeholders from many different parts of an organization to extract maximum value from a partnership.'

Large corporations in particular receive a steady stream of sponsorship requests. Even smaller firms may wonder how to think about where to invest their money to deliver value to the business. There are several questions to ask when thinking about how to assess sponsorship opportunities:

- Is sponsorship something that makes sense for us as a business—how can it help us achieve an unmet need? Collins noted, 'The sponsoring company needs to decide the role of sponsorship and agree internally what any partnership needs to achieve, whether that's driving awareness, whether it's building affinity with customers, building relationships, or driving sales.'
- What category of sponsorship would deliver us the most value? Should the company be focused on the arts, or sport, or philanthropy?
- Once the sponsorship type is agreed, what is the specific platform that is best aligned to our business?
- What would our stakeholders think about our support to the opportunity in question? Would it be easily explainable to them? Or would it create confusion? Would it create interest and enthusiasm? Or would it be met with indifference?

Answering questions like these will help establish an objective set of criteria against which the company assesses partnership opportunities.

Sponsorships and Employees

Entering a new sponsorship represents an opportunity to engage with employees. Their views on the sponsorship, good or bad, will play a role in its ultimate success. At the outset, a clear rationale for the new engagement should be provided to all colleagues that enables them to understand the company's involvement in it and to create excitement around it.

Many sponsorships offer a chance to further benefit the well-being of employees in some manner—whether through the joy of a new experience, the inspiration of supporting the recipient of the sponsorship, or the opportunity to become involved in something that has a positive physical or mental impact. In Hong Kong, the 'Oxfam Trailwalker' event has been held annually since the mid-1980s and is one of the largest sporting fundraising events in the city. Teams of four people complete a 100 km trail within a forty-eight-hour time limit. Not only does AIA Hong Kong sponsor the event, but it has also historically been the largest corporate participant.[3] The fact that employees enthusiastically take part in the event being sponsored provides multiple reputational benefits. It gives employees a memorable experience, it allows the company to showcase to its people its commitment to the community, and it reflects AIA's focus on healthy living.

Whatever happens, don't let the sponsorship become abstract to the employee base—or worse—a source of contention. If the company is sponsoring the F1 or the Australian Open, you don't want employees feeling like the benefits only go to the senior leadership and that they are not worthy enough to be part of the partnership experience. Not everyone can have a free ticket to a particular event, but there are plenty of ways to ensure people feel involved—staff days, luck draws, visits to the office by those being sponsored, free kit, digital content developed especially for employees—are just some ways to allow employees to feel good about a sponsorship.

---

[3] https://www.aia.com.hk/en/about-aia/environmental-social-and-governance-esg/community-engagement/principal-sponsor-of-oxfam-trailwalker.

Sponsorships and the Community

Collins said, 'The best sponsorship is a sponsorship that doesn't hinder the fans but enhances the fan experience. That's quite a lofty thing to say, but some brands have managed to achieve it. It's important for brands to engage with the audience, and typically, that starts with communities, particularly around team sports like rugby, football and cricket.'

Collins cited a sponsorship between SC Johnson and Liverpool Football Club. SC Johnson is a U.S. manufacturer of household cleaning supplies and other related products. As part of the partnership SCJ is helping to recycle more than 500,000 plastic bottles used at Anfield each season and turn that plastic into new Mr. Muscle bottles.[4] The partnership makes Liverpool the first UK professional sports team to link a waste-stream to a specific product. This is an excellent example of how a sponsorship/partnership can be entered into with an intent to not only make a community impact but in doing so, to highlight the sustainability credentials of both organizations.

On the subject of English football, one of the most vibrant aspects of AIA's long-standing partnership with Tottenham Hotspur FC is the community coaching programme run in Asia under the partnership.[5] Two fully qualified Spurs coaches are based permanently in Asia, and over a number of years have run a wide range of highly successful clinics and community activities in markets such as Hong Kong, China, Singapore, Thailand, Cambodia, Indonesia, and Vietnam.

---

[4] https://www.scjohnson.com/en/stories/sustainable-world/plastic-reuse-and-recycling/2021/september/sc-johnson-and-liverpool-football-club-score-with-plastic-reuse-partnership-to-tackle-plastic-waste.

[5] https://www.tottenhamhotspur.com/the-club/football-development/global-courses/asia/aia-partnership/.

The Potential for Reputation Risk

Companies enter sponsorship arrangements intent on creating reputational benefits. What is less considered is the potential for the partnership to produce reputational problems as a result of issues relating to the entity being sponsored—whether that is an individual, a team, an event, or even a nation. Sutherden noted that, 'Modern day sponsorship carries reputational opportunity and reputational risk in equal measure. I've been involved in many partnerships where you're reaching for an issues and crisis manual within a week of a new sponsorship being signed.'

Risk stems not only from something going wrong, but also from the ability—or lack thereof—of the company to extract itself from the engagement. This in turn, speaks to the way in which contract negotiations between the company and the rights holder are conducted. Sutherden said, 'I've been in Olympic contract negotiations, and I've been taken to Lausanne, I've been shown around the Olympic Museum. I've gone to FIFA, and I've touched the World Cup. I've gone to Chelsea and been handed a shirt with my name on the back. The seduction is utterly enthralling. If you get sucked into that, it will be a case of, "where do I sign"? Acting in haste. What that normally means is you are wide open to things going wrong because there isn't adequate protection in the contract to cover your reputation, because you haven't sufficiently thought about what might trigger a termination . . . or at least a path to resolution.' He went on to note, 'Clients often want to be in the contract meetings where high-profile sponsorships are being discussed and negotiated. What they sometimes lack is the ability to go through the "what if it all goes wrong" scenarios. What you need is a dispassionate, independent expert who can go through all the scenarios that could trigger a breach of contract and introduce remedies and mitigation strategies.'

A contract should never be entered into in a naïve fashion. Rather, the company needs to think through a range of difficult scenarios that could arise. What happens if the company sponsors a sports star who is filmed using cocaine? What happens if controversial statements are made on a particular social issue or political situation? What happens if a stadium collapses? And so on. The end result of this process should be a series of detailed clauses that are very clear and coherent about what will trigger a breach of contract. That can then be put into the proverbial drawer, to be pulled out if a situation arises that necessitates it. Sutherden emphasized that, 'The best contract negotiations minimise language like "best endeavours" or "in reasonable opinion"—it has got to be black and white.'

Assuming the company can exit, the question then becomes, will it? One high profile example of a sporting entity experiencing a major downfall was seen with the Yorkshire Cricket Club, which in 2021 was at the centre of allegations of institutional racism.[6] The serious allegations were sustained over a long period of time, resulting in legal actions, government involvement, and the national cricket board banning Yorkshire from hosting international matches. As a result, a host of sponsors exited their arrangements with the club, including Nike, which issued a statement that said: 'Nike will no longer be the kit supplier for Yorkshire CCC. We stand firmly against racism and discrimination of any kind.'[7]

This example aside, Collins observed that, 'Brands have two options in these circumstances. The natural response is to sever ties immediately and reinforce its position on any issues through a press statement. An alternative view is to continue to support

---

[6] https://yorkshireccc.com/news/statement-from-chair-lord-kamlesh-patel-obe/.

[7] Lawrence Ostlere, 'Nike ends kit deal with Yorkshire County Cricket Club over racism report', *Independent*, November 2021, https://www.independent.co.uk/sport/cricket/yorkshire-cricket-racism-azeem-rafiq-nike-b1951621.html.

the sponsored organisation or individual and work with them to ensure measures are in place to improve and evolve together. Sport fans respect longevity and some of the most successful sponsorships are those that have continued for many years.'

If and when controversy strikes the sponsorship property, the sponsoring company must make its decision based on the facts at the time. If the relationship between the two parties is strong, if the values they share remain consistent and if there are mitigating circumstances to the issue in question, then sticking by the team/individual/event in question is not a bad move. If the answer however to these points is negative, then it may be time to cut ties and move on.

Sportswashing

Sportswashing is the practice of an organization, a government, a country, etc. supporting sport or organizing sports events as a way to improve its reputation by diverting attention from social or environmental problems.[8] It reflects the hope of the sponsoring entity that their support for the sponsorship in question will generate goodwill among the fans of whatever is being sponsored—not only for that event or person but also for the entity itself.

Without going into an analysis of the moral implications associated with sportswashing, the reality is companies that produce legal products and services have the right to invest in sponsorships. The reputational consideration for such companies (and the entity being sponsored) is whether doing so could in fact generate more negative reaction than positive.

Santos[9] is one of Australia's biggest domestic gas suppliers and a leading LNG supplier in the Asia-Pacific region. In February

[8] https://dictionary.cambridge.org/dictionary/english/sportswashing.

[9] https://www.santos.com/about-us/.

2021, Santos was announced as the official natural gas partner for the Australian Open tennis tournament as part of a multi-year arrangement. The backlash was swift. Climate activists including 350.org Australia compared sponsorship with fossil fuel giants to 'doctors promoting cigarettes in 1930'[10] and launched an online petition against the sponsorship.[11] The partnership ended within twelve months.

Numerous examples of sportswashing exist, particularly stemming from global sponsorships launched from the Middle East. From a corporate viewpoint, the possibility of being accused of sportswashing must be a consideration should that company operate in industry sectors such as energy, automobiles, soft drinks, fast food, among others. For these companies, conducting a thorough analysis of how the sponsorship being considered will be received and how the sponsorship will be activated should be of heightened concern.

The Influencer

The advent of social media influencers has provided companies with another option on the sponsorship landscape. The concept of 'influencer marketing' is not new. Companies, and in particular marketing departments, are attracted to individuals who are perceived to have a large online audience that they have a degree of sway over. Striking up a partnership, or a sponsorship, with said influencer can be an effective means for drumming up increased awareness and interest in a business' products or services.

Sutherden said, 'If you decide to align yourself with an individual, whether an ambassador or influencer, there needs to be something very genuine and credible between what the individual represents and your business. Today, I think the public

---

[10] https://tennisthreads.net/australian-open-ta-cleans-up-its-act/.

[11] https://act.350.org/sign/tell-australian-open-say-no-santos/.

are infinitely more discerning to call out those that are just in it for the money and who are being somewhat disingenuous.'

The relationship between a company and the influencers is a delicate one. On a practical level, the two parties need to calibrate the way in which content is promoted by the influencer. Sutherden noted that 'From a company perspective, it's similar criteria—individual values, traits, the type of posts, and so on. Sometimes what will happen is the Head of Communications appears and says, ". . . we can't have an influencer say something that's not on brand". The influencer says, "Well, I'm not going to say that because it sounds as though it's straight out of a corporate brochure. It doesn't sound as though it's from my keyboard or my mouth at all." Then you can get into a dance over approvals, where the speeds of the company are too slow for the rate at which the influencer needs to publish content.'

What is the solution? Sutherden suggested, 'What you can do is provide the guidelines for content. Tell the influencer that we understand the importance of authenticity and we'd love for you to commentate authentically on these subjects. Send it to us for approval. And if we don't approve it within a certain timeframe, we have a "deemed approved" arrangement. That is, the brand will either say it's approved or not approved. But if nothing is said within an agreed timeframe, the influencer can deem it approved.' Sutherden concluded, 'What I have always done with influencers is ensure that there is an immersion session between both parties at the very outset. What are the red lights? What are the amber lights? What is the tone of voice? What is the style? That set-up is crucial.'

An immersion session is sensible, but to reiterate, the crucial first step is deciding to have a relationship in the first place. This is incredibly sensitive ground to tread. If a company skips over it—if it does not complete thorough due diligence *before* the partnership with the influencer is entered into, the likelihood for catastrophe is great. No company in recent memory has learned this the harder way than Anheuser-Busch InBev through its widely publicized and botched relationship with transgender-influencer Dylan Mulvaney.[12] Without litigating the entire episode here, in brief the controversy was sparked by an Instagram post by Mulvaney with some Bud Light cans as she celebrated 'her first year of womanhood'.[13] At least one of the cans featured her face. A boycott of the beer ensued, with sales of what had been America's number one beer, plummeting in the months that followed, and employees having to be laid off.[14] The company's leadership has stated that the beer sent to Mulvaney did not constitute a campaign and was done without management awareness or approval. This seems to be a classic instance of a company acting (two marketing employees were placed on administrative leave following the episode[15]) without investing the time and consideration required to properly judge whether the influencer in question was well matched with the company's stakeholders—and its aspirations for engaging with those stakeholders.

---

[12] Michelle Toh, 'Bud Light controversy cost parent company about $395 million in lost US sales', CNN, August 2023, https://edition.cnn.com/2023/08/03/business/anheuser-busch-revenue-bud-light-intl-hnk/index.html.

[13] Emily Stewart, 'The Bud Light boycott, explained as much as is possible', Vox, June 2023, https://www.vox.com/money/2023/4/12/23680135/bud-light-boycott-dylan-mulvaney-travis-tritt-trans.

[14] Stefan Sykes, 'Bud Light maker Anheuser-Busch to lay off hundreds of corporate staff', CNBC, July 2023, https://www.cnbc.com/2023/07/27/bud-light-maker-anheuser-busch-announces-layoffs.html.

[15] Krystal Hur, 'Wall Street Journal: Bud Light owner places two execs on leave after transgender influencer backlash', CNN Business, April 2023, https://edition.cnn.com/2023/04/24/business/anheuser-execs-on-leave/index.html.

Measuring Return on Investment

Measuring the value of a corporate sponsorship could be the subject of a separate book. Some brief thoughts, however, are as follows:

- Both the company and the sponsorship property need to collaborate to agree what metrics are required to measure the impact of the sponsorship. Both parties need to settle on specific benchmarks and targets at the outset. These can span a wide range of topics, including metrics relating to brand visibility, lead generation for new sales, stakeholder engagement, partnership relationships, and many more.

- Investing in research to build up a picture of how the company's customers and other stakeholders perceive the sponsorship will enable the proposition to be evaluated and further strengthened over time.

- The ability of the company and its sponsorship partner to have a transparent and trusting cooperation in the sharing of data provides the basis for productive assessment of the impact of the sponsorship.

- The company should have a list of questions that it can use data and intelligence to answer. These questions speak to the impact of the sponsorship on the company's brand, its business performance, and its commercial goals—all in light of the financial investment being made to secure the sponsorship.

Measuring the success of a sponsorship in large part relates to being clear about the reasons for entering it in the first place. Collins suggested, 'The industry has moved away from only looking at return on investment. It's more about a return on the objectives. A sponsorship has to perform in the same way as an advertising or marketing campaign. Are we trying to improve our brand values amongst our customers or engage more customers as part of sponsorship? Are we trying to motivate our workforce and engage with them more through sponsorship? Once we lock in objectives, we have a clearer route to a more accurate measurement.'

Summary of Principles

- Done well, a sponsorship can enable the company to showcase its purpose and values.
- Assessing (and supporting) sponsorships should not be the sole responsibility of the marketing team. The contribution of views and support from different parts of an organization is needed to extract maximum value from a partnership.
- Asking a series of questions helps to establish an objective set of criteria against which a company can measure the value of partnership opportunities.
- Making an effort to find creative ways to involve employees at all levels of the organization in the sponsorship will go a long way to maximizing the value of the investment being made.
- Sponsorships provide fertile ground for corporate engagement with the local community in ways that build tangible reputation building benefits.
- Risk stems not only from something going wrong, but also from the ability, or lack thereof, of the company to extract itself from the engagement.
- Before aligning with an influencer, make sure there is a very genuine and credible connection between what the individual represents and the values of the business.
- Measuring the success of a sponsorship in large part relates to being clear about the reasons for entering it in the first place, and having metrics agreed for gauging progress from the outset.

12

Corporate Brand Strategy

Conventionally, when companies think about 'brand', the usual association relates to how their products are marketed to customers. The teams responsible for 'branding' have mostly been housed in the marketing department, separate to the Corporate Affairs function. This does not always make a lot of sense. If an objective of branding is to help distinguish the company in the minds of consumers towards driving a competitive advantage, then this must be closely aligned with the *entirety* of a company's stakeholder engagement programme. In 2018, I was fortunate to be given the opportunity to oversee AIA's brand function. This chapter will include references to that time, as AIA transitioned to a new brand promise, which eventually would become its purpose.

Corporate branding helps customers understand what the company stands for and why it is different than the competition. In addition, the corporate brand is about more than customers— it should be how *every* stakeholder perceives and interacts with the company. This includes employees, for having a strong corporate brand goes a long way to attracting and retaining the best talent.

Marc Cloosterman is CEO of VIM Group, a firm that helps organizations implement rebrand and brand change programmes and optimise their brand management. He said, 'The brand is the most valuable intangible asset of any company. For the boards of directors that I work with and

CEOs of large companies, reputation is more risk-associated and brand has a higher standing because it is opportunity-associated, and something that can sit on the balance sheet. Reputation doesn't exist in the financial vocabulary. Brand does. There's no governance around reputation and there is governance around brand.' In response to a challenge that he does not think as highly of 'reputation' compared to 'brand', Cloosterman said, 'I love reputation, and if you are the head of Corporate Affairs, then reputation is very much front and centre of what you're doing, but if brand is also part of your remit, then you have more opportunity to work on what's ahead instead of the defence only. Brand is more associated with opportunity and reputation with risk.'

Pattie Kushner is an independent consultant who has previously held roles including chief public affairs officer at Mayo Clinic and chief communications officer at Labcorp. She and Cloosterman worked together on developing the Page Society's Brand Guide for Communications Leaders.[1] In response to how she thinks about brand compared to reputation, Kushner said, 'At the most basic level, when I think about brand and reputation, the brand is who we are, what we stand for, and what we aspire to be. Reputation is how we're perceived in the market on those aspects. Often there's a significant gap between them, but it boils down to what we say and do versus how we are perceived.'

There is typically some confusion when business executives start talking about brand. The discussion can quickly veer into the territory of discussing the merits of a logo or a tagline or a campaign. These subjects fall under the brand umbrella, but at its best, corporate branding is a driver of growth that supports strategic business objectives. The effective management of the corporate brand delivers a high level of consistency across every touch point

---

[1] https://about.page.org/en-us/page-cco-guide-corporate-brand-management-2023.

that stakeholders have with a company—it coordinates how the company looks, how it sounds in its dialogue with stakeholders and the actions it takes. This is not about being the 'brand police'. Cloosterman noted, 'Ten or twenty years ago you could play a policing role. The five elements of corporate identity were the logo, symbol, tagline, colour and font. Today there are hundreds of touch points and channels. So, the paradigm has changed from policing logos to orchestrating the brand experience.'

The concept of corporate branding has indeed moved far beyond logos and taglines. Kushner said, 'I always think about the brand in terms of a "say, do, think, perform" continuum because it's one of the simplest ways for people to understand a brand's core components more tangibly. While most corporate communicators have some experience and ownership in managing how a brand looks and sounds, they often have less ownership in its actions. Therefore, communicators need to understand the full aspects of the brand and be able to influence others to create brand alignment across the continuum.'

The way corporations think about their brand management varies around the world. Jacqueline Alexis Thng is Partner, Chief Experience & Growth Officer (Asia) at Prophet, a growth and transformation consulting firm. She said, 'What I've observed working with both Western brands and Asian brands is that Western brands manage the brands in a 360 manner. They look at everything. Asian brands tend to be still more sales and externally focused on driving and growing the brand. Most Asian companies will spend a lot of money in building the brand externally, be it in marketing, sales, advertising, and so on, but they do not invest as much in building their brand internally.' At the risk of generalization, this seems to be a fair assessment. Brand management has been decades in development in Western markets and is at an earlier stage of development in regions such as Asia (with some notable exceptions, particularly in markets like Japan and South Korea).

Establishing a Strong Foundation

The world of brand is littered with jargon, not all of which is helpful in the effort to work in a credible and coherent way on a corporate brand programme. With that said, some jargon is inescapable. Part of the foundational stage entails having a brand framework in place. The brand framework provides a definition of the company's brand position and ensures it marries up against the company's vision, mission, and values. Brand architecture on the other hand is the organizational framework a company uses to structure its brands, sub-brands, and products or services.[2]

Explaining her view of the difference between a brand framework and brand architecture, Kushner said, 'For me, the brand framework is the "what" – what does the brand stand for? How do we talk about it? What elements makeup how we express the brand? Brand architecture is more about the "how" – applying the brand in a structure or hierarchy that includes its application to subsidiaries, products, services, and growth within the company.'

Successful corporate brands are built on strong foundations. They sit over a well-defined mission, purpose, and set of corporate values. The company's brand framework defines the company's brand position and is a means of outlining these components, to make sure they're aligned and mutually supportive. Kushner said, 'Often people see the brand as just words on the page and the logo. To have a strong foundation for building the corporate brand, you must get beyond the basics and policing the logo to focus more on how audiences experience the brand.'

In 2018, when AIA transitioned from 'The Real Life Company' to 'Healthier, Longer, Better Lives', it did so by articulating an accurate and up-to-date reflection of what it stands for—and what it does as a company. The updated brand position took

---

[2] Katrina Kirsch, 'How to Develop Brand Architecture', *HubSpot*, January 2022, https://blog.hubspot.com/marketing/brand-architecture.

AIA from reflecting on who it was to explaining instead why it is valuable to its customers. The Group wanted to help address lifestyle-related diseases and non-communicable diseases in the Asia-Pacific region and could do so credibly through its Vitality proposition, which offers customers increased financial protection with tangible health and wellness rewards.[3] Since then, AIA has further extended and deepened its capabilities to help deliver health and wellness solutions. The adoption of Healthier, Longer, Better Lives was an expression of the Group's commitment to become a far more customer-centric organization. And it was done with great care—extensive research was undertaken across the Asia-Pacific region to allow the Group to understand how to bring the new brand to life in different markets with different cultures.

Employees as Brand Ambassadors

It almost goes without saying that employees as a stakeholder group are crucial to the power and longevity of any corporate brand. The people who work at the company encapsulate the corporate brand through their behaviour, attitudes, and actions.

As referenced earlier in the book, when AIA launched Healthier, Longer, Better Lives, it put a concerted focus on employees in the initial phase of the launch. This saw the introduction of a range of actions and initiatives to give as many employees as possible the opportunity be part of bringing the new brand promise to life. The reason? We knew we could not ask AIA customers to lead a Healthier, Longer, Better Life if AIA's own people were not committed to doing that themselves. In the first instance, it was a broad-based effort to engage with as many employees as possible. We launched competitions, we rolled out health and wellness initiatives, we held events—all designed to

---

[3] https://www.aia.com/en/health-wellness/vitality.

allow people to viscerally experience what the new brand was all about. The swell of pride and energy through the company in the months after the launch of Healthier, Longer, Better Lives was palpable.

Kushner said, 'When rolling out a new brand or changes to an existing brand, you must give employees the "why". We often give them the "what" and the "how" but not the "why." I always go down three why levels: why, why, why. Pare it back to what it means to the individual. When people understand what it means to them and their role, they are more apt to embrace it. That takes time, effort, and clear, consistent communication.'

At AIA, the brand team established what it called a 'brand champion network' to support and encourage cross market collaboration and adherence to the brand governance that had been established.

The Need for Internal Collaboration

As with many aspects of corporate life, effective collaboration between different internal functional areas is crucial to enabling successful brand management. Cloosterman said, 'The ownership for (corporate) brand sits in Comms or Marketing, mostly closely connected to the board of directors. You are overseeing the intellectual property that is the brand but if you look at touchpoints and channels, you are not the owner of those touch points and channels because the marketing channels sit in marketing. The website sits maybe in Communications. Digital apps where you communicate with customers sit in a commercial organization. ERP systems where you communicate with suppliers may sit in production. HR has portals which are branded. You have signage on the roof that's held by the Facilities team. You want to be the conductor of the brand experience across all these touch points and channels, but strictly speaking, it's not your budget. This is why you have to be extremely good collaborator. Training and education are a very important part of the process.'

Kushner elaborated by citing the need for cooperation with specific departments. She said, 'The topic of employer brand comes up often. HR often recommends creating an employer brand if the existing brand is not defined in a way that can translate meaningfully to current and prospective employees in a highly competitive job market. When that happens, you must ensure that any employer brand creation is truly an extension of the primary brand, not something wholly different, or you create a say-do disconnect that could result in higher turn-over.'

When asked about other relevant departments, she said, 'Finance is an often-overlooked group that needs to understand and embrace both brand and reputation because they can have a material impact on the company. When Finance understands and is aligned with the brand's inherent value, management conversations, including brand and reputation investment, become much more strategic. Similarly, Strategy and Business Development need to understand and embrace the brand. I have worked with several highly acquisitive companies where this was paramount. Brand architecture can run amuck without a clearly defined brand and activation plan, often in the form of decision trees. Last but not least is Operations. If the brand is conveyed through stakeholder experiences and touchpoints, the buck stops with Operations. Brand experiences can easily be undone by a seemingly simple efficiency or productivity change if the user's experience is not considered. So, when I think about internal collaboration, it is truly a team sport among leadership. While communications or marketing may "own" the brand, everyone should feel responsible for managing it. And when a brand gets isolated into one group, you start to see the erosion happen.'

Brand Governance

Brand governance is about how the company shows up in its interactions with its stakeholders in a way that consistently exemplifies its brand. An effective approach to brand governance ensures the corporate brand is understood and consistently used, across different business lines and geographic markets. Consistency is vital—when the corporate brand is communicated consistently, it becomes more recognizable, better differentiated, and more trustworthy. A big piece of this connects to employees. At AIA, we had a commitment to achieve a consistent brand identity across all of the markets in which the Group operated. This required an exhaustive audit of existing guidelines and brand materials, which in turn would provide the basis for a single brand standard to be adopted by all colleagues.

A set of brand guidelines (which in fact may be more than guidelines—they might be mandatory) will give employees an ability to understand how to use the brand to best effect in all of the company's outreach efforts. Such documentation can capture a wide range of information spanning things like the brand persona, the brand's tone of voice, wordmark do's and don'ts, colour usage, and so on.

Thng said, 'Making sure that what we do and what we say about the brand is consistent over time is critical, and governance is key to that. For companies operating in multiple markets, you need to be sensitive to the local culture and the ways that it's going to be implemented because otherwise some things will just not get implemented.'

Allowing flexibility in how the brand is expressed (but not what is expressed) is necessary when operating across multiple geographic locations. What resonates in Vietnam may not do the same in Hong Kong, or in the Philippines. Again, the 'what' cannot change. In AIA's case, this is Healthier, Longer, Better Lives. But how that is expressed can differ to recognise cultural differences across geographies. Kushner noted, 'At one organization, because they were in many geographic markets worldwide and resources were scarce, we provided clear guidance to give employees the flexibility to maintain consistency of message while implementing the brand in culturally relevant ways for their market. We did not define every element for them but provided the guard rails for applying the brand.'

The Brand as a Point of Competitive Differentiation

When the company is able to align its brand strategy with the experiences its stakeholders have in their interactions with the company—when the 'say' and 'do' that Kushner references are in sync, then real differentiation becomes possible.

Getting to this stage requires clarity of thought and the close internal collaboration described earlier in the chapters. Page, in its report on Corporate Brand Leadership, suggests a number of questions to ask in relation to using the brand as a differentiator:[4]

1. How is the brand driving preference?
2. How do stakeholders experience your brand? What do they expect, and how do they navigate your corporate portfolio?
3. Which brands have equity (if there are multiple in the portfolio)? How do you build around those brands and address/migrate the ones that do not?
4. Where does the company want brand equity to be?
5. Does your brand connect emotionally across audiences?
6. Do brand and reputation align? Where are the gaps?
7. Are there different audiences with different needs?
8. Are there risks to consider?
9. How do we organize and communicate our key capabilities, market segments, and offerings?
10. Does the brand story clarify the value you provide customers?

---

[4] Page 20, page-cco-guide-corporate-brand-management-2023.

Answering these questions will help to identify gaps in the corporate brand programme and assist with the development of a roadmap designed to progress brand management towards using the corporate brand as a true competitive driver.

Becoming a Fully Integrated Brand

When the corporate brand is fully integrated, at that point it becomes a driver for business growth and decision-making. Kushner said, 'Internally, when everyone understands the brand, the purpose of the company, and their role in it and feels empowered to own the brand experiences, that to me is a fully integrated brand because everyone has a role in making sure that they are living the brand.'

Page's report lists a number of questions to ask in this context:[5]

1. Are the brand, business strategy, reputation, and societal value all in alignment?
2. Does a shifting business strategy or changing market dynamics necessitate a fresh look at brand framework and architecture?
3. Do we need to reconsider brand due to organic and/or M&A growth?
4. How do we get investors to understand better the value proposition or change how they value our business?
5. Which are your key Brand Flagship Initiatives?

By asking—and having substantive answers to these types of questions—the company can start to harness the full power of its brand. Kushner noted, 'Having a fully integrated brand also means being able to identify brand and reputation gaps. Data and analysis are critical. Unfortunately, companies measure brand

---

[5] Page 29, page-cco-guide-corporate-brand-management-2023.

or reputation but don't see the unique value of measuring both. When you're measuring both, you have a better pulse on what's happening and can take action to address issues earlier and close gaps before they become chasms.' She went on to say, 'Finally, a fully integrated brand becomes a decision-making tool at the highest level. It can be a lever for transformation, culture, societal value, and business strategy because business strategies grow and evolve.'

Summary of Principles

- If an objective of branding is to help distinguish the company in the minds of consumers towards driving a competitive advantage, then this must be closely aligned with the entirety of a company's stakeholder engagement programme.
- The concepts of 'brand' and 'reputation' are connected but are not the same. One way to think about the difference between brand and reputation is that brand is what the company aspires to be; reputation is how the company is perceived by its stakeholders based on its behaviour and performance over time.
- Successful corporate brands are built on strong foundations. They sit over a well-defined mission, purpose, and set of corporate values. The company's brand framework defines the company's brand position and is a means of outlining these components, to make sure they're aligned and mutually supportive.
- Allowing flexibility in how the brand is expressed (but not what is expressed) is necessary when operating across multiple geographic locations.
- When rolling out a new brand or changes to an existing brand, colleagues need to understand what it means to them and their role—and that takes consistent communication.
- Effective collaboration between different internal functional areas is crucial to enabling successful brand management.
- A successful approach to brand governance ensures the corporate brand is understood and consistently used across different business lines and geographic markets. Consistency is vital.
- When the company is able to align its brand strategy with the experiences its stakeholders have in their interactions with the company, then real differentiation becomes possible.
- When the corporate brand is fully integrated, at that point it becomes a driver for business growth and decision-making.

Part Three

Protecting Corporate Reputations

13

When Crisis Strikes

The first time I worked on a full-blown crisis was in 1998. On September 25, an explosion occurred at a natural gas plant in Victoria, Australia, which was owned and operated by a joint partnership between Esso and BHP. Gas supplies to the state of Victoria were severely affected for two weeks. This meant no gas for hot showers (and the weather was cold) or for cooking. Businesses had to shut down. The state was in uproar. Working at Burson-Marsteller at the time, our client was not Esso, but the Victorian Energy Networks Corporation (VENCorp), a Victorian state government–owned entity. VENCorp had oversight for the system and had to coordinate both the stoppage of all gas use in the state as well as what would be the world's biggest relighting of gas appliances. I got a phone call the night it happened, which resulted in me turning up at VENCorp's office late that evening. Of course, this was well and truly pre-social media, so my immediate task was to sit by the radio and monitor the news stations for evolving media reports. I sat by that radio until 6.30 a.m. the following morning. There wasn't a lot that happened during that nightshift, but in the next two weeks, our team was a flurry of activity, organizing daily press conferences, dealing with incoming issues and queries, and developing a campaign to enable the relight programme to be done smoothly. It was relentless, exhausting, and exhilarating.

What Makes for a Crisis?

The term 'crisis' tends to be thrown around regularly in relation to corporate life. Sometimes the term is warranted but other times it is not strictly accurate. In the course of normal operations, companies will face a wide range of issues that need to be managed. These might include regulatory penalties, CEO changes, lay-offs, poor financial performance, and so on. There is usually more time available to manage an issue compared to a crisis. Business-as-usual can continue while managing an issue.

A crisis, on the other hand, requires the immediate and full attention of leadership and will impact business-as-usual operations until it is resolved. They take many forms—an environmental disaster, a bank run, a plane crash, a major product recall, are just a few examples. Andy Whitehead explained, 'A crisis materializes quickly and unexpectedly. It goes to the heart of an organization's licence to operate. To be defined as a crisis, I think it needs to put the organization into real peril.'

Ian McCabe is Principal, McCabe Advisory, LLC. He previously was the founding APAC Chairman of Edelman Global Advisory, and the Chairman, APAC Public Affairs of Burson-Marsteller. On the question of issues management compared to crisis management, McCabe said, 'One objective of every issues management assignment is to manage or contain the issue or issues to avert a crisis. However, a crisis is not necessarily a failure to manage an issue, a crisis can emerge without warning, but all crisis situations bring with them a range of issues that have to be managed during the crisis and during the important post-crisis rebuilding of brand strength or trust that was lost during the crisis. As such, issues and crisis management are different points on a company's radar screen, but they are inextricably linked.'

Crisis Management

The majority of this chapter will be devoted to looking at one particular type of crisis that has become exceedingly common— the instance of a company being the subject of a cyberattack that impacts its operations and its customers. Before this examination, it is worth making note of crisis management principles more generally. As defined by the Institute for Public Relations, crisis management is 'a process designed to prevent or lessen the damage a crisis can inflict on an organization and its stakeholders. As a process, crisis management is not just one thing. Crisis management can be divided into three phases: (1) pre-crisis, (2) crisis response, and (3) post-crisis.'[1] This chapter will focus on the first two phases. Recovering reputation after a crisis will be discussed in chapter fifteen.

A point here on terminology. The term 'crisis management' is sometimes questioned, given the implication that a crisis can in fact be managed! This is a fair observation given that in a crisis situation, there will be many variables outside of the company's control. Another way to think about it is that a crisis is a test of leadership, and the company must prepare, act, and communicate accordingly. Having acknowledged that, the term 'crisis management' remains valid when thinking about how the company can 'manage its response' once a crisis happens.

As will be discussed later in the chapter, a major element of work in this area takes place in the preparedness phase. Whitehouse said, 'My general philosophy for crisis management is that almost all of the work should go into preparedness. You should spend 90% of your effort on crisis planning and prevention. That prevention is around identifying potential crises and developing plans for them.'

---

[1] https://instituteforpr.org/crisis-management-and-communications/.

The detailed process that is entailed when a company responds to a crisis is the subject of many books. This book will not attempt to reflect all of the machinations involved in executing a response. However, before taking a more focused look at the instance of a cyberattack, a quick summary of some of the key principles of crisis management are as follows (with thanks to Ian McCabe for his insights):

- Assess your vulnerability and prepare for a range of crisis situations. Whitehead suggested, 'I recommend organizations build out a long list of the risks. Then, grade those risks by likelihood of coming to pass and degree of severity. You will see which are most severe and also most likely to happen. It is these risks that you should be scenario planning against.'

- Accurately define the crisis so you are responding to the issue or issues that triggered the crisis and the actions required to defuse or contain it. Do not jump to conclusions that might be incorrect. And it is not helpful or useful to immediately dismiss criticism of the company during these times. The company needs to take a dispassionate look at what has happened, understand the root causes, and then act accordingly.

- Stick to a structured framework of crisis response, reassurance, and rebuilding and determine the milestones that will enable you to move through these phases. Don't ignore the reassurance phase, you can't jump from response to rebuilding. It can be a short phase, but it is essential if the rebuilding phase is going to be successful. The company's stakeholders need to feel confident the company has taken action to address the issues that were at the core of the crisis in the first place.

- Control communication but make sure you communicate. A company can and should exert control over how it communicates in order to respond to the crisis, but this does not mean going to ground and not commenting at all. Doing so will just lead to more speculation and rumour which further erodes trust between the company and its stakeholders.

- You don't determine when the crisis is over, your stakeholders do, and you should work to drive to that point.

Making an Apology

Depending on the nature of the crisis, an apology can be a key requirement to enable the company to commence the process of rebuilding trust and its reputation. McCabe said, 'While it may seem alien in some cultures, in many an apology is expected and companies can't move on until an apology has been extended. There is a key role for an apology in many crisis situations because it shows the concern of a company's leadership and it can help frame and contain the issue or issues at the heart of the crisis. However, an apology needs to be well-framed, sincere, and credible and it needs to be delivered by the appropriate person or level within the company, organization, or government agency offering that message. Anything less can backfire and create an even bigger crisis.'

Whitehead reinforced this when he noted, 'I would argue for some form of apology in almost every situation, keeping in mind that sometimes, such as with crises caused by natural disasters, things are outside of the control of the organization.'

A Deeper Dive: The Instance of a Cyberattack

The issue of cybersecurity isn't a technology issue. It is a business one and a leadership one. It is also a major reputational concern. The attack and invasion of a company's networks can result in a blinding spotlight placed without warning on the company—on its executive team and on its ability to maintain trusting relationships with its customers and other stakeholders.

Antoine Calendrier is Vice-Chair, Corporate & Trust Services, APAC, at Edelman. He said, 'There is so much more now in terms of stakeholder expectations around cyber security. You can have your staff turning up at your offices and they are not able to work because the IT systems are all down. At the same time, customers are contacting you within hours to ask what is going on. So, your cybersecurity issue is not something you can deal with on the sidelines; it's about you being able to get your business back up and running while everyone is watching in real time.'

Sue Cato is partner at Cato & Clive and is recognized as one of Australia's leading issues management experts. Cato reinforced that a cybersecurity attack is very different to other types of crises. She said, 'If a bridge collapses onto a ship, we can determine that there were six cars that were on the bridge and there was one ship. You know the impact. This is not like that. In cyber incidents its far more complex and nuanced. A steady hand is needed in a cyber incident storm. You need people on your team with concrete backbones and a forensic lens in terms of how do we sort this out? Your customers matter the most and you must work out the solution, because that is ultimately how your reputation survives.'

The question of trust is never more to the fore than when a company is the subject of an attack. As Calendrier noted, everyone is watching you try to regain control, and the reality is that, even once a company finds its footing after an attack, that doesn't mean that its customers or observers of the business are going to trust that company, given its systems allowed a breach in the first place. Calendrier explained, 'If it is in your system, it's quite possible that your stakeholders, whichever way they are connected to you – whether through communications, orders, badging, processing and so on, might also be impacted by the issue. Your stakeholders will raise the question: could this also be in my system? The answer is that you have no idea. Your suppliers and others might start organizing into crisis teams so you end up being the nexus of a crisis surrounded by crisis teams who are thinking their systems may be impacted. The most basic reaction here is that stakeholders will cut ties with the company in question because you were the source of the infection in the first place. This is extremely challenging, because even with the best forensics companies involved, they cannot tell you for certain that the system is entirely clean. They simply cannot tell you without doubt that the system is entirely safe.'

The rest of the chapter will continue to examine the impact of crisis on corporate reputations through the lens of a cyberattack. It is apt to do so given the high degree of difficulty associated with responding to such attacks, the heightened impact on reputations that they can have and the frequency with which these attacks are taking place around the world.

The Need for Preparation

The ability to mitigate reputational damage in the wake of a cyberattack is in large part related to how much advance planning the company has done. Too often, crisis planning is pushed to the end of the to-do list and insufficient attention is paid to scenario planning. Being well prepared to face a cyberattack (or for that matter any crisis) is the bulk of the effort. A formal framework, encompassing governance procedures such as business continuity planning, crisis communications and incident management protocol, must be robust and kept current.

Technology system breaches and attacks come in many different forms. Cato noted, 'Companies need to war game best- and worst-case scenarios. These can be limited to, say, three key scenarios – you will never get them exactly right but they ensure you are not inventing it when something happens. These can be adjusted when you are actually in battle. It is important to know the answers to questions such as, if we need cyber professionals, who do we ring? Do we have them on retainer? Who is our team that we immediately bring into the war room?'

Mock simulations/drills should be conducted at least once a year, if not more, that allow procedures to be tested in practice and also to build more knowledge within the company about how to react to such a situation. The drills should include the involvement of the CEO and encompass the width of the company rather than selective functions. Game planning should consider the case where for regular communications platforms (email, Zoom, social platforms, etc.) have been knocked out and how to establish new means of communicating. In the case of a public company, the board should be kept informed as to the plans and preparations being made to counter a future attack.

The Need for Teamwork

Any type of crisis requires strong and effective collaboration within the company in response. Whitehouse said, 'I think good practice is to have the security team, the lawyers, the operations people, the finance team, all in the room in the context of a crisis, managing that crisis and the communications. What it is that we're going to say to all of our stakeholders as the matter unfolds, how are we going to listen to them, and then managing through the arc of the crisis as it hits.'

When facing a large cybersecurity issue, the quality of the response is essentially based upon the ability of the firm to marshal an ecosystem of actors to coordinate the response. A major cyberattack requires all hands-on deck, and who is designated to do what when attacks strike must be agreed well ahead of time. Is everyone clear on the roles and responsibilities of relevant members of the leadership team to ensure that the firm is ready to act quickly and effectively? Precious time can be lost if there is any hint of confusion regarding who is doing what on the team.

The company typically must engage specialist legal counsel. Calendrier noted, 'You need cyber security lawyers who really understand what's happening technically and can lay out the liabilities. That piece is important because once the shock of the announcement is absorbed, it's going to be about liabilities.' He also makes the point that 'Data privacy regulations tend to vary quite broadly from country to country. You need to have on-the-ground legal counsel that is specialized because they're going to be able to tell you what's happening from a regulatory perspective and then from a comms standpoint you design the appropriate response. You need to have absolute clarity of what is required and what is customary in the geography where you operate.'

A side note: traditionally there might be a degree of tension between Legal and Corporate Affairs regarding what can be said at various stages of the crisis. The challenge is to respond publicly to issues in defence of the company while not saying anything that creates legal risk. Communicators must be mindful of this risk, but at the same time, the best lawyers have a clear understanding of the need to operate with some level of transparency in the sense that we say what we know, and we say what we don't know from the onset, because it's material to the survival of the business. The lawyers help put the parameters around the language, what can and should be said, and the timing of it.

A notable reputational lever is also the quality of the IT forensics players employed to help with the response. A company that hires the best-in-class technology firms that specialize in this area will, in doing so, demonstrate they are investing in the preeminent resources available to respond to the situation.

Know Your Stakeholders

Being familiar with the expectations of its stakeholders allows the company to speak in a way that connects with the specific concerns of its various stakeholders. Much of this work should happen before any crisis strikes. Trust must be established, including not only with customers but also stakeholders such as government and regulatory officials. Government is a critical player because it can essentially direct the nature of the reputational impact. If the company described by the government as being a responsible player that is doing whatever it takes to respond, that's a major benefit. But things can quickly become very politicized. Cato noted, 'Although you may not be legally required to disclose a certain level of detail to the Government, you do not want the Government or authorities to feel they have been misled. You need to behave in a manner that gives you the right to be trusted.'

There are times when there will be political rhetoric that's critical or hostile to the company as it attempts to traverse the fallout of the crisis. Talking generally on this subject (not necessarily in the context of a cyberattack), McCabe said, 'This is a very sensitive area because a company is often impacted by political issues or developments that are not directed at them and any response can make them the poster child for that issue or development. If they are being singled out by a government or a politician, they need good intelligence to determine if they are being singled out to send a message to an industry or wider group of companies or if they have done something that needs to be quickly addressed in order to end the attacks by officials who often control the company's ability to operate. Companies need to think carefully before getting into a political debate, there is often little upside and usually significant downside. Communications teams need to work closely with legal and government relations advisors in these situations to determine the best course of action.'

Another key stakeholder group are employees, and the company needs to take care to ensure its people do not feel as though they're bearing some of the consequences of the cyberattack. Calendrier said, 'How you engage employees depends on the set up and size of the organization but in general in the case of large, multi-market organizations, it tends to work well to have daily briefings with management that cascade a message through the company. This can be safer than relying on written emails, which might go outside and backfire. I remember a time when there was an email from HR to employees which the threat actor saw, and thought was too reassuring and so heightened the attack.'

Providing a Response

Is the attack credible? What ransom was demanded? Will or did the company pay it? What information has been taken and/ or exposed? How are you keeping customers informed? These questions among others require coherent, considered, and consistent answers. Companies must also find the right balance between taking unequivocal responsibility for areas where they are at fault, but also pushing back when faced with inaccurate finger pointing.

Cato observed, 'One of the ways some people are getting it wrong is trying to behave as they would in a traditional crisis, which is to throw their arms around it, apologize, say we are on top of it, explain this is why it won't happen again. This is a normal response to a crisis, but cyberattacks require a very different response. The one thing we know is that there has never been a cyberattack yet where in the first 24-48 hours, which is when people want to respond, that they have any reliable idea about what has happened. So, when you double down, and tell people about the attack and that it is under control you open yourself up to a world of pain. Invariably when you have the specialists in, they find it's so much worse than you thought. Then you have to come out and say, we know we said it was under control but in fact it wasn't actually 100,000 customers impacted, it was a million people impacted. Then you have to say either, we had no idea, or we misrepresented the situation. Then you make what is already a bad situation far worse.'

Cato suggests an initial response along these lines:

We believe there has been a cyber incursion. We believe there is a possibility there may have been a breach that has impacted customers. We have appointed experts to look at it. We have notified the appropriate regulators and authorities, and we will keep you updated.

She said, 'At least you are giving people the confidence that you're on it and you [are] dealing with all the appropriate people to get a hold of it. This is not saying in any sense that "we know that" because you don't.'

Providing context to the situation should not be seen as making excuses. Calendrier made the point, 'It is very tempting to play the victim because it is a criminal act, but this just doesn't stand. The position of being a victim might resonate internally but the moment you're speaking out, people will not tolerate that because it means that maybe in the future it can all occur again. People understand and know that you've been a victim but there is also a reason why you were attacked and not another company B. Maybe your systems were more vulnerable, maybe you didn't do the right thing – and when review[ing] the forensics reports you realize that [there] have been vulnerabilities in the system.'

Cato agreed, 'The company should never play the victim card. Your customer is the end loser – you are the channel for your customers to become vulnerable and the ultimate victim.'

Lead Rather than Manage

When an attack happens, particularly at a large scale, there is fallout in all directions, much of it is out of the company's control. Cato said, 'Lesson number one is in the first day and days you don't know what you don't know. And it might take many weeks to know. A company with a good culture wants to be transparent and especially if it's material you know you have disclosure obligations. You know your stakeholders, you know morally and ethically that if you were the person affected, you would want to know immediately. Where it gets legally and ethically challenging is where you have no way of verifying or guaranteeing what details have been taken and whether or not we should be worried about it. You could be throwing people into a spin and creating liabilities that you don't need to and then you've got your obligations in terms of reporting to the various cyber regulators and authorities relevant to your jurisdiction. There is the legal overlay in terms of questions like what you do have [to] disclose, what do you have to do, etc. It is enormously complex when you are in the middle of the storm. So, anyone working in Comms has the instinct to throw their arms around it, but sometimes it is like a MASH unit – do you initially save the patient but unleash gangrene, making the damage worse. It is incredibly nuanced and there are so many different voices – moral rights, ethical rights, commercial rights, regulatory rights – so it is much harder than it looks and if you wade into it with one lens, it is incredibly dangerous.'

External variables simply cannot be controlled, but they can be addressed with strong leadership. Be authentic and have your values consistently on show as you act with intent. Act quickly but avoid acting through panic. Demonstrate your care for your customers, your understanding of the impact of the attack and the actions you are taking to respond to it.

Cyberattacks are increasingly common and are not going away. Companies will continue to invest in IT security to guard against attacks, but it is immensely difficult to counter all attacks all the time. Companies must not only be ready with the right level of technology, but also have the investment made ahead of time in professional crisis communications planning and preparedness.

A Case Example: The 2015 Experian Data Incident

Experian is a multinational data analytics and consumer credit reporting company. In October 2015, Experian North America announced it had been subject to the unauthorized acquisition of information from a server that contained data on behalf of one of its clients. The data included some personal information (names, addresses, social security numbers, birth dates, etc.) for approximately fifteen million consumers in the United States. Experian discovered the breach itself and proactively announced it via a press release. The breach highlights the trust issues that a company's clients and partners have in relation to its ability to protect sensitive information.

After Experian announced the breach, the then chief executive of the client in question issued a statement, which in part said, 'I am incredibly angry about this data breach and we will institute a thorough review of our relationship with Experian.' Experian took decisive and comprehensive action to address the fallout from the breach. It is notable that in 2023 the company affected remains a client of Experian.

Gerry Tschopp is SVP, Head of Global External Communications and Chief Communications Officer, North America, at Experian. Tschopp was at the firm in 2015 when the breach occurred and provided his insights on the experience and shared his experience of the episode. The following passages are in his own words.

Finding Out

The thing with data breaches is that by their nature, they are ill-defined and there is a lack of information. I was first alerted to this breach by our General Counsel, who called me to say that we have seen an anomaly in the system, and we need to get together with our Security team and talk about it.

The Challenge of Getting the Facts

We sat around a table with our CEO, with Legal, with our head of the business unit that was impacted, with our security people, government affairs, investor relations, compliance, and comms. At the early stage the focus is all about investigating what has happened. The thing is, on day one you are not sure what it is or how widespread it is. Initially it might be, for example, 100 people affected. Then it's 250. And then it's 1,000 people. We wanted to get the facts straight and it took some time to figure it out. We confirmed what it was, how big it was, we discussed it with the client. It was critical to ensure we were in lockstep because we knew the client was going to be a part of this as well.

Making the Announcement

We did feel pressure to make a public announcement as soon as possible, but we also wanted to get it right. Our CEO, to his credit, as we were talking about what to do, made it very clear that we had to do right by the consumer. We must help them. And he meant it.

We put out one press release. The media wanted to do deep interviews. They wanted to get more information. We just took the position of being transparent, providing the facts, letting them know this is what we know and now we are focused on taking care of the consumers. And we're ensuring that our systems are locked down.

Stakeholder Engagement

We also knew this wasn't just a media relations exercise. We had to dig deeper and consider our employees, policy makers, consumer advocacy groups ... and think through when and how we communicate with them. And how do we maintain trust with our other clients? We had to engage with this range of stakeholders in a way that provided a consistent message so that they were informed by us and not just by the media coverage.

We knew there would be a reputational impact and that we needed to be proactive with all the audiences. We knew everyone in the company needed to be speaking with one consistent voice. We kept it to key messages around what it was, what we're doing and how we're helping.

Impacted consumers were given a series of recommendations. They would go to our website and could put in their information to check if they had been affected by the breach. If they were, then they were given access for credit monitoring, fraud alerts, and then specific steps to protect their identity. It was a step-by-step process.

The Role of Corporate Communications

We were focused on employee communications, managing incoming media calls, monitoring social media, making twice daily reports to management, and constant contact with the client comms team to make sure we're being consistent.

We are a global company and we listened closely to the coverage generated around the world, in the press and online. We were very disciplined about our public comments.

Being direct and calm with everybody in the room is important because in times of high stress, people can get hot under the collar quite quickly. Keeping calm helps with having conversations and with thinking a little more clearly. Some people don't like to share bad news with leadership, but it is far better to do so than have them ask or see something.

The Importance of Teamwork

Everybody needs to work together. There can be no silos. Nothing happens without proper integration with Legal, Marketing, Business Unit leaders, Security, and our executive teams.

* * *

Whether it's a cyberattack or another form of crisis, the resulting period time will require the company to navigate a period fraught with challenges to its reputations. While the type of crisis to be faced is uncertain, the appearance of one for a company of any reasonable size is almost inevitable. Investing time and resources to plan ahead, to agree a means of response and to rehearsing with colleagues will pay dividends in enabling the company to endure what is to come and even to move forward in a stronger position than before.

Summary of Principles

- The term 'crisis management' refers to how the company can manage its response once a crisis happens, rather than an ability to manage the crisis itself.
- A crucial element of crisis management is the devotion of time and effort to being prepared ahead of time through scenario planning and the development of plans.
- In most instances, an apology is a key requirement to enable the company to commence the process of rebuilding trust and its reputation.
- A cybersecurity crisis is not exactly the same as other categories of crisis given the high degree of difficulty in establishing the facts and the capacity for trust issues to quickly permeate through the stakeholder ecosystem.
- Conducting drills focused on two or three likely scenarios is a necessary element of preparing for the eventuation of a cyberattack.
- A huge part of getting the response done well is the company's ability to have a team in place that spans both key internal stakeholders as well as external advisors.
- The company should never attempt to suggest that it understands all the facts if this is not the case.
- Never position the company as the victim.

14

Mitigating the Reputational Impact of Litigation

Litigation poses a severe threat to corporate reputation. Not only is there the legal case itself to contend with, but there is, alongside it, the court of public opinion, an age-old concept that has been turbo charged by social media and smart phones. Legal action can be launched into the public spotlight fast and everyone can have an opinion on that action, whether accurate or not. Simon Pugh is Partner, Litigation Communications and Disputes at Portland. On the broad impact of litigation on reputation, Pugh said, 'Companies very rarely are unscathed by litigation, even if you're the one bringing the claim. There is always something that probably is going to be uncomfortable as disclosure exercises often yield something that you don't want in the public domain. There is definitely the potential for, at one end of the spectrum, things to be uncomfortable or embarrassing, but at the other end of the spectrum for it to have a massive impact on your business.' He went on to elaborate, 'Some particular types of litigation, for example, class actions or regulatory breaches, may cause customers to shy away from, or boycott, your products. It may impact your ability to retain talent or to find new talent. If you're a listed business, it might impact people's desire to invest or hold shares in the company. If you're a private business, it might impact the ability to raise capital.'

The ability to balance the constraints demanded by the legal process with proactively protecting reputation is tricky to achieve, but very necessary when the company is faced with a high-stakes legal situation that could last for months if not years. How the litigation is managed by the company can have a lasting influence on the perceptions of customers, employees, investors, and other stakeholders. Depending on the type of litigation, some or all of these stakeholders will have questions about it and how the company is responding to it. Jamie Moeller is Founder and Principal of JWM Strategies, and previously was Managing Director, Global Public Affairs Practice at Ogilvy Public Relations Worldwide. He said, 'During the litigation and then coming out of litigation, win or lose, you presumably will still be in business. You'll still be selling products and or services, and you still want your stakeholders to think positively about you, which is why communications is so critical to protecting your brand.'

Of course, the reputational impact of litigation will in large part depend on the nature of the case in question. Commercial litigation is a story that could be very pertinent to business partners or to employees. Criminal proceedings are in a different court system, with a different set of allegations and potentially serious implications. They deliver heightened risk to the company, although business litigation can generate its own impact on corporate reputation.

This is no longer a U.S. phenomenon—international markets have become far more litigious than in the past. In this regard, McAndrews noted, 'We have seen the export of class-action style litigation from the U.S. to other markets, including Europe, Canada and Australia.'

A 2022 report by law firm Clifford Chance, talking about the occurrence of class actions, noted, 'In the UK, for example, very significant group actions have been filed across a range of sectors, including: the RBS Rights Issue litigation and the Lloyds/ HBOS claims following the GFC in the financial sector; the

VW diesel emissions action in the consumer sector; the Tesco accounting error shareholder action; the Google iPhone litigation with respect to data privacy; and a raft of competition-related claims, including the MasterCard fees litigation and the FX market group actions. Environmental claims, such as the CO_2 emissions litigation brought by a group of NGOs against Shell in the Netherlands, is another fast-developing area.'[1] These are but a few examples. Corporate litigation will continue to spread and change internationally, reflecting the intricate interactions taking place that encompass legal, economic, social and regulatory elements around the world.

Aligning the Communications Strategy with the Legal Strategy

Moeller said, 'First and foremost, the communication strategy has to support the litigation strategy. You can't have two separate tracks.' In a separate discussion, Pugh reinforced this principal. He said, 'The first principle is that the legal strategy has to come first. The things we want to do from a communications perspective, need to make it easier for you to do what you're doing in the litigation process and at the very least, not making it harder.'

Having acknowledged the communications programme must always be in support of the legal process, the communications strategy must also be holistic and comprehensive. Moeller said, 'You have an audience in the courtroom, which is the judge and sometimes the jury. You have an audience outside the courtroom, which are shareholders, customers, employees, and none of them care about the nomenclature of the law. They care about what's

---

Clifford Chance, 'The Growing Risk of Group Litigation and Class Actions', April 2022, https://www.cliffordchance.com/content/dam/cliffordchance/briefings/2022/04/the-growing-risk-of-group-litigation-and-class-actions.pdf.

happening and why it's either going to impact them or not impact them. It's the same story it just has to be told differently for different audiences.'

What the company must avoid is a communications strategy that is disconnected from the legal process in-flow. The high-profile controversy in 2023 over the relationship between the PGA Golf Tour and the Saudi's Public Investment Fund (PIF)-funded LIV Golf Tour is a case in point. When the LIV Tour launched and started poaching PGA Tour players, the PGA sued and initiated a very aggressive PR campaign—essentially accusing LIV of 'sportwashing' for the Saudi government. Then, without warning, the PGA and Saudi Public Investment Fund announced that they had reached an agreement in principle to join forces and drop all litigation. Players, media, sponsors, and policymakers all expressed shock, leading to a backlash against the PGA Tour's leadership. There was an acrimonious hearing in the U.S. Senate and media reports that the U.S. Department of Justice was looking to open an investigation. The PGA's ferocious communications campaign in the first instance was very effective, but it seems to have been launched without due consideration of the possibility that they would drop their litigation in the manner that took place.

As with other categories of issues and crisis management, managing the reputational impact of litigation is a team undertaking. The worse outcome occurs when those within the company's executive team have not planned ahead and had the conversations necessary to understand what needs to happen when a case is launched. Jeff McAndrews is a partner at FGS Global and co-leads the firm's global Crisis and Issues Management practice. He has extensive experience in the field of litigation communications. When I asked McAndrews about the best approach to mitigating the reputational issues associated with litigation, he said, 'So much of this [good litigation communications strategy] depends on the relationship between communications and legal, both inhouse and your outside advisors. You have to start there. You have to have those relationships, and have a consensus on an approach, because when litigation is filed against you it can be very intense, and the allegations can generate a lot of scrutiny very quickly.'

For the company that is the target of litigation, being ready and having everyone on the same page becomes even more critical. Often the person or company launching the action will have advisors who are adept at media relations to proactively frame the lawsuit using emotive and easily understood language. McAndrews said, 'The allegations always generate much more attention than the defence. If you're the one bringing the litigation, you have that freedom to tell your story, be the first mover and put the opposing side on the back foot. You have a lot more options in terms of controlling the narrative and getting in front of stakeholders. From a defence perspective, this really emphasizes the need to have a plan in place and having a close relationship between communications and legal, so that when something comes in, you've got that muscle memory that allows you to quickly assess the issue and respond appropriately.'

Taking a Comprehensive Approach to Stakeholder Engagement

By its nature, people across the board are curious when they hear about disputes of any kind, and this is certainly the case when it comes to legal action. A company cannot expect to be engaged in a litigious dispute without it receiving attention from a range of stakeholders, including employees. Pugh said, 'Often information needs to be kept confidential because that's what's required by the legal process, but I think businesses need to explain either why they are bringing the litigation or why they are going to defend it, and that employees understand how that aligns with the values of the business.'

McAndrews agreed with the principal that coordination of the litigation response must extend to all aspects of stakeholder engagement. In reference to regulatory discussions he said, 'What you say in the regulatory sphere will impact your litigation position and vice versa. Everything needs to be coordinated. The communications team needs to be working with the lawyers and government relations, it's very indicative of how the circle of people involved can grow, and communications will typically act as a coordinating hub. It points to the need to have the proper processes in place and think through your scenarios ahead of time and establish those working relationships. This helps ensure you are not creating new problems [in] the course of defending yourself, whether through having wrong information or inaccurate information or saying something that wasn't public before. The stakes are typically just too high to make those mistakes.'

As with many other dimensions of reputation management, litigation communications should employ the use of research. Carefully designed and executed research will help to generate nuanced insights into stakeholder perceptions and sentiments on matters relevant to the action. Pugh said, 'One limitation is confidentiality, given much of the work before the legal action is out of the public domain. And from a budgetary point of view, doing a focus group for every single stage of the litigation is expensive. What you usually end up doing is tying the research to the elements of the case that are most likely to attract media interest.'

There is also a place for testing key messages. Pugh noted that, 'We use a lot of message testing in a way that you would with conventional or political campaigning. That can help when trying to condense messaging into things that resonate and are easy to understand.' He added that, 'You might want a quite focused and targeted message that is not aimed for the general public, but rather a fairly small sector of industry stakeholders or politicians.' Pugh went on to stress that this process is not designed to attempt to impact the litigation itself but rather to support the company's reputation in the context of the litigation taking place.

Making Public Comment

The traditional approach to corporate litigation is clear cut. Inside the courtroom, legal teams contest the matter at hand via detailed and extensive debates. Outside the courtroom, the communications strategy is simple: no comment. Today, more sophisticated companies understand that 'no comment' alone is a one dimensional and potentially damaging approach to the effort to build stakeholder support for the company's position.

Of course, great care is necessary about what is said and when. The company does not want to get ahead of the litigation process. It does not want to speak out of turn. It does not want to speculate or issue unchecked information and create more problems for itself. Pugh said, 'There are various points where documents become public, but when they are not public then you must respect that. A judge won't be impressed if he or she is reading things in the FT that they would expect to be hearing firsthand in the courtroom. So, you risk annoying the judge and, at the very serious end, you could be in contempt of court and the penalties of that are serious for all involved.'

McAndrews emphasized that, 'Litigation communications need to mitigate future risk and not generate any new risk. It's that moment when litigation or another crisis hits and a company, or a person, feel the need to defend themselves and respond very quickly, but maybe they don't have all the information they need, or maybe the information they have isn't accurate. That is a very dangerous moment, one when it's very easy to create new risk. What you want to be doing is clearly articulating your position, defending your reputation and supporting your legal strategy. You can't do that on a dime, it's something that you need to think through with your legal partners ahead of time.'

When I asked him for his further views on the issue of making public comment, McAndrews said, 'I understand there are circumstances in litigation when a company may not want to or shouldn't say anything. But, in general, every time you say no comment, you're giving the other side carte blanche to establish the narrative and paint the entire picture however they want. It really behoves you to be able to say something, even if it is "we will answer those specific claims in the appropriate forum, but what I can tell you is that these are our core values, this is how we approach a situation, we may not have all the facts yet, but we're dedicated to addressing this issue, etc." There is always something you can say to reflect what type of company you are, what your position is, even if it's just to say we reject these claims outright, we think that they are spurious – that's better than nothing in my view.'

There is also a capacity to talk to journalists on a background basis, to ensure the company's position—and the legal process itself—is accurately understood. Pugh said, 'Often litigation is really complicated and there's lots of difficult issues at play, both in substance of the case, but also in terms of the legal process. Most court reporters will have a good understanding of the process. But court reporting is one of the things that is shrinking. Often what you find is you're either talking to a sector journalist, who understands the issues, but they won't necessarily understand the process. Or you're just talking to the news reporter who's been farmed the story that day, and there's probably quite a lot of explaining to do.'

Avoiding Personal Attacks

An aggrieved party who takes legal action against a company can make things nasty, making allegations that the company may strongly oppose. The same applies to other stakeholders. The temptation is there at times to get personal, whether it's in relation to an employee or a business partner. But the company's other employees and business partners are watching what it does and says during these times. This is where there is a place for sophisticated communications running alongside the legal arguments being made in court. Moeller said, 'When you're on the defence, it is important to tell your side of the story to the extent you can through the legal process. The one line I don't think you can cross is you don't want to disparage the plaintiffs. You don't want to question either their motivations or their honesty, as tempting as that sometimes might be. You don't want people looking at that and saying, Well, that could be me. And does this company really care about doing the right thing?'

McAndrews echoed this viewpoint when he said, 'You can never forget your customers are watching. When litigation involves a customer, too often companies do forget. Even if it's a heated moment during litigation, they should assume that all their other customers are watching. You should not forget to express sympathy for them as appropriate, and there are ways to do that without accepting blame or guilt, or at least not attack or blame them outright.'

When Judgement Is Made

A stakeholder engagement plan is required ahead of time, so when the judgement lands, the company is ready to move quickly, and everyone internally is on the same page. Scenario planning needs to have been done, encompassing the various outcomes—a win, a loss, or a mixed result. A suite of materials needs to be prepared, including draft media statements, question and answer documents, employee messages, and so on. Pugh noted that, 'What we will commonly do is, once the hearings are finished and the judgement is being written up, we will scenario plan for different outcomes. It's not always the case that it's a complete win or a complete loss, sometimes there can be a kind of middle ground. We will think about that in advance.'

If the company wins, then the options for how to react to that are more expansive. The type and scope of response will also depend on the case in question. Moeller said, 'I had a client that was involved in a very large, high-profile patent infringement case. Once they won their case, they wanted to promote their victory very heavily because they wanted to send a signal to any other competitive companies, that if you come after our patents and our intellectual property, we will come after you and there will be a price to pay. Once we won, there was a global media campaign to talk about the verdict and the impact of that verdict.'

If the result goes against the company, the question becomes one of how to respond. McAndrews said, 'It's okay to disagree, and to show a clear path of what you're going to do to appeal, even if it's just to say we're exploring our options. Sometimes you just need to take the hit, but you can still make sure that your position [is] heard, and your stakeholders understand that there are next steps.'

Pugh made the point that, 'Even if you have lost, there might still be positive things in the judgment that you can draw attention to. For example, if the judge says something like, you had a good case, but you failed to overcome a high legal bar.'

Companies will more likely than not have to, at some point, contend with litigation of some variety. This might range from an intellectual property issue, antitrust investigations, through to alleged fraud, data privacy, discrimination claims, labour matters, or cross-border disputes, among many other examples. The company, if it is to manage its way through complicated issues related to the litigation, must remember that while its legal strategy comes first, it ignores the outside world at its peril. Win or lose, its reputations will be better protected if it plans for how it will engage with all relevant stakeholders in a manner that protects its reputations to the fullest extent possible.

Summary of Principles

- Litigation poses a severe threat to the reputation of a company and an effort must be made to manage the reputational impact of litigation as well as the legal process itself.
- The communications strategy has to support the litigation strategy, always, and cannot be pursued as a separate exercise.
- It is critical to have a close relationship between communications and legal teams beforehand to enable the company to quickly assess emerging issues and respond appropriately.
- A company cannot expect to be engaged in a litigious dispute without it receiving attention from a range of stakeholders and it needs to be ready to respond accordingly.
- Research can help to generate nuanced insights into stakeholder perceptions and sentiments on matters relevant to the action.
- Litigation communications need to mitigate future risk rather than generate any new risk, however, there remains room for the company to make comment that builds understanding for its position.
- Always avoid the temptation to get personal, whether it's in relation to an employee or a business partner. Other stakeholders will be watching closely.
- A stakeholder engagement plan is required ahead of when the judgement lands, so the company is ready to move quickly, and everyone internally is on the same page.

15

Rebuilding Lost Reputations

In the aftermath of a crisis, the question becomes, how to move forward and regain trust that has been lost between the company and its stakeholders? Technically, this chapter belongs in the 'Earning Reputations' section of the book; however, it seems apt to have it directly follow the chapters that speak of reputational loss. While it can take only one big 'wrong' to create reputational damage, it can take a lot 'doing the right thing' over a long period of time to address that 'wrong' and regain the lost reputation in question. Just ask Wells Fargo, the U.S. bank that was derailed by scandals starting in 2016 in relation to the opening of millions of fake bank accounts to meet sales targets. In the years that followed, the bank was fined repeatedly and 2018, the Federal Reserve placed a cap on Wells' ability to grow its business until it could demonstrate it had addressed past issues.[1] In September 2022, in a hearing before the U.S. Senate, it's CEO stated that 'We

---

[1] Press Release, 'Responding to widespread consumer abuses and compliance breakdowns by Wells Fargo, Federal Reserve restricts Wells' growth until firm improves governance and controls. Concurrent with Fed action, Wells to replace three directors by April, one by year end', Federal Reserve System, February 2018, https://www.federalreserve.gov/newsevents/pressreleases/enforcement20180202a.htm.

began a process nearly three years ago to change our company's culture and priorities, and we have taken strong steps in that direction.'[2] Achieving true recovery in the wake of a crisis takes an accurate understanding of what went wrong, an appreciation of how the company is really perceived by its stakeholders and a roadmap that allows the company to move forward.

Making a Damage Assessment

The severity of damage to a company's reputations will differ depending on the crisis or scandal it has endured. A company that has been the subject of a cyberattack will face a different set of issues compared to the company that has been involved in widespread fraud, or a company that has had to undertake a product recall. Before the process of regaining reputations can take place, the company needs to have an informed understanding of exactly what reputational damage has taken place, and with which stakeholders.

Doug Dew is Regional Managing Director, Corporate and Public Affairs, Asia-Pacific, with Burson. He is based in Beijing. Dew noted, 'The starting point has to be having a precise handle on just how much the organization's reputation has been damaged. This requires an evidence-based diagnosis of the problem based on qualitative and quantitative research.' He went onto say, 'Sometimes we've worked with clients where they've realized they didn't have as big a hit to their reputation as they first thought.'

A formal assessment is required that enables the company to have an educated understanding of when the timing is right to move on from the crisis that has taken place and what needs to be done in order to do so effectively.

---

2 https://www.banking.senate.gov/imo/media/doc/Scharf%20 Testimony%209-22-22.pdf.

When to Switch Gears

Jamie Moeller said, 'In my experience, the thing that often gets forgotten is the recovery piece. Smart companies spend a lot of money preparing for crisis and then you're forced to manage a crisis. But you've only done two thirds of the job. Recovery to me is absolutely critical because it is a brand protection and enhancement exercise.' He suggested that, 'There is a danger of reintroducing people to how you messed up before and you have to at some point, cut it off. I think research can play a big role in determining when it's time to move on from crisis recovery communications.'

Dew said, 'You can often organise it in a phased approach where you have the initial crisis response, and then there's a reassurance phase where you're looking to reassure your stakeholders that you're taking the actions to address the issues that have caused the reputation to be negatively impacted. Then, you want to move into a recovery or renewal phase. In this phase, you will pivot towards positive stories about the company and stakeholder engagements that help you build back goodwill equity and trust.'

On the issue of the appropriate time to pivot towards the future, Dew said, 'One key determinant is the degree to which you are still being asked those questions about whether you have done the right and responsible thing. Are your stakeholders still demanding more actions to address those core issues of concern? Are they still indicating they are very much concerned about what caused the crisis and your company's conduct? Once that dies down and they seem to have been reassured, once for example your consumer hotlines are no longer ringing on the subject, then you can move on to recovery.'

The company cannot make the unilateral decision that it's time to move on. Rather, it needs to accept this decision in the hands of its stakeholders; listening to their concerns and understanding their mindsets will help the company make the decision to enter its recovery phase.

Will Harvey is Director of the Social Purpose Centre and Professor of Leadership at Melbourne Business School, University of Melbourne, and author of *Reputations At Stake*. Harvey said, 'You've got these multiple reputations that exist within, but also between stakeholder groups. You need to understand what their sentiments are and then ensure that your strategy is appropriately engaging.'

The Imperative to Engage Employees

As with so many aspects of corporate reputations, the employee base is a critical stakeholder group in the programme of rebuilding lost reputations. Both during and also well after the crisis, it is critical that the company connects with its people to ensure they know what is going on and what is being done to address the situation.

A review of the health of a company's relationship with its employee's post-crisis should include an examination of company culture and whether the values the company has in place are supporting how it operates. A reputational rebuild may entail a reassessment of the company's culture and consideration of changes that need to be made to that culture to enable it to move forward. Harvey made the point, 'There's a whole body of literature in business and management known as organisational identity, which is how members of the organisation collectively perceive it. In the context of a threat, take the BP Gulf of Mexico crisis, suddenly, you've got this big, ongoing crisis and people are really starting to attack BP. This becomes an identity crisis at an organizational level because those employees of BP start to wonder if they are comfortable staying because it has an impact on their individual identity. People don't want to work for a stigmatised organisation because others people make judgments about them and what they do.'

Re-engaging employees who feel a sense of disenfranchisement or even shame working at the company that has been through a crisis or scandal is easy to understand but difficult to do. Understanding the values and culture that need to be instilled or updated is one part of the equation. The other is working tirelessly every day to make it happen. It encompasses every aspect of corporate life, from the people that get hired, to the training employees receive, to how performance is evaluated and compensated. It also means taking exception to those within the company who do not uphold its values and taking swift action to discipline or fire those people who do the wrong thing. An environment where employees feel safe to speak up is also critical. The executive leadership team must be visible, confident, and credible role models who set the tone for the entire company—they also must be united in presenting a vision about what the future of the company looks like, and the role of its people in getting it there.

Above all, it requires instilling employees with a sense of purpose—either existing or refreshed—that generates (or regenerates) a sense of pride in being part of the organization.

Demonstrating Action

Of course, words are hollow without deeds to give them meaning. Nothing impedes the recovery of reputational damage more than issues arising from not addressing previous decisions, policies, or initiatives that led to the damage in the first place. Dew said, 'Actions are the foundation for any words. You have to do the right thing and be seen to be doing the right thing. And then you communicate that. You've also got to convey the right attitude of humility or an apology, or whatever is appropriate to the specific situation. So, words do matter, but messages need to be centred on doing the right thing.'

These actions need to be more than a marketing activity. They must go to heart of the company's operations and how they engage with their stakeholders. Dew elaborated that 'Companies that have had these big moments where their reputation has taken a hit in the market, they often double down on investing in stakeholder engagement and they become more focused on corporate reputation management. But it's not just about that. It's also about the investments the company needs to make to show that they're a good company that is meeting stakeholder expectations. That could be core business decisions, like a new joint venture or an R&D centre or something else that shows that you're committed to contributing to that market to an extent that is commensurate with the opportunity they have to profit from the market.'

For many people, McKinsey has long represented the pinnacle of professional services firms—the gold standard. And yet, even McKinsey is not immune from reputational damage. It experienced at least two high-profile controversies over the past decade. One of those was in the U.S., where the firm advised Purdue Pharma, the pharmaceutical company that manufactures OxyContin, a highly addictive opioid painkiller. This work coincided with the opioid crisis in the United States. A statement on the firm's website reads, in part, that, 'In 2019, McKinsey committed to no longer advise clients on any opioid-related business anywhere in the world. We also continue to support organizations working to combat the opioid crisis.'[3] The firm reached a settlement of approximately US$600 million

---

[3] https://www.mckinsey.com/about-us/opioidfacts.

settlement with all 50 states, the District of Columbia and five U.S. Territories.[4]

Emerging from this episode, and also the scandal it experienced in South Africa[5], the firm has invested heavily with the intent of ensuring such crises do not repeat themselves in the future. McKinsey's Ramiro Prudencio said, 'Over the past several years, we have built clear criteria for what engagements we should take on and which ones we should not. This has been an important journey for the firm. We see reputation as the responsibility of every single individual in the firm – and every firm member participates in risk training, which includes training on external communications policies. Risk management, which I think is part of reputation building and management, is critically important to the firm today.'

McKinsey launched a new risk management framework, requiring its partners to assess client projects across five interrelated dimensions: Country, Institution, Topic, Individual, and Operational considerations. Referred to as 'CITIO', this framework is embedded in the way the firm gauges risk relating to all its client work. Prudencio said, 'We assess across five primary dimensions: the country in which the potential engagement is taking place, the institution we are serving, and the topics we are addressing. We also consider the individuals we will be working with and the operational implications for the firm and its teams. We look at these five dimensions and ask a series of questions within each. If there are indications that there is risk across any of these dimensions, the engagement is reviewed by our client service risk committee, comprised of partners and colleagues who are independent of the proposed engagement. The committee

---

* https://www.mckinsey.com/de/news/presse/settlement-funds.

* https://www.mckinsey.com/za/our-work/speech-by-kevin-sneader-at-gordon-institute-of-business-science-seminar.

determines whether the engagement can go ahead, if it should be modified to manage risks, or not go forward at all.'

This is a prime illustration of the substantial investment of both money and thought needed to allow a company to showcase to its stakeholders the serious steps it has taken to avoid future crises of a similar nature.

Keep the Drumbeat Going

Despite a temptation to bunker down and stay quiet in the aftermath of a major crisis, silence is not an option in the programme to regain and strengthen reputation. As the company takes action to address past issues, it should be open about past issues and mistakes and take a proactive stance to letting its stakeholders know about the progress it is making. The development of campaigns provides the company with a steady stream of content to be used across all communications platforms and in particular via the company's social media footprint. Thought leadership that generates useful, relevant, and digestible content can be used to supplement the communication of company milestones, product launches, events, community initiatives, and so on. Customer testimonials and stories also help to reflect the positive impact the company is making in its industry.

Harvey said, 'Often reputation threats relate to one of either character reputation or capability reputation. If you've done something unethical or that might be legal but is not socially acceptable, that relates to character reputation. The capability reputation is about your kind of financial performance, or the quality of your products and services. If any of those things come into question, then that's when your reputation can be lost. I have suggested in my *Reputation. At Stake* book a third aspect of reputation which is known as contribution reputation. If you think about capability and character, both of those things are about people making judgments regarding what you've done in the past, and people will make judgments about whether they're going to hire you, or they're going to work with you or buy a product based on that past. The contribution aspect is future oriented and saying, my perception of contribution will be linked to the past, but it's also related to how much value I feel can be provided by you in the future.'

This is a pertinent insight—the ability to consistently highlight its commitment and ability to deliver value now and into the future is key as the affected company goes about rebuilding its reputations. Mistakes may well have been made in the past. The company, having addressed those mistakes, must communicate a pathway forward that enables its stakeholders to support its 'contribution reputation'. Generating a sense of optimism about the company's outlook is vital.

Third-Party Advocates

As an individual, having friends who stick up for you makes life a lot easier when trying to get back on your feet. The same goes for companies. Nurturing relationships with stakeholders who will proactively support you and even speak out publicly on the company's behalf pays significant dividends. This cannot be done only when times are difficult. On the contrary, it is a long-term undertaking.

Penta's Whitehead gave me an anecdote that sums this up well. 'My father would tell a story where he'd be at the Tower of London. And a tourist would ask, how do you get the wildflowers in the moat around the Tower of London to look so beautiful? And my dad would say it's really simple. All you need to do is have rain fall for 1,000 years. The point is that investment in building reputation over the days, weeks, months and years is needed ahead of the crisis. Having good relationships with your stakeholders, having friends before you need them is essential so that when the crisis comes, you've got all of that in place.'

As it earns reputation when times are good, the company needs an effective stakeholder engagement programme in place to connect with the people and audiences relevant to its business. Developing relationships where these stakeholders become familiar with—and supportive of—the company's purpose and values, via interactions with the company's leadership, will help generate an ecosystem of valued advocates. This in turn will provide huge power to the company's efforts to renew its reputation post-crisis.

Summary of Principles

- Achieving true recovery in the wake of a crisis takes an accurate understanding of what went wrong, an appreciation of how the company is really perceived by its stakeholders and a roadmap that allows the company to move forward.

- The company cannot make the unilateral decision that it's time to move on. Rather, it needs to accept this decision in the hands of its stakeholders; listening to their concerns and understanding their mindsets will help the company make the decision to enter its recovery phase.

- A review of the health of a company's relationship with its employees post-crisis should include an examination of company culture and whether the values the company has in place are supporting the work it does and how it operates.

- Nothing impedes the recovery of reputational damage more than issues arising from not addressing previous decisions, policies, or initiatives that led to the damage in the first place.

- Despite a temptation to bunker down and stay quiet in the aftermath of a major crisis, silence is not an option in the effort to regain and strengthen reputations.

- Nurturing relationships with stakeholders who will proactively support you and even speak out publicly on the company's behalf cannot be done only once times are difficult.

16

Government Relations and Geopolitics

Seven years working in Mainland China instilled a strong appreciation in me for the importance of government relations. When talking about stakeholders in China, whether customers, employees, business partners, universities, or charitable organizations, among others, the stakeholder that connects all of them is the Chinese Communist Party. While China might be at one end of the spectrum in this regard, the reality is that governments everywhere exert varying degrees of influence on the way companies operate. Whether it's China or elsewhere, the government is a key stakeholder for any company. The ability to earn positive reputations among this stakeholder is a key component to the organization's sustained success.

The Remit of Government Relations

Jake Siewert is Head of Global Public Policy and Political Risk at Warburg Pincus. Siewert's career has spanned the private and public sectors, including as Press Secretary at the White House. On the question of how government relations has changed over the years, he said, 'In the old days, government relations was very much about building personal relationships around a shared interest. If a company had a plant in a town in Iowa, you had to know the congressman, the mayor, the senator, the governor, and there would be a shared interest in making sure that the plant was successful. If there was an issue that you wanted those people to advocate on your behalf, then you invited them to the plant, you might hold a fundraiser for them, it's all about building those relationships. That's still important and you can't neglect it. What's dramatically changed today is the lawmakers are as responsive to what's going on in social media as any other stakeholder.'

This raises a theme that is consistent throughout this exploration of corporate reputations, which is that every move a company makes is interconnected in a world where the flow of information is not controllable. Jake provided an anecdote that illustrates the shift that's taken place. 'I remember back to a time when I worked for a company that wanted to build a new facility in a small town in the Amazon. It was a good project for the town. What was interesting is that when we went to these tiny, remote villages in the Amazon, where people had to come in by boat, they had laptops, and they were asking questions about our operations in Iceland, Texas, Australia, and places like that. People can punch the company name into Google, and if any negative stories pop up, there's only so much the politicians can do for you. The world has become radically more transparent, and you need to have a strong narrative in place around the world to support your government relations.' Politicians are highly sensitive to public commentary around a particular company and any controversies must be solved before the company can expect support.

What Constitutes an Effective Approach?

As the landscape around which government relations continues to shift, what makes for an effective approach to engagement? Donough Foley has had a long career in government relations, with a primary focus on the Asia-Pacific region. Among other roles, Foley was Managing Director Government & Public Affairs at Moody's Asia-Pacific and Head of Government, Asia-Pacific, at Philips Electronics. In relation to what makes for effective engagement with the government, he suggested, 'The common feedback I get from regulators in Asia is that people don't listen. Companies don't look behind the need for a policy change. They don't look behind what's happening, what the regulator needs. Nobody asks, what more can we do for you? You get more from the last 15 minutes of the meeting, when you ask the "what more can we do for you?" question because it's open ended. Versus just saying that this policy is not going to work for us.'

In Asia, there is a close relationship between large local businesses, state-owned enterprises, and political stakeholders. An awareness of those stakeholders, their goals, and what it may mean to the company's advocacy or commercial goals is vital. There are also a web of business associations and chambers of commerce in countries across the region. Foley said, 'From a government relations perspective, if you want to be successful your focus isn't just entirely on the government space. If you look at Asia as a whole, whether it be Japan, Singapore, Malaysia, or China, business is closely aligned with government. There are organizations across each of those multiple markets where if you don't have a seat at the table, if you're not building a network, then you don't really get to know what's going on before it's too late.'

Steven Okun is CEO of APAC Advisors and Senior Advisor to McLarty Associates. An American citizen, Okun has lived in Singapore for many years, where he's held a range of prominent public affairs roles. On how to think about a proactive framework for government relations, Okun said, 'The five P's of Public Affairs are global. They are: Policy, Public Interest, Process, Politics, and Partnership.' Okun elaborated on each, which are summarised as follows:

1. Maintaining an informed understanding of policy is an obvious starting point. Before you can advocate for a change in a regulation or law, you need to know the

policy arguments both for and against. Public affairs practitioners must know both sides of the argument and be able to articulate your company's position clearly and in depth.

2. The company must be able to explain why implementing the policy it is advocating advances the **public interest** from the government official's vantage point. Okun notes that every government—from multi-party democracies to one-party states—considers the public interest from their own point of view before making major policy decisions in some fashion. On a related note, Siewert said, 'You need to design a narrative that feels local and makes sense in a local context. In the past, a lot of big American multinationals tended to centralize communications. They ran everything through headquarters and there was a process for approval around media interviews, around branding and marketing campaigns and the like. For a global company today, if you put a powerful person in the headquarters, that is fine, but their perspective becomes the perspective of headquarters. So devolving communications to local leaders is critical.' This has led many companies to be a lot more proactive in rotating staff from Asia into headquarters.

3. The **process** upon which this policy is going to be decided varies from governments, is usually complex, and varies in transparency. A detailed understanding of the local decision-making process allows you to lobby the right audience at the right time. You need to know what you don't know. Retaining experts who understand your objectives and can leverage their 'local-ness' on your behalf gives you a greater chance of success.

4. What are the **politics** behind a particular law or regulation? Politics can derail even the most coherently argued policy position that meets the local public

interest test. To meet this challenge, you need to look far beyond newspapers and policy briefs. Talk to experts and understand the trends and events in local markets. Peel back the rhetoric and really look at what issues are driving the decision-making process. Only after you map the stakeholder landscape can you connect the dots, understand who supports whom, and develop a battle plan.

5. The importance of **partnerships** recognizes that effective government relations includes engagement with workers and customers, shareholders, banks, NGOs, and *the media*. Developing local partners who will willingly articulate your position across the entire stakeholder map often provides the greatest impact. Building these partnerships can be accomplished regardless of one's nationality if it is based on shared interest. That said, there is a school of thought that while well accepted in the West, the role of grassroots campaigns and media-lead initiatives to support government advocacy has been less of a priority in Asia.

Okun explained, 'The 5P model works everywhere. What has changed more recently in its execution is that geopolitics impacts the "politics" and the "public interest" points more than it had previously. You need to be aware of the geopolitics far more today compared to 20 years ago. Back then, for example, when you came to the Singapore government, public interest would very much focus on how much FDI you were bringing, how many jobs you were creating, how many expats are we bringing in to pay taxes. Now, you talk about those things, but you also talk about what are you doing for the Singaporean workforce, how you will be training them, offering them opportunities and how your presence will benefit Singaporeans directly.'

The Critical Impact of Geopolitics

In past eras, government relations was a comparatively sedate corporate function, carrying out technical and mundane work in the backwaters of corporate activity. Companies could go about their business with little concern about what was going on in the public sector. How things have changed, under the influence of a volatile and interlinked geopolitical landscape. Corporate missteps, whether through action or inaction, can be punished quickly and forcefully.

Geopolitics is not new. The term 'geopolitics' is considered as having been used by Swedish political scientist Rudolf Kjellén around the turn of the twentieth century.[1] Awareness of geopolitics has always been relevant to companies, even if only to know the legal basis for being allowed to operate in another country. What is new is the magnitude of the impact of geopolitics on corporations around the world. Okun put it this way: 'Twenty years ago, trade and economics were in one bucket, and national security and diplomacy were in a second, and there wasn't a lot of overlap. Then, in managing public affairs, you did not have to consider how what you did in China would be received in Washington. While there were certainly issues between the U.S. and China geopolitically and from a national security perspective at the turn of the century, these were often separate to business matters. Today, trade and economics have merged with national security, so you have to be thinking about both U.S. and China when you're conducting business in China.'

When asked for an example, Okun said, 'When I was at UPS, the first UPS aircraft to land in China happened in 2001. It coincided with the time when a U.S. military aircraft had been grounded on Hainan Island with its crew detained, resulting in an international crisis. The event commemorating that arrival went

---

[1] https://www.newworldencyclopedia.org/entry/Rudolf_Kjell%C3%A9n.

forward. Today, whether to go forward with such an event would be considered very differently.'

In the past, it was far easier to separate business dealings from international politics. It was also a simpler exercise for an MNC to do and say something in one market and feel reasonably secure that it would not impact the company to any notable degree in another market. Today, this is not possible. Okun made the point, 'If you are an American company, it is no longer the case what you are doing in China is going to be treated completely differently from what you are doing in the States – they are now intertwined. You must be aware of both markets and try to balance them. China will also act against U.S. companies for what they say in the U.S. You saw that with the Houston Rockets General Manager a few years ago when he made comments about Hong Kong, which ended up costing the NBA a lot of business in China.'

While it is impossible to predict what will happen in future years, it seems things will get worse rather than better. Looking at the global environment in which governments are operating, Okun said, 'I use the term "poly crisis", which has been popularized by Adam Tooze, a professor at Columbia University, to describe the coming together of multiple crises. Governments can barely handle one crisis at time. But when you have not one, but four or more global crises as we have today, those crises bump into one another. Governments cannot effectively handle. You have the U.S.-China crisis, the Russian crisis, the climate crisis, a supply chain crisis and a post-pandemic crisis. The climate crisis is leading to food shortages and the Russian invasion of Ukraine is also creating food shortages. Those two then bump into one another, making the food shortage crisis worse.' Okun went on to note that the U.S. Inflation Reduction Act was introduced to help finance the climate transition, but this has also caused trade tensions internationally. He concluded, 'So, you have to be aware of this poly crisis and what that means for governments.'

Corporate Narratives and Geopolitics

What is the impact of this complex and unpredictable environment on the reputations of corporations?

In some respects, the fundamentals of reputation remain the same irrespective of geopolitics. The components of corporate reputations such as your customer service, the way you look after your employees, your environmental track record, and so on, will be the same whether your company is doing business in the U.S. or, say, China. However, the way that a company talks about its business in one market is not confined to that market. Aggressively promoting your commitment to China might be perfectly legitimate, but if done clumsily, could create problems in Washington.

It goes the other way too. Okun said, 'An interesting issue relates to those companies that take stances on social issues in the States, whether it be abortion, gun control, voting rights, etc. They might want to do that in the U.S., but then when a social issue comes up in China, the same company says, "We don't talk about politics." That opens the companies to charges of hypocrisy. Now, will that lead companies to being less active in this sense in the U.S.? We already see this on the environmental side, with "green hushing". Will "geopolitical hushing" be next?' As discussed in chapter seven, this is a weighty challenge. As companies become more public and active on these issues, it becomes harder for them, when confronted with questions about a political or policy matter, to suggest they are just a company and do not operate in the realm of political issues.

The Need to Monitor and Solicit Perspectives

Dr Lindsay Shorr Newman is Practice Head, Global Macro-Geopolitics at Eurasia Group and at the time of writing this book was Head of Geopolitical Thought Leadership at S&P Global. When asked about particular signals companies need to be looking out for as they monitor the geopolitical environment, she explained, 'What are the signs or signals to watch for to understand whether a particular risk is becoming more or less likely to hit? These indicators will be pathway dependent. What to watch for on a potential conflict escalation pathway will be different from an economic or security partnership being agreed. With conflicts – are there military exercises upcoming, reservists being mobilized, troops amassing at the border? On diplomatic developments the signs to watch could include upcoming multilateral meetings, bilateral meetings on the side line of a summit, planned state visits, domestic economic outlooks.'

Newman went on to make a point that reflects Okun's assessment economics and national security considerations have intertwined. She observed, 'That all being said, we also find ourselves in a moment where countries are adopting policies that put business at the centre. These policies are *intended* to align commercial decision-making with national priorities. Tracking domestic policy developments and budget implementation plans have a further relevance for business at this time.'

The ability to better understand and hopefully mitigate geopolitical impacts on the corporation requires active engagement with a range of external stakeholders (in this sense, the value is the same as for all types of systematic engagement that enable the company to operate sustainably). In the context of geopolitics, the most relevant external stakeholders include government bodies and regulators, industry associations, supply chain partners, non-governmental organizations, international bodies and customers.

A systematic and comprehensive approach to external stakeholder engagement will allow the company to build a more accurate picture of the wider landscape. Engaging with stakeholders allows companies to gain diverse opinions, document relevant information, and build relationships.

The Importance of Employees

Employees may not be the first stakeholder group that comes to mind when thinking about geopolitics, but they must be considered. Companies with an international footprint will have employees from a range of cultures and with a diversity of viewpoints on social and political issues. What resonates in the U.S. doesn't necessarily hold sway somewhere like China or even other Western countries.

The level of pressure on a multinational company will ebb and flow around geopolitical developments and the onus should be executive leadership to act in a way that mitigates internal conflict or backlash. On big decisions regarding major initiatives, colleagues from all relevant geographies should be included and views heard. As well as helping to cultivate a feeling of togetherness, doing so is just smart business. Newman summed it up perfectly, when she said, 'Geopolitics is about perspective building – to understand current dynamics and anticipate how they might progress we cannot just look at policy or economic figures or industry trends or regulation. We need to consider all of these factors in combination. Internal corporate functions are watching and tracking indicators of stability and change, that together contribute to building an understanding of the geopolitical landscape and how to navigate the way forward.'

Empowering the local management team to contribute local insight as decisions are made is a crucial element of multinational companies navigating geopolitics in different markets around the world. Newman said, 'Geopolitical developments are not removed from the local. This is underappreciated. The geopolitical "layer" cannot be added on at the end of analysis or considered independently of country and regional trendlines. It is impossible, for instance, to understand the Russia-Ukraine war, and its likely trajectories, without the context of the historical relationships between the two and between Russia and the North Atlantic Treaty Organisation, without a sense of Russia's economic outlook, domestic policy, regional ambitions. We can say the same for the push on industrial policies or reshoring—in many instances domestic dynamics are driving foreign policy. Geopolitical analysis and forecasting is most useful when informed by local, national, and regional insights.' The imperative for local insight means companies cannot assume any common baseline of what different geopolitical issues mean for the business. Local employees must continue to invest time in helping those at headquarters understand what is happening on the ground, and vice versa—those in the local markets must have an appreciation of the environment in the company's home market.

How to Think about Geopolitical Risk

Company boards and their leadership teams are accustomed to deliberating on risks facing the company, including geopolitical risk. There is an opportunity to strengthen this area by ensuring a highly thorough and regular analysis that may or may not be connected to specific decisions the company needs to make. Keeping a close watch on the horizon means looking out for budding geopolitical risks material to the company's operations, whether these involve people and facilities, compliance with local regulations, human-rights considerations, and so on.

Newman said, 'In this period out of equilibrium, throwing off unanticipated risk, a big question for business is how to identify, manage and mitigate exposure. With an expanded remit, it can be hard to know where to look and how to safely proceed. If Russia's invasion of Ukraine taught us anything, it is that the speed at which change unfolds can confound. To remain on firmer footing, businesses need to incorporate advance warning systems into their commercial strategy. Setting out the likelihood and impact of risks that could impact their operations (including their supply chains) and investments. Scenario planning is a critical tool to identify risk pathways and for risk mitigation planning.'

When asked about how companies can be proactive in the management of geopolitical risk, Siewert offered the following observation: 'It's very important to build geopolitical considerations into your investment process. There is a tendency for capital approvals to be made based on a relatively narrow model. And the people making those decisions are super smart, but they usually have gone to similar business schools, have similar world experience and have been taught in a similar way to do things like stress test a macroeconomic shock to the business. But today, the world has the first land war in Europe since World War II, the most significant energy crisis since the 70s, the highest inflation since the 70s and a huge looming conflict between the two largest economies in the world. Plus, the global pandemic. All those things are interacting in complicated ways, and you can't look at a potential investment in a bubble to one side. You need to think more broadly about risk. You also cannot model a capital-intensive project on the basis everything will be the same for the next 30 years. Governments change, policies change. Even in places like Canada and Western Europe, we have governments with very different views of the same project. If you don't model those things in, you're putting yourself enormously at risk.' He went on to elaborate, 'You also have to assess probabilities to different potential outcomes. A probability might be only 10%, but it would have a huge impact on the business. You cannot say that is a 5% risk, when it could be that a 5% risk has an 80% impact on the business. So, you can put a number into a model, but there is a tendency to underestimate the ways in which the politics will affect these investments even in very stable political regimes.'

The insight that Siewert provides speaks to the importance of having executives in the company with the mindset to be able to keep these considerations top of mind around the Boardroom table. On the issue of internal capabilities, Siewert said, 'A lot of firms might have diversity, but if you look closer, what if the executives are all trained at Harvard Business School, and Wharton or Oxford and Cambridge? Then you need to recognize that they tend to think alike about things. They may have all grown up in an investment bank, and then they were hired by a PE firm, or they worked at McKinsey. They haven't had to think about these broader risks, or they certainly don't understand the way in which political people make decisions. So, you need to have the right skillset inside a firm and on your investment committee.'

Okun said, 'American companies now consider the scenario of a cross-Straits Taiwan. Various signals could indicate a cross-Strait conflict becoming more possible, for which CEOs would consider taking steps to protect their workers and mitigate risks to their business, either directly or to their supply chains. Twenty years ago, the two biggest risks most U.S. businesses considered were (1) an operational disaster and (2) a terrorist attack. War across the Straits was not on the list. Today, it should be, albeit recognising that the probability of an attack without any warning is extremely small.'

Newman concluded, 'As we look forward, we can expect more rather than less volatility in the years ahead. For businesses planning over the multi-year horizon, it is essential to know your timelines. What are the risks you are most worried about and how likely are they to hit in the next quarter, six months or 3-5 years. Part of building an advance warning system is also identifying the relevant risk pathway and what indicators to look for to help understand if a timeline is accelerating or the radius of impact is expanding. Finally, business needs to be adaptive with plans, A, B, C, through Z on hand, because headwinds remain, and business finds itself at the nexus of unfamiliar risk.'

Dealing with geopolitical risk will be, to some degree, different for every company. As is the case with social advocacy, some companies will have a larger risk appetite than others when it comes to geopolitical events. Some will feel more comfortable continuing to operate or making investments in more turbulent and sensitive markets. Others will have no comfort at all with such possibilities. While there is a spectrum of risk appetite in this regard, what seems to be certain is that global relationships will remain tense and even precarious. Cyberattacks with State backing, trade wars, energy and food security, ongoing tensions between the U.S., China, and Russia (not to mention other conflicts throughout the world), and international arguments over the process of transition to a sustainable future are some of the factors contributing to a highly charged landscape. Companies that fail to take a proactive and thoughtful stance regarding these disruptive forces face elevated chances of negative hits to their business—and reputations.

Summary of Principles

- Given the transparent nature of the world, companies must have a strong and credible narrative in place to underpin their government relations effort.
- When interacting with policymakers, it is constructive to look at the issue from their perspective. Position the company as a source of support rather than a problem to be navigated.
- The five P's of Public Affairs are global. They are: Policy, Public Interest, Process, Politics, and Partnership.
- Trade and economics have merged with national security issues, making geopolitics a major source of pressure and risk on corporate activity.
- Monitoring signals helps the company to understand and prepare for risks. These might be military developments (military exercises, reservists being mobilized, etc.), diplomatic developments (upcoming multilateral meetings, bilateral meetings, planned state visits), as well as domestic economic developments.
- Empowering the local management team to contribute local insight is important. When making decisions regarding major initiatives, colleagues from all relevant geographies should be included and their views heard.
- Businesses need to incorporate advance warning systems into their commercial strategy. Scenario planning is a critical tool to identify risk pathways and for risk-mitigation planning.
- It is important to always assess the probability of geopolitical change and risk over different timelines when making decisions regarding investments the business plans to make in international markets.

17

Responding to Investor Activism

Investor activism is an emotive term. For some, just hearing it churns up notions of an outsider agitating for change and with the power to cause major disruption. For others, shareholder activists are a force for good, holding companies and their boards to account.

Investor activism is highly relevant to the themes of this book because of its ability to impact corporate reputations, particularly when the argument goes public. Hard questions being raised about various aspects of the company's strategy, operations, and/ or leadership will generate reputational issues. Other investors, customers, and business partners may lose confidence in the way the company is being managed or feel negatively about an aspect of its performance. Employee morale can be badly affected. And regulators might, as a result of the activism, take a closer look at the company, placing further pressure on its reputation. The degree to which shareholder activism affects corporate reputation will be dependent on a range of factors, including the validity of the issues being put forward and also the way in which the company responds to the situation.

Andrew Honnor is Managing Partner at Greenbrook, a London headquartered firm that provides strategic communications advisory services to the investment industry. Greenbrook has a strong track record of working with activist investors. Honnor suggested, 'Investor activism is an entirely healthy part of the system of shareholder democracy. When someone who pays their own money to take a significant shareholder position challenges the company, the leadership of that company can find it quite uncomfortable. But that is part of being a publicly owned company. The heads of these businesses are not owners, they are akin to managers of a football club. And if the manager doesn't perform, the manager gets sacked.'

Activism represents a broad spectrum of activity, ranging from completely friendly to hyper aggressive and stemming from large firms to much smaller ones. Certain firms will have a track record of pursuing specific investment strategies, which are different to others. Regardless of how you think about the subject, shareholder activism is not going away. Many public companies will experience some type of shareholder activism and depending on how it is navigated can have major implications for corporate reputation.

Activism is also global. With a noteworthy number of Japanese-listed companies trading below their perceived value, Japan has become one of the key locations in the world for shareholder activism. This has been triggered by the government's proactive support for governance reform. One notable example of shareholder activism in Japan was seen with Olympus, the manufacturer of optical and digital precision technology. In 2011, Olympus experienced a major accounting fraud scandal, which sparked a drop in its share price.[1] Since 2018, international shareholder activists pushed the company for major change. The U.S.-based ValueAct Capital Management took a stake in Olympus in 2018, and in 2019, Olympus brought a ValueAct

---

[1] 'Olympus Used Acquisitions, Deal Fee to Hide Losses', *CNBC*, November 2011, https://www.cnbc.com/2011/11/08/olympus-used-acquisitions-deal-fee-to-hide-losses.html.

partner, Robert Hale, onto its board.[2] The company has subsequently experienced strong progress and success. This is not a one-off by any means. Several activist fund managers have been appointed to the boards of large Japanese companies, including Elliott Investment Management's Nabeel Bhanji to the board of Toshiba.[3] Japan continues to be a focal point for international activists, who see plenty of upside in cash rich Japanese firms that have the perceived capacity to be more profitable and deliver better returns to shareholders.

Discussions Behind Closed Doors

There are numerous high-profile cases of corporates having to contend with activists agitating for change and of course the public fights have the greatest reputational impact. That said, a large portion of activist initiatives are kept private. Honnor explained, 'We are not interested in having a public fight, we do not do communications for the sake of communications, and the vast majority of these actions never go public. The activist may not even appear on the share register if they do not breach a certain threshold. They will make a private engagement with the Board and if the Board is sensible, it will listen carefully, and a win-win can be created.' This is a good point. Many activist campaigns can be termed 'friendly' in nature, with negotiations conducted behind closed doors. The shareholder will approach the company with a perspective about capital deployment, ESG-related issues, or

---

[2] Rintaro Shimomura, 'Olympus names activist investor to board to boost reforms', January 2019, Nikkei Asia, https://asia.nikkei.com/Business/ Companies/Olympus-names-activist-investor-to-board-to-boost-reforms.

[3] Makiko Yamazaki, 'Toshiba board gains two directors from activist funds in historic shift', Reuters, June 2022, https://www.reuters.com/article/ toshiba-shareholders-idCAKBN2O905X.

other views on how the company can lift its performance, leading to private discussions.

Dr. Jochen Legewie serves as Kekst CNC Japan Head and Chairman in Asia. He stated, 'The public campaign of an activist is always their last resort – and obviously the most threatening one to any corporate. Usually, any such campaign is preceded by extended background negotiations or proceedings. It is during these and other investor meetings where companies benefit from talking in the language that activist understand. Japanese companies typically talk about growth and revenues, but less so about profits or value creation. The concepts might be similar, but shareholders, in particular activists, are all about value creation and ultimately share price increases. Hence any equity story that overemphasizes growth is likely already bad in their eyes.'

However, with that noted, no company should be complacent. When I asked Gary Sheffer about the importance of preparation, he responded, 'During that period where there is some détente going on, you should be preparing for the talks to break down and to have a war in many cases with the activist. When they arrive at your doorstep, even quietly, you should be scenario planning.'

Fail to Prepare, Prepare to Fail

Pat Tucker is Head of M&A and Activism, Americas at FTI Consulting. When I asked Tucker about being prepared, the first thing he said was, 'The preparation for activism is really understanding the different angles of attack. What does it look like when the activist attacks you? It might be a generic 13 D filing. It might be a nasty public letter. It might be a leak to the media. Each one of those actions calls for a different type of response.'

By the time they act, the activist will have completed a thorough analysis of the company, will have identified areas of weakness and put its case together for what change is needed and why. Honnor made this point very clear when he said, 'We tend to work activist investors for months before anything goes public if it goes public at all. We look at how to escalate pressure. What is the engagement with board going to look like? What is the content of the message to the Board? What we care about is winning the campaign. That starts with how you approach the board, how you engage with the board, how you run this escalation and pressure campaign, that at some point, may or hopefully may not go into the public domain.'

The larger investment firms have been in dozens, if not hundreds, of these situations. They know what they are doing. Given the level of planning undertaken on the activist side, the company itself had better have already undertaken a similar level of effort into a response plan should an activist come calling. Gary Sheffer, reflecting on his GE experience, said, 'We didn't have anybody on our doorstep, but we knew they would be there eventually and so we put plans together for dealing with activist investors and who they might be. And if you're doing risk management, as a communicator, this should be on your list.'

Being prepared means the company has a plan in place that is agreed upon, at board level, that ensures that all relevant executives understand the protocols in place to respond to shareholder activism. This includes the identification of an external advisory team spanning financial advisors, lawyers, and a public relations firm. On this, Sheffer said, 'I highly recommend hiring a financial communications firm, as good as you think your team may be. You need somebody who's been through the fight is previously and so to me, if you're going to oppose an activist investor, it's all hands on deck.'

In practice, as with crisis preparedness, many companies neglect to get ready. Legewie alluded to this when he said, 'We differentiate in our services between two things, one is preparation. And the other one is actual support. A company may have no activist on its shareholder roster but feels that they should prepare because you never know when somebody might arrive. This is

the most proactive approach. More commonly, companies notice
that an activist has acquired a 1–3 percent stake and then gets
nervous. The company wants to improve its equity story and find
out where its vulnerabilities are out of the eyes of an activist.'

Tucker outlined four factors that, in his experience, need to
align for a company to be targeted by an activist:

1. There is value to be had at the company, given it is trading
    lower than people perceive it's worth. There can be a wide
    range of reasons behind this, and it does not necessarily
    mean the company is being badly run. For example, there
    might be a value assessment that if you break up the
    company into two companies, a tremendous amount of
    value would be unlocked.

2. There needs to be some sort of action that can be taken
    to unlock that value. Tucker pointed out that this is why
    activists did not seize on the energy sector when oil prices
    went down. That is, an activist can't solve for oil prices.

3. Which shareholders support this action to unlock that
    value? A board has to act on behalf of all shareholders.
    An activist can feel the company is undervalued and see
    an action it wants taken, but unless other shareholders
    feel the same there is unlikely to be change.

4. Is there a path to force the company to follow this plan?
    A public company board should always be responsive to
    shareholders, but an activist will typically want to know
    that proper mechanisms are in place to hold the board
    accountable to shareholders. On a simple level, a board
    that is annually elected is then fully subject to shareholder
    pressure while a board that has staggered elections may
    be able to resist shareholders over time, thus reducing
    an activist's ability to realize a short-term win.

Tucker then summed up what this means for preparing a defence. He said, 'There's value, there's an action to take, there are shareholders who support me, and I can see a path of change. If there are those four factors, you have a problem. And then what we do with companies is flip it. How does the market understand your value? Are there misperceived actions that could be taken? Do they think a breakup would be super easy and unlock value but fail to account for dis-synergies, or tax liabilities? You can walk down that line, and when you do that, you really realize where your defence messaging best lies.'

Know Your Shareholders

What is your company's reputation among its shareholders? Are there any divergences between how the company sees its strategy and progress compared to how its shareholders see it? These are questions that require steady attention over time. Irrespective of any activist programme, all public companies should ensure they have a robust investor relations programme. This requires systematic shareholder engagement to communicate the company's progress and outlook, to explain its strategy, and to seek feedback on a regular basis. This can be done via one-on-one engagements, investor conferences, earnings calls, and investor days. A professional approach builds relationships as well as enabling the company to nip emerging issues in the bud. Honnor put it to me in plain terms, 'Understand your shareholders. Know your owners. And if your owners are unhappy, do something about it. Don't wait to be whacked over the head by an activist who's only a manifestation of the discontent that a lot of other people have.'

Such a proactive stance also applies in Japan. Legewie said, Japan is very different from other countries where this type of pressure stems pre-dominantly from the private sector. Here, there has been a top-down political decision to encourage companies to come up with regimes that strengthen the rights of shareholders. And if you have stronger shareholder rights, this opens up new opportunities for an activist. Like elsewhere, a single activist in Japan usually is only taking a maximum of 5% of the company. You cannot force decision-making with a 5% stake, but an activist can be effective by convincing other including "long-only" investors to align with them. We tell our clients, it is not about the activist, it is about the other shareholders. You need a business strategy and an equity story that is convincing to the other 95% because they will be the decisive force.'

The Role of the Board

The board has a crucial role to play, as it examines the challenges facing the business and how it is being perceived by the market. Such an examination may give rise to several outcomes, including gaps in understanding between what the company has actually considered and how it has acted accordingly, and what the external view is regarding what it has done or not done. If the corporate strategy is not well defined externally, that should be rectified as a matter of priority.

The board also needs to find a way to encourage frank feedback from the management team and the investor relations team in particular. Tucker explained, 'One of the biggest challenges is the board's ability to get honest, up-to-date information about how shareholders perceive it. Even good Investor Relations Officer's will know their shareholders, but they will typically only know their shareholders. It's important to make sure you're asking questions of the people who don't hold your stock – the folks that are looking at you and deciding not to invest. You want to know what they think and that takes some humility to go out and say, why don't you like me? Management teams and boards are just not good at doing that. But that's exactly what an activist is doing. Want to get ahead of it. You've got to ask those questions.'

Well run boards have thought through the various scenarios attached to an activist approach at length before one comes knocking. One outcome from doing so is the ability for the company to effectively adopt part or all of the activist playbook early on and promote it as their own. Discussing this with Tucker, he offered the following anecdote: 'I was working with a client on their investor day. We wanted the investor day to solve for the street's misperception of recent transactions that depressed margins coupled with a long-term guidance that seemed to indicate the financial profile would remain static. We knew we were solving for something big that would mitigate activism. At the time we were developing our deck, a major activist shows up privately and hands us 65 pages about everything we're doing wrong. However, notably, the last five pages of their deck almost matched identically to the five pages we were working on for the investor presentation: we have the exact same idea. Because we had reached the same conclusion, the board understood where its position was and what it needed to do. There was no debate about "are we properly valued?" or "are their arguments right or wrong?" We knew exactly where we were. Tactically, the activist's incentive was to own the story. That's why activists leak their investment all the time, because once it's leaked, they're in the stock and every action that company makes after that is defensive and reactive to the activist. Therefore, all value creation from those actions are seen to be accrued to the activist. In this instance, the activist leaked it to the Journal on a Sunday and the story ran on Sunday night. And we said, no-one should trade without our updated guidance in the market. The investor day was not happening for another two weeks, but we finished the CEO portion of the investor presentation and put it out on Monday morning. We said it was such an important investor day we wanted shareholders to have time to digest this information in advance, but the real goal was to make sure that our updated guidance was in the market ahead of time and we got full credit for that. And the activist could not disaggregate the trading that day from them being in the stock versus our guidance. The board retained full optionality to do what it wanted to do by being prepared and ultimately the activist went away without asking for board seats or critiquing the company publicly.'

Communicating with Activists

Before deciding on how to engage with the activist, the company needs to understand exactly who they are dealing with in the discussions. Doing some homework entails asking a number of basic questions, such as:

- What is the activist's track record of success?
- Have they targeted similar companies in the same industry?
- What strategies have they employed in the past?
- What is their negotiation style?

Once it has an informed view of the activist, the board can make the decision about if and how to enter communications with them. Before the decision is made to communicate, the company should be clear about its objectives for doing so. In the end, entering discussions is often regarded as the best means of negotiating a deal, but it should be done on a considered basis at a time that makes sense for the company.

Tucker made the point, 'The management and some representatives from the board should always be inclined to engage with the activist like you would with any investor. Leave it to the activist to show they're unreasonable, erratic, irresponsible, etc. that would make the board think differently, but until they do that, treat them like a regular investor because other investors will view that interaction in the same way, asking themselves, what if I had a problem? And is that how you will treat me when I have a problem? And if the investor breaks the compromise, fine, other investors will get it like hey, they were unruly, they were irrational. But if the board immediately shuts the door, then you know, Vanguard is going to say, Oh, I could have a problem someday and you're just going to shut the door on me?'

When Things Go Public

The prospect of a dialogue or debate with an activist investor has major ramifications for the company. A public discourse can represent a major distraction for both the management team and the employee base. Typically, scrutiny of the company will go up, media coverage will intensify, and volatility can engulf the company.

When asked how companies should think about their options for a public response, Tucker said, 'There's the generic statement of, we respect our shareholders and we will engage; there is the reflection of where you might be in the moment with the activist engagement (if it's the first time they've ever reached out, you might comment on that, if you've been talking for that with them for six months, you might comment on some perspective of that). And then there is the defence messaging aspect of it. I boil that down with companies to think about three questions: What value have you created? What value will you create? And how do I know that you have the right board to ensure you can achieve that value creation? If you can frame your messaging in those buckets, then you'll be golden.'

Sheffer said, 'Activists have access to journalists and are very sophisticated about telling their side of the story. You are starting at a deficit, vis-a-vis, the story of the activist.' He went on to say, 'Activist investors are very good at telling simple and persuasive stories. Cut corporate costs. The current leadership team is underperforming. The board of directors is asleep at the wheel. They're simple. They're clear. And they're focused. So, there's an activist investor playbook.'

Activist investors, and their PR advisors, have a notable tactical advantage. There are activist beat reporters at all the major financial publications. These journalists to a large degree rely on the activist team for their sourcing. On the corporate side, the action is likely to happen just once, so the journalist will not repeatedly need to go back to that company for sourcing. The activist has a leg up when it comes to setting the narrative.

Tucker reinforced this point of view. He said, 'When you're attacking an incumbent, calling for change, everybody in the world loves that type of story. The activist will have the tactical advantage of timing and a deep relationship with a reporter. They can use that very effectively to create news value in the headlines they want. On the other hand, it's always "the company responds to" or "the company work towards" and it is very hard to be proactively interesting on that front. When the activist blames the management team or Board, that is not a boring headline.'

When things spill into the public domain, it's invaluable to have independent allies the company can lean upon, including financial journalists and sell-side analysts. These relationships should be in place well prior to any issue arising. If the company is convinced it has a meritorious case to argue, then it should be making that case to key opinion leaders that can support the company's position.

Engaging with Employees

At many listed companies, employees are also shareholders. Being an owner of the company, as well as an employee, provides staff with additional leverage if they are unhappy with the state of play at the firm. Honnor said, 'Employees might be as annoyed with management as we are. They may well agree this is a great company, but it has lost its way.'

Employees can become shareholder activists in their own right. Employee share schemes means power via equity ownership. Although it would be unusual for institutional investors to side with employees, any type of employee-led shareholder action makes for good media fodder, causing embarrassment for the executive team. It is therefore necessary that board and senior management are supplied with accurate and timely insights into employee sentiment on any number of topics and to be ready to act accordingly to address any material levels of dissatisfaction.

At the least, a public interaction with an activist has the capacity to be incredibly disruptive internally. Tucker said, 'You want to assure employees that the board's acting in the company's best interest, that the board has this situation well in control. It is useful to normalize it. This is life as a public company. We interact with our shareholders. Some shareholders have perspectives and some of them have more passionate views than others. This is just how the world works.'

The Role of Retail Investors

Conventional wisdom is that retail shareholders don't vote. Some estimates place retail shareholding voting at around 30% of total shares owned, compared to institutional investors voting at 92% of the shares they hold.[4] There are a range of factors behind this trend, including a general lack of appreciation by retail investors of the impact of their vote and a low understanding of shareholder resolutions.

While traditionally retail investors may be reluctant to vote, they do represent a potentially significant voting bloc at many public companies. In the U.S., retail shareholders owned 31% of the 'street-name' shares of the 'average company in 2022, up from 29% in 2021.'[5] In Asia, Hong Kong traditionally boasts a large percentage of retail investors.[6] Tucker suggested that 'Retail

---

[4] 2020 Proxy Season Review | Broadridge.

[5] https://www.broadridge.com/_assets/pdf/broadridge-engage-and-mobilize-your-retail-shareholder-base.pdf.

[6] Staff Reporter, 'Hong Kong tops list for number of adult share retail investors', *Hong Kong Business*, https://hongkongbusiness.hk/markets-investing/news/hong-kong-tops-list-number-adult-share-retail-investors.

investors are probably the most overlooked and confounding group of investors for any company. Retail investors tend not to vote. When it comes to a proxy fight and an activist engagement, you're thinking about votes. And if the investor doesn't vote, they're not relevant to the equation. But there's research that shows that younger retail investors are more interested in voting as part of their investment.'

If a company has a large retail shareholder base, then it is worth the investment of time to develop content that is specific to this investor segment. Tucker said, 'If you're a large company with a meaningful retail base, every dollar you spend on teaching your retail shareholders the process of voting and getting them comfortable with voting on a clear-day basis, will pay dividends in a potential proxy fight. Because we know that retail shareholders disproportionately support management. A retail shareholder whom you teach to vote, is a vote for management, and therefore is a better block of defence against an activist. What we find is large companies with big retail shareholder bases usually have completely ignored them until their proxy fight, and then they are panicked. It's only then they spend huge amounts of money mailing and digital targeting and trying to get the vote. One of my big mantras right now is telling companies to spend the money now on teaching retail shareholders to vote, because its invaluable in a crisis.'

In closing, it is safe to say that activist investors will continue to target companies around the world, agitating for change. Whatever the view on the merits of such activity, the fact is that companies will need to keep their guard up. It's not sufficient to have a defence protocol on file. Company board and their senior executive teams must be actively committed to understanding where they might be vulnerable to an action, to engaging with their investors on an ongoing basis, and to regularly reviewing their plans so they are ready and able when the proverbial knock on the door is made.

Summary of Principles

- Many public companies will experience some type of shareholder activism and how it is navigated can have major implications for corporate reputations.

- Being prepared means the company has a plan in place that is agreed upon, at board level, that ensures the leadership team understands the protocols in place to respond to shareholder activism.

- Public companies should ensure they have a robust investor relations programme that builds relationships as well as enabling the company to quickly address any emerging activism issues.

- Well run boards have thought through the various scenarios attached to an activist approach at length before one comes knocking.

- Entering discussions with the activist is the best means of negotiating a deal, and the management and the board should always be inclined to engage with the activist like they would with any investor.

- A public discourse can be a major distraction for both the management team and the wider employee base, and investor activists typically are very sophisticated about how they run public campaigns.

- The appropriate approach to employee communications needs consideration when there is a public dialogue taking place with an activist.

- If a company does have a large retail shareholder base, then it is worth the investment of time to develop content that is specific to this investor segment.

18

Navigating the Reputation Risk of Mergers and Acquisitions

In November 2006, I was in Guangzhou, in southern China. It was a big occasion. For more than a year, Citigroup had been in the race to acquire a controlling stake in Guangdong Development Bank (GDB). In order to be allowed to take control as a foreign bank, Citigroup had assembled a consortium of investors, which included Chinese enterprises such as China Life, State Grid, and CITIC Trust. Once approved, it would be the first time an international financial services company had been permitted to assume a significant management role in a Chinese financial institution. The process had been a taxing one, with numerous roadblocks and negotiations taking place amid global media attention and a domestic debate over foreign ownership of Chinese State assets. Even former President George H. Bush had gotten involved, reportedly sending a letter to China's Ministry of Foreign Affairs. The pressure on the deal team, led by the late and great Richard Stanley, was immense.

We had finally received the news that we had won the bidding process. The plan was to keep the signing ceremony private, with a press release to go out afterwards. True to the unpredictable nature of the deal, on the day of announcement, we discovered that the local government had informed some Guangzhou media outlets about the signing ceremony. Of course, that meant the word was out, not only among the local press but with the international media who have strong connections with China's domestic media outlets. Bloomberg's Hong Kong bureau had even called Citigroup's Hong Kong office to ask if they could get a lift to Guangzhou! We ended up with a large media contingent on-site, and had to deal with some further twists and turns before the deal was signed that day.

The year it took for the deal to come together, and the process after signing it, was an unforgettable experience, with both highs and some lows. It gave me a vivid insight into the impact of mergers and acquisitions (M&A) on corporate reputations.

The Reputation Risk of M&A

Yes, there is power to earn reputations from successful M&A. But there are many risks if the M&A process does not go well. There is in fact a level of bravery that goes into M&A. A large, complex deal means that the company will likely to be buffeted by many different challenges. The M&A process shines a spotlight on the company—one that might question its standing on ESG issues, the strength of its investor case, its track record as an employer, its compliance standards, and so on. All of these things will get scrutinized like never before.

Consistent with the principle that any organization has multiple reputations with different stakeholders, M&A planning needs to take a holistic yet tailored approach to reassuring and nurturing confidence among the company's stakeholders. Employees often represent two stakeholder groups in this context, the employees of the acquiring company and those of the company being acquired. External stakeholder including investors, customers, regulators, and supply chain partners, will have their own distinct views of what the deal means for them.

How the company interacts with all of these stakeholders, at different phases of the deal, will go a long way to deciding the success of the deal. The right messages are required at the right time, to mitigate any anxiety that change might produce, to build enthusiasm for the merger, and to address any misconceptions that might exist. Simon Pangrazio is Managing Partner at WATATAWA, an Asia-based stakeholder engagement consulting firm, and is someone who has worked extensively on M&A deals. Asked about the impact of M&A on reputation, Pangrazio said, 'I think it's down to how clear the rationale is for the M&A that's on the table and who benefits from it. There are many different circumstances under which an M&A can take place. It could be a distressed asset, or a merger of equals or it could be more of an innovation-driven M&A where you have a company trying to push into a new space. Those dynamics have a big impact on how the deal is seen.'

To the point about different circumstances, it is true that reputational implications will vary depending on the deal itself *and* whether the reputation being considered is that of the bidding company or the target company. For the purposes of this analysis, much of this chapter is predicated on the scenario of an acquisition that both parties want to go ahead with, and looks at the process primarily from the perspective of the bidding company.

Pre-Deal Announcement

The pre-announcement phase of a deal is the time to think—at length—about not only the narrative that will accompany the announcement, but also about elements of the deal that might get questioned by stakeholders. Scenario planning is required to ensure the team is ready should problems arise. The overriding goal should be to achieve understanding and support for the company's value proposition which is driving the transaction in the first place. Pangrazio said, 'Usually, the first and the most important question that we ask, is what is the business case for being better together? If you put one plus one together, how do you make sure people understand that actually equals three, not two and make the whole greater than the sum of the parts. And that is a theme that has to run right through the entire process. Both for positive positioning reasons, and also for anticipating and inoculating against naysayers. It sounds simple, but to me, communications wise, everything hinges around how well you can express and prove that point.'

Despite the importance of devoting time to thinking about the reputational implications of the deal, this often is neglected. Those involved in the transaction naturally gravitate towards subjects such as the internal rate of return, the legal structures, the viability of a transaction, the regulatory-related issues when sizing up a transaction. Companies put an enormous amount of effort on the theoretical value of a combination of synergies of entering into a deal. They think about the reputational impact of the transaction itself, much later—often too late.

The days of companies thinking about M&A as primarily corporate finance-led have been superseded by the imperative to think about the company's reputational and regulatory exposures. The external landscape is complex and in the case of international deals, one that has a lot of geopolitical sensitivities. In that environment, the story that you're going to tell needs to be rigorously stress tested in relation to every stakeholder and every potential scenario that the company might face. A case can then be developed at the outset that helps the company to navigate through the process, rather than just trying to respond real time.

The preparations in the pre-announcement phase need to go well beyond planning for a successful announcement. A credible narrative also must be designed for use in the event that the acquisition does not actually come to fruition. Deal making can easily fall apart due to many factors, often outside of the company's control.

The work to develop key messages that produce a desired set of behaviours requires more than a brainstorming session around the boardroom table. To do this in a professional, robust, and substantial way, an investment in research is needed. Some deal elements will not be able to be tested because of confidentiality issues, but there is still a lot that can be tested. Questions such as:

- How are people going to react to a particular set of outcomes?
- How do they feel about your different stakeholders?
- How do they feel about your business?
- To what degree do they respect you and trust you?
- How might your company be strengthened or weakened by various developments?
- What messages will land and why?

Ultimately, the pre-announcement phase must include preparations not only for an announcement, but for the lead up to that announcement and then what happens after the announcement is made. Businesses need to consider whether they have a completely clear, well-thought-through narrative case, and not just an investment case, but a holistic case for why they are doing the deal and how it fits into the broader corporate strategy. As in the case of a crisis scenario, during deals, the company cannot afford to be slow reacting to queries and emerging issues. It needs to be nimble on the spot of course, but it also needs to have developed its core case beforehand to avoid drifting and stumbling when interactions with stakeholders enter dangerous territory.

Dealing with Leaks

M&A by its nature is confidential, and yet, the process is also a magnet for speculation and gossip. There is a contingent of financial journalists' hotly intent on tapping into deal rumours to break news that positions their particular publication ahead of the rest. Secrets in the world of dealmaking have a habit of being discovered on a frequent basis.

Leaks in M&A have the power to adversely impact the deal as the company's stakeholders react to being surprised by the news. If not handled with care, leaks can be a distraction and even destroy the best-laid plans. Despite attempts to avoid leaks, often details including both parties in the transaction as well as pricing details will become public ahead of any planned announcement date. According to a 2022 report by H/Advisors Abernathy, 75% of leaks correctly named both merger parties and 60% of leaks reported the transaction value within a 10% margin.[1] The report also found that when deals leak, they are doing so earlier than ever before. In 2022, leaked deals (in the U.S.) appeared in media coverage an average of twenty-eight days prior to an eventual announcement.

Leaks can spark prominent media coverage and a spike in social media attention on the companies in question. Sam Turvey is Managing Partner at H/Advisors Maitland. He said, 'Those first 24 hours after a leak are usually critical because that's when you can confirm the issues and underlying topics that are going to dominate the conversation around that transaction. It could be price or structure of the deal, national security, job security, plans for the company, management, etc. You don't have huge amounts of time to engage the most influential reporters, usually columnists, to help shape their thinking. If you've prepared well, you should be in a pretty good place for those first 24 hours, rather than scrambling around trying to work out who needs to do what, when and where.'

---

[1] H/Advisors Abernathy, 'When A Deal Springs a Leak' Vol. 3.

This is far from a U.S. phenomenon. H/Advisors Abernathy's Global Report on M&A leaks showed that in 2022, 55% of deals in the Asia-Pacific region leaked last year ahead of any announcements, ahead of Western Europe where 48% of deals leaked. In fact, both Asia-Pacific and Europe had a greater number of deal leaks than in the U.S.[2] On why the Asia-Pacific region leads the world for such leaks, the report stated, 'Any attempt to pin reasons on this phenomenon would be speculative, but factors could include the fact that the investment professional communities are smaller and work in close proximity within the financial centers there, hounded by an especially lively financial press.'[3]

Turvey suggested, 'There are about four different types of leak. The personal leak is where an individual is aware of a potential deal and provides a nugget of information that might be useful to a reporter, with the expectation of a future favour. The publicity leak tends to happen towards the start of a process and the advisers either want to raise awareness or set some boundaries around a process and start to shape interest in it. The strategic leak might happen to try and address factually incorrect information out in the market, for example around the price range. And then there is of course just human error – where inside information is shared by mistake.'

The likelihood of leaks requires the development of a leak strategy as well as draft materials, including media statements, question and answer documents, regulatory-related statements, an update to the board, and so on. Of course, it is not possible to predict the precise nature of a leak, but doing this foundational

---

[2] https://h-advisors.global/news/h-advisors-report-reveals-a-third-of-all-na-global-deals-leak/.

[3] Page 3, https://h-advisors.global/wp-content/uploads/2023/07/global-eaks_booklet_20230712_spread.pdf.

work enables the company to act more quickly and effectively when one does happen.

Finally, while leaks are difficult to prevent, nonetheless, the CEO and executive leadership team must be firm and vocal with those involved in the deal from the very first moment about the critical importance of confidentiality.

Media Relations and Social Media

The topic of leaks begs the question, what can and cannot be said publicly during the M&A process. The company and its advisors need to be well aligned. Traditionally, the approach is to decline to comment on all media enquiries. For an ad hoc media call, that is a reasonable default position, however not commenting on all queries is not the optimum approach. Pushing every query away with a 'no comment' can be taken to mean the company either doesn't know what to say, that it is not truly invested in the issue, or even that it is feeling weak in relation to a potential outcome.

Pangrazio said, 'The parties usually need to set their stall out in an offer document and in Board recommendations to shareholders. That may include an independent advisor's view. However, that doesn't preclude other third parties from commenting on the deal. So, as you're preparing your offer document, we usually suggest that you need to decide who the influencers are that you want to come out with a good assessment of the rationale for the deal. They're not as restricted in what they can say, and you want reinforcement and validation from analysts, market commentators, journalists, etc.'

Providing key reporters who are covering the deal with guidance on a background basis remains a useful means of encouraging accurate reporting. This is not about trying to put a spin on things. Rather, it is about helping the journalist hear through all the noise to get to the core of what the issue in question is really about.

Similar to traditional media relations, how social media is used during the deal process is to a large degree dependent on timing. Confidentiality and compliance issues mean that before the deal closes, the use of social media should be approached with discipline. When used well at the right time, then social media provides a means of reaching the right people. Turvey said, 'It's not enough to look out for official filings to an Exchange or company statements for important deal information, you also need to be aware of key deal participants using platforms like LinkedIn. This is not common but some people with a large follow count can see merit in using social media. Matt Moulding is an example of a CEO who has used LinkedIn to offer his perspectives on transactions involving his company, THG Group. Social media posts should still be vetted by the legal and advisory team and can provide a means of amplifying a particular view on the deal.'

With that said, it might be that the aim is to use social media not to reach 100,000 people, but in fact to be seen and understood by just, say, ten people—and taking a considered approach to social media can enable this to happen. Digital strategy is helpful both in terms of tracking and understanding sentiment, tailoring messages to different audience groups and understanding the ramifications of the deal. The corporate website also remains relevant. According to H/Advisors Abernathy's report, for M&A transactions announced in 2022, corporate-owned websites were the top-ranked referring domain in 88% of the largest deals.[4] The company must do its housekeeping and make sure its own content is up-to-date, accurate, and contains the messages relevant to the M&A in question.

Of course, the rise of digital has meant changes in the way deals are covered, given the rise of digital newsletters and other platforms that are focused on breaking news. Turvey said, 'The media has really changed in the last 20 years with the rise of online

---

[4] Page 4, https://h-advisors.global/wp-content/uploads/2022/12/Deals-Leaks-Report-HAdvisors-Abernathy-Dec-2022.pdf.

versions of newspapers, blogs and blogger platforms, and of course social media. For example, Betaville in the UK is a deals-focused blog run by someone who used to be a successful M&A journalist at a traditional media outlet. The blog, which started in 2014, has broken some big scoops. At first, when there were spikes in a share price, people didn't necessarily know where it was coming from, which was this site behind a paywall. Outlets like Bloomberg now monitor Betaville. My point is that leaks can pop up in places that either didn't exist in the past or are harder to spot and monitor. It is part of the reason leaks are more common than they used to be.'

Regulatory Pressure

M&A transactions involve material risks across a range of areas, including regulatory risk. Companies that launch an acquisition process may also be forced to undertake lengthy and complicated regulatory engagements. Anti-trust authorities can knock down or require new solutions to be found if they see the transaction as concentrating market power in a manner that could stifle competition. Further, if the deal involves multiple international markets, then the process is further complicated given that individual jurisdictions will have their own regulatory authorities that will require being part of the review process. And increasingly, many countries are taking a more protective approach to foreign investment, particularly in those sectors considered to be sensitive to national interests. For example, China's first Foreign Investment Law (FIL) came into effect on 1 January 2020,[5] which subjects foreign investors to national security reviews and blocks investment in certain industries.

---

[5] https://www.gdeto.gov.hk/en/doing_business/doing_business. html#:~:text=for%20foreign%20investments.-,The%20Foreign%20 Investment%20Law%20of%20the%20People's%20Republic%20of%20 China,treatment%20plus%20negative%20list%20management.

The mitigation of regulatory risk requires a very proactive and constructive engagement with government and regulatory stakeholders. Underlying this engagement is a thorough understanding on the part of the company regarding all relevant regulations and monitoring for any regulatory updates that could impact the transaction. A cross-functional approach, involving legal, compliance, risk, finance, and communications is required.

At the heart of the deal, the question must be answered as to whether this a navigable transaction? Answering in the affirmative means being able to find a narrative case for that transaction that will sustain the company not just through to winning day one. Transactions can now take years of negotiations in a multi-jurisdictional context. A company operating in multiple markets globally needs to traverse through complex regulatory processes. These regulatory processes of course must be approached carefully from a legal point of view. But actually, it's the environment around those decisions—political, social, and structural—which impact the deal at least as much as the laws themselves.

Pangrazio said, 'There are M&A deals [that] get 90% of the way through the process only to fail to get regulatory approval. That can actually backfire on the parties and leave them looking like they didn't understand or manage the process properly. Along the way, it's about what companies can do to proactively remove or address potential regulatory hurdles on their respective sides of the deal to give the highest chance of success.'

Announcement Day

The announcement of a merger is a critical opportunity to share the company's vision behind the deal, and what it means for different stakeholders. It usually arrives after a period of intense negotiations and preparations, and it is a high-stakes moment, as the company only gets one chance to get the news out there in the best way possible.

A highly coordinated approach is required, which may span both companies in question as well as multiple geographic markets. The approach to an announcement can typically include the following elements:

- A video or conference call with the company's most senior leaders (just prior to the announcement), including those on the ground in relevant geographic markets, to let them know the details of the deal on a confidential basis.
- The lodging (in the case of a public company) of the relevant documentation with the Stock Exchange (outside of trading hours).
- The distribution of a message to all employees explaining/ celebrating the deal and providing some insight into the path ahead. This can help set the tone for the deal from Day One, encouraging employees in a manner that is authentic and open about what it means for them.
- The distribution of a press release to all key journalists following the company. This would be accompanied by whatever media strategy has been developed, which could include a range of one-on-one interviews for the CEO.
- A series of analyst briefings (or a group session) to explain and reinforce the merits of the deal. The CEO and senior leadership team must be able to very coherently layout the rationale behind the deal and why it will drive future value for shareholders.
- Town Hall meetings for employees of the companies involved in the deal to reduce any anxiety and to allow colleagues on both sides of the deal to feel engaged with the process ahead.
- Talking points for senior leadership to enable them to convey the details of the deal to their respective stakeholders.

Announcement Day cannot be fumbled. If stakeholders are left unconvinced by the unveiling of the deal, the share price can drop employees can be underwhelmed and uncertain, and partners can be wondering what to expect next. Any and all of which put the deal behind the eight ball from the very start, placing a strain on the reputations of the acquiring company.

Post Announcement, Pre-Close

Once the deal has been announced, there can be a relatively long period until it actually closes. This is a period of time that's fraught with danger, and yet, the ability to say much during this time is usually limited. This can prove awkward in the face of stakeholder demand for information.

Things can be further exacerbated by the actions of competitors, who might see the transaction as an opportunity to cause some kind of disruption. Talented employees may get restless and start to leave on both sides if they become overly uncertain about what the future holds in store. Employees will have worries about job security and this is not just at the middle and lower level of the company. This can easily lead to management distraction because people are thinking, 'Do I have a long-term future here? What's that going to look like?'

If the company doesn't engage with customers, employees, and other stakeholders, then a vacuum will be created for others to fill. Even a general reassurance that the company is committed to keeping people informed and a reiteration that they are valued by the company will help to maintain and build trust. The leadership team will also use this time to further shape the integration path. Feedback can be gathered about how employees want the integration experience to feel, and about how employees think customers and partners would want to feel (and how they would feel if the process wasn't handled well).

Finally, Turvey suggested a sense of balance is needed, when he said, 'When it comes to M&A, it's okay not to have proactive communications all the time. It is okay to tell people you will update them when the timing is right. Again, it really depends on the situation, the industry and the level of influence or reputation management needed around a transaction.'

After the Deal Closes – Integration Communications

The integration phase has real implications for the success of the deal and the reputations of the company. Often it is not done very well. After the bright lights fade away, the truly hard work begins. Brian Lott at Mubadala, talking about integration, said, 'Good M&A is additive, bad M&A is destructive both reputationally and in real business value. I think it is tremendously underestimated the amount of human emotion that goes into change, and it is a classic challenge to the corporate world to really understand that once the papers are signed the hard part begins.'

Pangrazio said, 'The initial rationale for the M&A will be scrutinised as of course will the price versus market value. But the success of the M&A won't really be judged until you get to the integration and execution stage. And that's where many M&As come undone. I think a lot of people wait on assessing reputational impact until they see whether both companies are good to their word in what they actually achieve and whether they can execute actual integration.'

At the point of commencing integration, its vital to achieve clarity and agreement among those involved in the process. Here there is a need to explain to stakeholders in as much detail as possible, the integration road ahead, including timelines for key milestones and the corresponding impact on relevant stakeholders. By doing so, the company is setting itself up for the best chance of success. The most effective leaders fully commit to the integration process in a number of practical ways, including:

1. Providing a clear and compelling vision for the organization's future; and linking the importance of employees to achieving that future.

2. Being visible—investing time and effort to interact with employees, not only talking to them but also listening and responding to questions.

3. Addressing difficult issues, and having tough conversations, in a timely and genuine manner.

4. Being hypersensitive to ensuring actions match words—there can be no discrepancies in this sense if credibility and trust is to be maintained.

5. Celebrating the wins along the way and rewarding those who exemplify the behaviours the organization is striving to adopt.

It is especially important to set clear expectations for those managers and leaders on the 'frontline' of the integration—and to support them in meeting those expectations.

Finally, the merger will, to some degree, involve a need to rebrand at least one side of the party, if not both. While that is the subject of a separate analysis, the approach and execution to this effort will be dependent on a range of factors, including the nature of the transaction and the industry itself.

When thinking about turning aspirations into reality around an M&A deal, there is nothing of higher importance that a systematic and comprehensive approach to integrating the companies involved. How this is done, and what is achieved, can have a potent impact on the reputations of the company. Done well, with the strong support and involvement of senior management, the integration should be positioned to deliver an energised employee base, engaged customers, supportive business partners, and happy investors.

Summary of Principles

- The M&A process places a sharp focus on the companies involved, and this scrutiny has significant reputational implications.

- The pre-announcement phase of a deal is the time to think— at length—about not only the narrative that will accompany the announcement, but also about any elements of the deal that might get questioned by stakeholders.

- Preparations in the pre-announcement phase need to go well beyond planning for a successful announcement. A credible narrative also must be designed for use in the event that the acquisition does not come to fruition.

- Leaks can spark prominent media coverage and a spike in social media attention on the companies in question and must be prepared for accordingly.

- Care must be taken about providing on-the-record comments while the deal process is underway, but the value of providing comment within what is permissible from a regulatory viewpoint should also be considered. Providing key reporters who are covering the deal with guidance on a background basis remains an effective means of encouraging accurate reporting.

- The mitigation of regulatory risk requires a very proactive and constructive engagement with government and regulatory stakeholders. Underlying this engagement is a thorough understanding on the part of the company regarding all relevant regulations and monitoring for any regulatory updates that could impact the transaction.

- A highly coordinated approach to announce the deal is required, which spans both companies in question as well as multiple geographic markets.

- Post announcement and pre-close, if the company doesn't engage with customers, employees, and other stakeholders, then a vacuum will be created for others to fill.

- A systematic and comprehensive approach to integrating the companies involved is paramount when thinking about turning aspirations into reality around an M&A deal.

Part Four

Tracking Progress

19

Measuring Impact

The announcement has been made. It was months in the planning. Things went well. A full house of journalists attended and asked a lot of questions. The CEO seems happy. A report is produced in the days after the announcement, containing a summary of media coverage achieved. The centrepiece of the report is a dollar figure, known as the 'AVE', or Ad Value Equivalency. The AVE refers to the dollar value of an advertisement that's the equivalent size and circulation to the earned media coverage. Widely used for many years, the AVE has been discredited by prominent industry associations, such as AMEC, as 'flawed'[1] as it attempts to compare two very different things: the cost of taking an advertisement and the value of the activity undertaken. The value associated with earning reputations is ingrained with far more benefits than the expense of paying for advertising. The same goes for many metrics associated with social media programmes. Does a big number attached to 'impressions', or the number of people who were assumed to be exposed to your content, matter at all? No—it just speaks to how many people might have seen it and that in itself does not provide insight into the effectiveness of the effort to help the company achieve its objectives.

---

[1] https://amecorg.com/2017/06/the-definitive-guide-why-aves-are-nvalid/.

Chapter one alluded to the fact that conversations around reputation, communications, and stakeholder engagement traditionally have not been supported with data, unlike other areas of corporate operation. An examination of the business value of reputations, or the activities stemming from reputation building, cannot be complete without an attempt to answer the critical question of how to measure the effort.

Much of this chapter is guided by the expertise of Dr. Jim Macnamara, a Distinguished Professor of Public Communication at the University of Technology Sydney. Macnamara also worked closely with the World Health Organization (WHO) during the Covid-19 pandemic to help WHO use measurement, evaluation, and learning to increase health outcomes for people across the world. Extensive reference is also made to a report produced by the Institute for Public Relations (IPR), 'The Communicator's Guide to Research, Analysis, and Evaluation'.[2]

Measuring Reputations

The majority of this chapter is devoted to how a rigorous approach can be taken to measuring programmes and activities designed to help the company earn more positive reputations. There is a nuance here between measuring such efforts in comparison with measuring reputation itself. Some would argue that the latter is almost impossible, given that reputation is in the mind of the beholder! It is a perception and as such is inherently qualitative in nature.

Alan Sexton said, 'I think it's extremely difficult to quantify reputation and requires custom models to be built for

---

[2] Mark Weiner, 'The Communicator's Guide to Research, Analysis, and Evaluation', Institute for Public Relations, March 2021, https://instituteforpr.org/communicators-guide-research-2021/.

different organisations. There are so many variables that go into it. My team is very focused on cultivating belief in the future of the firm, and we're looking at whether stakeholders believe our company's best days are ahead or behind it. Maybe that one measure is an oversimplification, but it could be valuable to have a simple focal point around which to coalesce everybody: whether people truly believe you have a bright future and quantifying and tracking that over time.'

Andrew Walton said, 'We have an insatiable desire for insights and data, which we put at the heart of our reputation planning. My predecessor built a fantastic dashboard that we call the reputation tracker, which has a variety of quantitative and qualitative metrics that feed into it. We measure by polling and by sentiment tracking—where people are on the awareness-to-advocacy spectrum. We measure quarterly, and we also get monthly tracker data because media sentiment is instantaneously measured. This system is built for the corporate brand and our marketing teams have a separate set of tracking for our consumer brands.'

Walton's reference to the marketing team having separate tracking reflects the distinction between reputation measurement and brand measurement, the latter speaking to the value of the company's brand or brands. In its annual study, Kantar BrandZ examines the world's most valuable brands. In 2023, it listed Apple at number one with a brand value of US$880bn, followed by Google (No.2; $578bn) and Microsoft (No.3; $502bn).[3] Although brand value, as an intangible asset, is not included on corporate balance sheets, it will be a significant factor in the case of, for example, a company being acquired.

---

[3] https://www.kantar.com/campaigns/brandz/global.

Macnamara provided his own view on the definition of corporate reputations as:

A. **What the people who matter** (it is the perceptions of people who are really important to an organization that matter—not the views of a general survey sample)
B. **Think** (reputation is perception—not always reality)
C. **About what they think matters** (many reputation surveys measure against criteria the organization considers to be important, or the survey company considers to be important. This is wrong. We should (i) ask key stakeholders (the people who matter what they think matters in relation to the organization), and then (ii) ask them their perceptions of the organization on those criteria).

Measuring corporate reputation will always entail a high degree of difficulty, given those reputations are ultimately the sum of what individual stakeholders think of the organization. Nonetheless, tools are available to achieve a nuanced and insightful understanding of the effectiveness of different programmes. Companies are responsible for understanding and using them in a manner that helps optimize the effort of earning and protecting reputation. The remainder of this chapter will look at how this can happen in practice.

The 'MEL' Model

Measure, Evaluate and Learn, or 'MEL', is a model used in the context of programme evaluation and the measurement of performance. The three elements can be summarized as follows:

• Measurement involves monitoring and taking measures of various factors and conditions.

- Evaluation involves analysis to compare the measures obtained with baselines, objectives, and KPIs—and to reflect on whether they indicate a value, such as an increase or improvement.
- Learning is gained from analysis-based insights that help refine strategies and create a path of continuous improvement.

Using the MEL model, companies can analyse what happened, and then more systematically plan for the path ahead, in a way that supports continuous improvement.

Landscape Analysis

At the outset of a new year, or prior to the launch of a new initiative, there is a need to avoid making unfounded assumptions and to take a fresh look at the wider environment in which the company operates. This can be done through a landscape analysis. The IPR report[4] states, 'A landscape analysis begins with a dispassionate look at past performance, performance vs. competitors, conventional wisdom, and what has come before. At the same time, environmental factors and emerging issues that affect the enterprise should also be examined including regulatory action, societal trends, and popular opinion.' The report identifies a number of questions that can be asked in order to advance the analysis:

1. What is the current environment? What factors are affecting and will affect the organization externally and internally? What changes are happening to the industry?

---

[4] Mark Weiner, 'The Communicator's Guide to Research, Analysis, and Evaluation', Institute for Public Relations, March 2021, https://instituteforpr.org/communicators-guide-research-2021/.

2. What does the organization seek to achieve, and how does our environment reflect our position?
3. Who are our friends, competitors, and opposition, and how do they operate?
4. What place does the company hold within the current environment? Why is this? Is it likely to continue?
5. What does the organization need to know to improve its position?

The insight this approach generates about the organization and its external environment helps to ensure that—at the outset—the objectives, strategies, and tactics of the organization are well informed and backed by research.

Setting Objectives

A basic and yet sometimes overlooked stage prior to launching any initiative or programme that needs to be measured is the process of setting objectives. If credible goals have not been established at the outset, then leaders can't effectively evaluate the success of a campaign, initiative or the corporate function itself.

According to IPR's report, 'Objectives should follow the SMART (specific, measurable, attainable, relevant, and time-bound) format, which allows for the creation of strategies and tactics that clearly align with each objective and the ability to later demonstrate a return on expectations.'[5] This starts with setting a baseline, such as where the current level of knowledge or behaviour of the intended stakeholder audience, and then setting specific measurable objectives of what the change should be based on increasing awareness, changing attitudes, and/or changing behaviour.

---

[5] Page 14, https://instituteforpr.org/wp-content/uploads/IPR-Guide-to-Measurement-v13-1.pdf.

Inputs and Activities

Once objectives have been set, then a list of relevant inputs and activities can be produced. Inputs and activities are not the same. Inputs are the elements required to actually do the work, both in terms of information and also resources. They can include:[6]

- Existing research data that is relevant to the programme at hand
- Background and context information
- Budget—the setting of a budget and identification of the most cost-effective approaches (e.g., through Cost-effectiveness analysis)
- Resources—what skills do you need? Are there partners that could add value to the effort?

Activities are the actions that will be undertaken as part of the function's remit or the specific initiative in question. They could be things such as the drafting of key messages or the training of company spokespersons, and so on.

Outputs, Outcomes, and Impact

There is a distinction between an output, outcomes, and impact when thinking about how to measure programmes designed to earn reputation. In summary:

- Outputs represent the most basic 'ingredient' when thinking about measurement, identifying what materials or products are produced and distributed. This could include things like media releases, blogs, social media posts created, events, etc. However, if no one sees the output, then it has no impact.

---

[6] AMEC Framework.

- Outcomes are quantifiable change in awareness, knowledge, behaviours, and so on—among the target audience—that result from the particular initiative or programme.
- Impact represents the business outcome and may take some time to achieve. Communications will be one factor contributing to impact, but it may not be the only factor.

Knowing how to use these terms correctly is an important prerequisite to having an effective measurement programme.

Program Logic Models

A logic model is a graphic depiction (road map) that presents the shared relationships among the resources, activities, outputs, outcomes, and impact for your program.[7] Macnamara said, 'Program logic models are planning tools used to explicate and illustrate the proposed pathway to change (called the theory of change).'

Macnamara uses the program logic model to reinforce the imperative of connecting value to reputation-earning activities. If the Corporate Affairs team only concentrates on inputs, activities and outputs, then it can only be viewed within the company as a cost centre. However, if outcomes and impact can be captured, including changes in behaviour or desired business results, then the function becomes a *value* centre.

The additional rigour that these models bring, Macnamara pointed out, is that, 'To be logical, inferences and conclusions need to be rational and reliable – not assumptions or mythical mantras.'

The Challenge of False Logic

False logic speaks to the issue of relying on metrics with faulty reasoning. For example, some evaluations of corporate

---

[7] https://www.cdc.gov/evaluation/logicmodels/index.htm.

programmes will cite the number of media mentions the programme has received as a measure of impact. Macnamara said, 'Of course, media relations and publicity remain important. But in program logic terms, they are outputs. We "put out" information into the media – same with websites, publications, etc. But we don't know and can't assume that target audiences consume the content or, even if they do, whether they believe it, remember it, or do anything as a result.'

This is a common issue in the area of measuring communications programmes. Substitution error occurs when metrics (numbers), or qualitative indicators of successful activities or outputs, are presented as evidence of outcomes or impact. In particular, output indicators are frequently substituted as outcome indicators. For example, in public relations, the widely used metrics of reach, impressions, and sentiment are examples of those that are erroneously claimed to be indicators of outcomes.

Macnamara also noted, 'Substitution error involves substituting a measure from one stage of a logic model as claimed evidence of achievement of a more advanced stage. Media impressions (the number of people who potentially could see media content based on media circulation or audience ratings etc.) is a good metric to show outputs were broadly circulated. But impressions is not the number of people impressed. Impressions is a measure of output. Outcomes required evidence of audience reception and response.'

Evaluation and the Need for Multiple Data Sets

Measurement and evaluation that shed insights on the outcomes, impact, and value of a particular initiative must go well beyond media metrics. Macnamara said, 'Integration of multiple data sets is essential to demonstrate progress through activities and outputs to outcomes and impact. There can be no single metric or method for the very different things we do and the different stages that we progress through.'

On a practical level, this speaks to the importance of taking an integrated approach. IPR's report states that, 'Instead, breaking down the silos and creating an integrated measurement and evaluation system can provide clearer data about what stakeholders say and do. With an integrated research, analysis, and evaluation approach, departments share gained insight about stakeholders to best track the consumer journey and measure combined success. For instance, information about stakeholders can be found through web analytics, customer relationship management data, call centre data, mobile app data, social media analytics, blogs, news, forums, investor reports, and especially in the big and "little" data that companies collect as technologies increasingly become more sophisticated.'

A wide range of instruments and tools can be employed to assist with the evaluation process. With the number of variables involved and the need to take a holistic and integrated approach, the company needs to consider custom-made models that are well suited to their particular situation. At a basic level, actions that can be taken include:

- Surveys that generate qualitative, open-ended responses and quantitative numerical data
- Traditional media monitoring and analysis
- Social media listening
- Website traffic analysis
- Focus groups
- Employee interviews
- Mobile app tracking

Whether these actions or others, taking a well-rounded approach will enhance the accuracy of the evaluation process, which in turn will foster more informed decision-making regarding future improvements that can be made.

The 'Learning' Phase of MEL

The third element of the MEL model is 'learning'. Macnamara said, 'Learning takes us beyond the descriptive to inferential and predictive findings. MEL is therefore a positive concept. It is about planning and designing the future—not just reviewing the past.'

Typically, this effort is not done particularly well and is usually skipped over without much rigour. Yet, an investigation of what went right as well as wrong, delivers real impetus to the company's ability to improve its reputation work in the future. More specifically, learning from measurement and evaluation provides the basis for refining future strategies, sharing insights that are helpful to other departments and teams across the organization (including in different geographic markets) and encouraging a culture of innovation where new ideas based on past experiences are welcomed.

Macnamara makes a useful point that it is crucial to learn by listening to people, rather than only listening to media. He notes that this can be achieved via surveys, interviews, focus groups, textual analysis of submissions to consultations, complaints, and correspondence; customer journey mapping; and direct stakeholder engagement.[8]

Building Capability

Macnamara, in a paper on the topic of MEL, laid out, as part of a comprehensive case study of his experience with the World

---

[8] Jim Macnamara, 'Vanity to Value: Demonstrating the Impact of Comms', 2023 AMEC Global Summit.

Health Organization, some of the actions that occurred to facilitate learning about evaluation.[9] These included:

- Developing written guidelines: Developing written guidelines for distribution to relevant colleagues provides a clear and comprehensible overview of MEL. Macnamara explained that at WHO, these guidelines were in the form of a manual, which had modules 'MEL for Media Publicity'; 'MEL for Social Media'; 'MEL for Websites'; 'MEL for Publications'; 'MEL for Videos and Films'; 'MEL for Events'; and 'MEL for Internal Communication'.

- Train staff through workshops: Macnamara wrote that, 'In addition to an introductory workshop covering key principles, theories, concepts, and models, workshops focussed on each of the modules in the WHO MEL Manual. MEL workshops of 1.5 to two hours duration including interactive sessions and Q&A were conducted online via Zoom and Microsoft Teams. Each was repeated in different time zones to gain wide participation. Participants completed pre-tests to identify their knowledge about the topic and post-workshop surveys of participants were conducted to gain feedback and measure knowledge change.'

- Macnamara noted the use of short video clips, stating that, 'To further enhance learning in today's attention economy in which busy people prefer "sound bites", GIFs, and short videos, a series of MEL microlessons were produced as videos and posted online. These contained key tips via narration and illustrations in 7-10-minute formats.'

---

[9] Jim Macnamara, 'Expanding M&E to MEL for strategic communication insights, outcomes and impact: A breakthrough case study', University of Technology Sydney.

The Practicalities of Measurement

One challenge when conducting programme measurement and evaluation is a practical one—money. Many companies are unwilling or unable to allocated budget toward this effort.

Macnamara contended, 'Frankly, don't bother doing communication if you can't incorporate some MEL built into it. If you do, you are working off assumptions and guesswork. It's time for the comms industry to grow up and become professional. Simply distributing information based on personal intuition, gut feel, or past experience is not enough. We live in an ever-changing and fast-changing world.' He offered some practical advice:

- Start small – Do pilot projects or even trials (when management sees effective, valid results, they usually find budgets).
- Use low-cost methods and tools – Google Analytics is cost-effective as are survey tools such as Survey Monkey. There are many other low and no cost methods.
- Prioritize – Apply MEL to priority projects (you don't have to measure everything).

Measuring Reputations of Value

As previously noted, the reputations of a company exist in the minds of its stakeholders. How someone perceives anything is intangible by nature. There will always be gaps between the perception, whether good or bad, and the reality of the entity, person or situation. One of the underlying themes of this book is that the existence of noise, particularly online, is not always an accurate indicator of any impact on the actual reputations of a company. This is not to say that it isn't important to monitor such noise and act accordingly, but it is worth remembering that a spike in chatter online about a company, even if dramatic, does not automatically equate to a shift in how that company is perceived by its stakeholders in reality.

In addition, a company that is 'famous' does not necessarily have reputations that help it advance its business agenda. The brands of mighty companies are known around the world, but this does not always mean they have an accurate and trusting reputation in the minds of their specific stakeholders. Those stakeholders will each have their own priorities and agendas when thinking about the company in question. Famous or not, an analysis of reputation must be tailored to different stakeholder groups accordingly. Furthermore, different reputations have differing degrees of value at different times, as stakeholder contexts, norms, and expectations change; and as business needs, priorities, and models change. Therefore, measurement and tracking need to be specific and prioritized and subject to review and course correction.

The effort to measure reputations is complex and requires careful planning. It can, however, be accomplished and in doing so, provide a valuable return on investment as it allows the company to witness how its effort to earn and protect reputations is connected to the enablement of substantial business results.

Summary of Principles

- The value of Measure, Evaluate and Learn, or 'MEL', is that it allows companies to not just look back at what has happened, but to help them systematically plan for the path ahead, in a way that supports continuous improvement.

- A landscape analysis helps to ensure that—at the outset—the objectives, strategies, and tactics of the organization are well informed and backed by research.

- Developing objectives using the SMART (specific, measurable, attainable, relevant, and time-bound) format allows for the creation of strategies and tactics that align with each objective and the ability to later demonstrate a return on expectations.

- It is useful to understand the distinction between an output, outcomes, and impact when thinking about how to assess programmes designed to earn reputations.

- The programme logic model can be used to reinforce the imperative of connecting value to reputation-earning activities.

- False Logic speaks to the issue of companies relying on metrics with faulty reasoning.

- Measurement and evaluation that sheds insights on outcomes, impact, and value must go well beyond media metrics.

- A specific focus on learning is crucial in the effort to refine and improve the company's stakeholder engagement programmes.

- Companies should have the proper skillset within their ranks on the topic of evaluation before they can properly evaluate their functions and programmes.

Conclusion

At the start of this book, I noted that I didn't have all the answers and I gladly offer that by the end of it, I still do not! Far from it. Further, I do not claim that all of the principles laid out in the book are particularly groundbreaking in nature. I do hope however, they provide a useful jumping off point for those interested in some of the pertinent means by which companies must earn and protect their reputations.

I also hope this book provides the reader with an appreciation of why leading companies invest immense time and effort in safeguarding their reputations. Despite those who (sometimes with valid reasons) accuse corporations of making a negative impact or being exploitative for their own profitability, I believe the vast majority of companies want to do the right thing. They want to be around for a long time and in doing so, they want to take pride in their reason for being and their contributions to their customers, employees, and local communities. Yet, companies cannot go about their business as they have in the past. To fulfil their strategic aspirations requires a concerted effort that consistently speaks to every aspect of their operation, including how they conduct themselves, how they respond when mistakes are made or crises occur, how they find and keep talented people, what they are doing to contribute to society or how they stand up for their values. These things, among others, are all elements of a company's existence that many people today consider as important as the product or service that it provides.

Chapter one laid out that the company does not have a singular reputation. Which reputation the company wants to achieve for what with which stakeholder (and even within each stakeholder grouping) is something its leadership needs to consider. Not all reputations are equal, and trade-offs will need to be made as companies conduct business in an unpredictable world. Companies, like people, do not have full control over their reputations given that a reputation for anything is held in the minds of others. This is why the book talks of 'earning' reputations rather than 'managing' them.

Further, corporate reputations are earned on far more than the act of communications alone. Being able to assess the landscape in which the company operates, the capture of useful insights, the ability to inform and persuade in an honest fashion, and taking actions that generate trust between the company and its stakeholders are all key elements of earning valued reputations. And, yes, the ability to communicate is also vital. The act of earning reputations requires a company-wide effort that is proactive and forward-looking in nature. Those companies that choose to be reactive in this context can expect to be buffeted by turbulent forces to the point of distraction and potentially the destruction of value.

Protecting reputations is as important as earning them. Reputations will inevitably be challenged periodically through a range of circumstances. Some of those circumstances have been covered in this book, such as cyberattacks, legal disputes, geopolitics, investor discontent, or a transaction gone wrong. There are many other sources of strain on reputations, but whatever the example, it is important to recognize the significance of thorough planning and preparation towards mitigating the fallout and to enabling the company to maintain or regain trust between it and its stakeholders.

For those involved in corporate life, it is worth asking the question, does your company have the means to earn and protect reputations of value? Can the company identify insights and intelligence of importance to the business? Can it connect the dots between different people, agendas, priorities, and actions? Is it willing to have honest conversations about the decisions it needs to make and the values it has? Does the company consider reputational impacts as a critical component of its strategic decision-making process? Is it properly engaged and supporting its employees? Are investments being made to measure progress and impact of efforts to engage stakeholders and earn reputations for specific things with specific audiences? These are the types of questions worth asking and answering by any company striving to win on a sustainable basis.

As time goes on, some of the topics in the book, such as purpose, ESG, geopolitics, investor activism, among others, will continue to ebb and flow as influences on the shaping of corporate reputations. Social media, for example, although already indelibly ingrained into our lives, still remains at a relatively nascent stage in the scheme of things. It arguably only became mainstream in the last twenty years. Newspapers have been with us for hundreds of years. What social media looks like in another twenty years, let alone another hundred years, is anyone's guess, but as it evolves, no doubt will the opportunities and challenges it poses for companies also change. Perhaps some basic tenets will remain in place—social media will remain a highly influential and impactful force, companies will need to attempt to monitor online conversations and claims relevant to it, companies will continue to use social media to help them communicate their positions and progress, and they will need to be prepared for the rise of backlash. While the channels may evolve, the principles of earning and protecting reputations will remain consistent.

As I mentioned in the introduction, I did not attempt to tackle the impact of Artificial Intelligence (AI) on corporate reputations. We remain early in the new era of AI and there is no question that it is presenting implications for companies that are yet to be fully grasped. There will continue to be a range of positive and powerful applications of AI to help companies make better decisions and engage with their stakeholders in ways not before possible. On the flip side, AI does pose reputation risk. Disinformation and also misinformation are far from new concepts, but AI will continue to drive their proliferation and not just in the political area. Weaponized information that is both credible and viral poses substantial risks to companies, who will need to find ways to respond effectively. The spread of false information misleads people and creates distorted perceptions. The Covid-19 pandemic provided many examples, such as the debunked claim that the vaccine contained microchips for tracking people's movements. There are a range of other areas where AI technology has the ability to cause reputational risk for the company, including in relation to customer privacy. The potential for AI to create bias that puts a particular group in society at a further disadvantage is another problem that companies will need to address in their decision-making process. These are indicative examples of how companies will need to grapple with AI in the context of their reputations. Many more examples exist and will emerge in the years ahead.

I also noted at the outset of the book that the approach to, corporate reputations varies in different geographic regions of the world—and within those regions. The social, political, and media landscape for companies doing business in the United States is a world away from those operating in China. And there are marked differences for a company earning its reputation in China compared to a company doing so in say, India or Thailand. In one part of the world, transgender issues might be high on the agenda of companies to talk about. In another, it is people's ability to access clean drinking water. Making definitive observations about topics such as speaking up on social issues must then be approached with caution. What is expected in the West does not necessarily follow suit in the East. As companies with an international footprint strive to meet and exceed the expectations of their stakeholders, they are tasked with a tricky path to tread. One size does not fit all.

In the final analysis, what does not change around the world is a desire for trusting relationships, in this case, between a company and its various audiences. If a company has a strong understanding of its purpose and values, if it makes decisions in an informed and thoughtful manner, if it does not shy away from difficult issues but rather tackles them with integrity, and if it can communicate its progress towards making a positive impact on those it touches, then its reputations should be of great value indeed.

Acknowledgements

This book is the realization of a long-held ambition. My heartfelt thanks goes to Nora Nazerene Abu Bakar at Penguin Random House SEA for the faith that Nora showed in me to allow me to write the book. Nora gave me a brilliant opportunity—to be published by Penguin Random House, one of the world's most reputable publishing houses. It has been a joy working with Nora and her amazing team.

I am fortunate to have been supported by individuals smarter than myself throughout my career. This book was also an effort to further educate myself on the subject of earning and protecting corporate reputations. On both fronts, I have a number of people to thank.

There are several people in my life that I consider to be career mentors, and I would like to single out three of them. Stu Spencer was my boss at AIA and is one of the most intelligent and articulate executives I have known. Even better, Stu is also someone who genuinely cares for others, and I am grateful for his encouragement and counsel. Basil Towers is not someone who has been a colleague but has been amazingly generous to me over the years. Bas has always given me time to lend his considerable intellect and to help me in any way possible. Ian McCabe was my boss at Burson-Marsteller and is one of the sharpest minds in the field of public affairs. Ian is someone who deflects the limelight, always operating in service of his clients. Over the years, Ian has been a constant source of support. I thank Stu, Bas, and Ian for their friendship and their willingness to share their wisdom with me, including in the context of writing this book.

Many people gave me informal feedback on particular chapters of the book or put me in touch with people to interview. My sincere gratitude goes out to: Katrina Andrews, Charlie Butcher, Alexander Chan, Louise Clements, Sarah Crawshaw, Peter Debreceny, Myriam Khan, Karen Khaw, Lapman Lee, Tom Lenon, David Gallagher, Susan Ho, Patrick Humphris, Mark Jackson, Mike Klein, Michelle Madamba, Marshall Manson, Mark McCall, Tina McCorkindale, Paul Meathrel, Jasper Meyns, Chris Moon, Time Payne, Stephen Ries, Parker Robinson, Ishtar Schneider, Matt Stafford, Samantha Stark, Arun Sudhaman, Richard Tesvich, Nicholas Worley, and James Wright.

I also extend my heartfelt thanks to each of the superb subject matter experts who spoke to me for the book and who are quoted in each chapter. As the reader will appreciate, I could not have written this book without their insights. I am humbled by the calibre of people who gave me their time and attention.

I would like to take this opportunity to warmly thank my amazing family and my large tribe of friends. I am so grateful for their enduring support. Finally, this book is dedicated with love and admiration to my sons, Robert and James. They are more wonderful than I ever could have dared to imagine.